Microsoft Press

W9-BLI-965

Microsoft Visual Basic 6.0 Development

Microsoft

Mastering

PUBLISHED BY
Microsoft Press
A Division of Microsoft Corporation
One Microsoft Way
Redmond, Washington 98052-6399

Library of Congress Cataloging-in-Publication Data
Microsoft Corporation.
    Microsoft Mastering : Microsoft Visual Basic 6.0 Development /
Microsoft Corporation.
      p. cm.
   ISBN 0-7356-0900-4
   1. Microsoft Visual BASIC.   2. Application software--Development.
I. Title.
QA76.73.B3M542   1999
005.26'8--dc21
                                      99-33876
                                      CIP

Printed and bound in the United States of America.

1 2 3 4 5 6 7 8 9   WCWC   4 3 2 1 0 9

Distributed in Canada by Penguin Books Canada Limited.

A CIP catalogue record for this book is available from the British Library.

Microsoft Press books are available through booksellers and distributors worldwide. For further information about international editions, contact your local Microsoft Corporation office or contact Microsoft Press International directly at fax (425) 936-7329. Visit our Web site at mspress.microsoft.com.

Acquisitions Editor: Eric Stroo
Project Editor: Wendy Zucker

Acknowledgements

Authors:
Teresa Canady
Pete Harris
Susie Parrent

Developed with Training Associates, Inc.

Program Manager: Pete Harris

Lead Subject Matter Expert: Pete Harris

Lead Instructional Designer: Susie Parrent

Instructional Designers:
Teresa Canady
Cris Morris
Melanie Christensen (Training Associates, Inc.)

Subject Matter Experts:
Janet Robinson
Sean Chase (Training Associates, Inc.)
Dave Perkovich (Training Associates, Inc.)

Production Manager: Miracle Davis

Production Coordinator: Gale Nelson (Online Training Solutions, Inc.)

Editors:
Ed Harper (MacTemps)
Reid Bannecker (S&T OnSite)

Library: Marlene Lambert (Online Training Solutions, Inc.)

Graphic Artist: Stephanie Lewis (Training Associates, Inc.)

Media Production: Jim Larkin (Resources Online)

Build and Testing Manager: Julie Challenger

Localization: Audrey Guidi

continued on next page

Additional Management: James Gower

Book Production Coordinator: Katharine Ford (ArtSource)

Book Design: Mary Rasmussen (Online Training Solutions, Inc.)

Book Layout:
R.J. Cadranell (Online Training Solutions, Inc.)
Jennifer Murphy (S&T OnSite)

Companion CD-ROM Design and Development: Jeff Brown

Companion CD-ROM Production: Eric Wagoner (Write Stuff)

About This Course

This course is designed to teach you how to use Microsoft Visual Basic to create database applications using components.

This course assumes you are familiar with basic programming and relational database concepts and have experience developing applications with a previous version of Visual Basic.

Course Content

The course content is organized into the following 10 chapters.

Chapter 1: Visual Basic Essentials

This chapter provides a brief review of the skills you need to create Visual Basic applications.

Chapter 2: Using Visual Data Access Tools

In this chapter, you will learn how to use the visual data access tools that come with Visual Basic 6 to create applications that connect to a database.

Chapter 3: Using Class Modules

In this chapter, you will learn how to use class modules in a Visual Basic project to create COM components that are available only within that project.

Chapter 4: Building ActiveX Controls

In this chapter, you will learn how to create ActiveX controls.

Chapter 5: Using ActiveX Data Objects

In this chapter, you will learn how to write code that uses ActiveX Data Objects (ADO) to connect to a data source, retrieve and manipulate data, and disconnect from a data source. You will also learn how to build and manage disconnected recordsets.

Chapter 6: Advanced Data Access Issues

In this chapter, you will learn about database concepts for creating advanced client/server applications. You will implement features such as client-side or server-side cursors and support for Microsoft SQL Server stored procedures. Additional topics include managing referential integrity errors and ensuring data integrity.

Chapter 7: Using COM Components

In this chapter, you will learn how to use external COM components to extend the functionality of your application.

Chapter 8: Building COM Components

In this chapter, you will learn how to build COM components that can be shared by many applications. You will learn how to compile a COM component both as a separate executable program and a dynamic-link library (DLL).

Chapter 9: Optimizing and Deploying Applications

In this chapter, you will learn how to optimize the usability and performance of an application, and how to use the tools provided with Visual Basic to develop applications more efficiently. You will also learn about security issues involved in using ActiveX controls on HTML pages, and how to ensure the security of the controls you distribute. In addition, you will learn how to create a Setup program using the Visual Basic Package and Deployment Wizard.

Chapter 10: Building Internet Applications

In this chapter, you will learn how to use Visual Basic to create different kinds of components and applications for the Internet.

Labs

Each chapter in this course includes a lab that gives you hands-on experience with the skills that you learn in the chapter. A lab consists of one or more exercises that focus on how to use the information contained in the chapter. The labs for this course build upon each other from Lab 1 through Lab 9 to create a single application. Labs after Lab 1 contain code to get you started and code for the lab solution. Lab 9 has no code for the lab solution. For detailed information about the design of the labs in this course, see "Overview of the State University Bookstore Application" on page 28 in Chapter 1, "Visual Basic Essentials."

In order to complete Lab 2 through Lab 9, you will need to set up the State University Bookstore database using Microsoft SQL Server. For detailed information on how to set up the State University Bookstore database, see Lab 2, Exercise 1: Creating the StateUBookstore Database.

> **Note** The lab solution code throughout this course uses a SQL Server named MSERIES1. To run the lab solution code with a different server name, replace all occurrences of MSERIES1 with the name of your SQL Server.

Lab hints, which provide code or other information that will help you complete an exercise, are included in Appendix B. You will see the following icon in the margin, indicating that a lab hint is given.

Lab Hint Icon

To complete the exercises and view the accompanying solution code, you will need to install the lab files that are found on the accompanying CD-ROM.

To complete the labs, you need:

◆ A PC with a Pentium-class processor; Pentium 90 or higher processor

◆ Microsoft Visual Basic 6.0 Professional Edition

◆ Microsoft Internet Explorer 4.0 Service Pack 1 or later

◆ Microsoft SQL Server 6.5 recommended

Self-Check Questions

This course includes a number of self-check questions at the end of each chapter. You can use these multiple-choice questions to test your understanding of the information that has been covered in the course. Answers to self-check questions are provided in Appendix A. Each answer includes a reference to the associated chapter topic so that you can easily review the content.

CD-ROM Contents

The *Microsoft Visual Basic 6 Development* CD-ROM that is included with this book contains multimedia, lab files, sample applications, and sample code that you may wish to view or install on your computer's hard drive. The content on the CD-ROM must be viewed by using an HTML browser that supports frames. A copy of Internet Explorer has been included with this CD-ROM in case you do not have a browser or do not have one that supports frames, installed on your computer. Please refer to the ReadMe file on the CD-ROM for further instructions on installing Internet Explorer.

To begin browsing the content that is included on the CD-ROM, open the file, default.htm.

Lab Files

The files required to complete the lab exercises, as well as the lab solution files, are included on the accompanying CD-ROM.

> **Note** 7.1 megabytes (MB) of hard disk space is required to install the labs.

Multimedia

This course provides numerous audio/video demonstrations and animations that illustrate the concepts and techniques that are discussed in this course. The following icon will appear in the margin, indicating that a multimedia title can be found on the accompanying CD-ROM.

Multimedia Icon

In addition, at the beginning of each chapter is a list of the multimedia titles that are found in the chapter.

> **Note** You can toggle the display of the text of a demonstration or animation on and off by choosing **Closed Caption** from the **View** menu.

Sample Code

This course contains numerous code samples.

Sample code has been provided on the accompanying CD-ROM for you to copy and paste into your own projects. The following icon appears in the margin, indicating that this piece of sample code is included on the CD-ROM.

Sample Code Icon

Internet Links

The following icon appears in the margin next to an Internet link, indicating that this link is included on the accompanying CD-ROM.

Internet Link Icon

Sample Applications

Visual Basic 6 contains a large selection of sample applications. These samples demonstrate everything from simple programming operations for beginners to more advanced topics that will be of interest to the experienced Visual Basic programmer.

For detailed information about the sample applications that are provided with Visual Basic, read the article "Samples" in Visual Basic Help.

Conventions Used In This Course

The following table explains some of the typographic conventions used in this course.

Example of convention	Description
Sub, If, Case Else, Print, True, BackColor, Click, Debug, Long	In text, language-specific keywords appear in bold, with the initial letter capitalized.
File menu, **Add Project** dialog box	Most interface elements appear in bold, with the initial letter capitalized.
Setup	Words that you're instructed to type appear in bold.
Event-driven	In text, italic letters can indicate defined terms, usually the first time that they occur. Italic formatting is also used occasionally for emphasis.
Variable	In syntax and text, italic letters can indicate placeholders for information that you supply.
[expressionlist]	In syntax, items inside square brackets are optional.
{While | Until}	In syntax, braces and a vertical bar indicate a choice between two or more items. You must choose one of the items, unless all of the items are enclosed in square brackets.

`Sub HelloButton_Click()`
`Readout.Text = _`
`"Hello, world!"`
`End Sub`
	This font is used for code.

ENTER	Capital letters are used for the names of keys and key sequences, such as ENTER and CTRL+R.
ALT+F1	A plus sign (+) between key names indicates a combination of keys. For example, ALT+F1 means to hold down the ALT key while pressing the F1 key.

table continued on next page

Example of convention	Description
DOWN ARROW	Individual direction keys are referred to by the direction of the arrow on the key top (LEFT, RIGHT, UP, or DOWN). The phrase "arrow keys" is used when describing these keys collectively.
BACKSPACE, HOME	Other navigational keys are referred to by their specific names.
C:\Vb\Samples\Calldlls.vbp	Paths and file names are given in mixed case.

The following guidelines are used in writing code in this course:

◆ Keywords appear with initial letters capitalized:

```
' Sub, If, ChDir, Print, and True are keywords.
Print "Title Page"
```

◆ Line labels are used to mark position in code (instead of line numbers):

```
ErrorHandler:
Power = conFailure
End Function
```

◆ An apostrophe (') introduces comments:

```
' This is a comment; these two lines
' are ignored when the program is running.
```

◆ Control-flow blocks and statements in **Sub**, **Function**, and **Property** procedures are indented from the enclosing code:

```
Private Sub cmdRemove_Click ()
    Dim Ind As Integer
    ' Get index
    Ind = lstClient.ListIndex
    ' Make sure list item is selected
    If Ind >= 0 Then
        ' Remove it from list box
        lstClient.RemoveItem Ind
        ' Display number
        lblDisplay.Caption = lstClient.ListCount
    Else
        ' If nothing selected, beep
        Beep
    End If
End Sub
```

◆ Intrinsic constant names appear in a mixed-case format, with a two-character prefix indicating the object library that defines the constant. Constants from the Visual Basic and Visual Basic for Applications object libraries are prefaced with "vb"; constants from the ActiveX Data Objects (ADO) Library are prefaced with "ad"; constants from the Excel Object Library are prefaced with "xl". Examples are as follows:

```
vbTileHorizontal
adAddNew
xlDialogBorder
```

For more information about coding conventions, see "Programming Fundamentals" in the MSDN Visual Basic documentation.

Table of Contents

Chapter 1:
Visual Basic Essentials

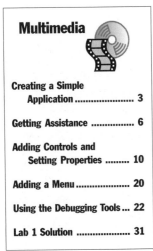

Multimedia

To complete this course successfully, you should have a basic understanding of how to work with Microsoft Visual Basic. This chapter provides a brief review of the skills you need to create Visual Basic applications.

Objectives

After completing this chapter, you will be able to:

◆ Use Visual Basic to create a simple application and an executable file for users.

◆ List the files that comprise a Visual Basic application.

◆ Use the Visual Basic debugging tools.

◆ Add run-time error handling to a procedure.

Understanding Visual Basic Development

This section introduces you to some of the fundamental concepts of Visual Basic development. It lists the steps necessary to create a Visual Basic application, and provides a brief summary of Help resources for Visual Basic.

Understanding Event-Driven Programming

Visual Basic is derived from the Basic language, which is a structured programming language. However, Visual Basic uses an event-driven programming model.

Procedural Applications

In traditional or procedural applications, the application controls which portions of code run and the sequence in which they run. Application execution starts with the first line of code and follows a predefined path through the application, calling procedures as needed.

Event-Driven Applications

In an event-driven application, execution does not follow a predetermined path. Instead, different code sections run in response to events. Events can be triggered by the user's actions, by messages from the system or other applications, or from inside the application itself. The sequence of events determines the sequence in which the code runs. Therefore, the path through the application's code can differ each time the program runs.

An essential part of event-driven programming is writing code that responds to all the possible events that may occur in an application. Visual Basic makes it easy to implement an event-driven programming model.

The following illustration shows some actions that generate events to which you can respond by writing code. These events can occur in any order.

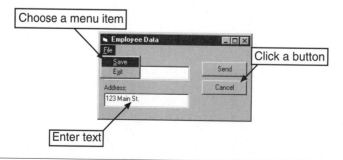

Creating a Simple Visual Basic Application

You use the following steps to create an application in Visual Basic:

1. Create the user interface of the application.

2. Write code that responds to events that occur in the user interface.

   To see the demonstration "Creating a Simple Application," see the accompanying CD-ROM.

3. Create components.

4. Test the application.

5. Compile and distribute the application and components.

Understanding the Files in a Visual Basic Project

As you develop an application, you work with a project to manage all the different files that make up the application. A project can include the following files:

◆ Group Project File (.vbg)   *Project = Application*

The group project file is a list of all the projects contained in one group.

◆ Project File (.vbp)

The project file is a list of all the files and components associated with the project, as well as information about the environment options you set. Visual Basic updates this file every time you save the project.

◆ Form Module (.frm)

A form module contains textual descriptions of the form and its controls, including property settings. A form module can also contain form-level declarations of constants, variables, and external procedures, event procedures, and general procedures.   *L?*

◆ Form Data File (.frx)

Visual Basic creates one binary data file for each form. The file contains binary properties such as pictures or icons. Binary data files are automatically generated and cannot be edited.

◆ Class Module (.cls)

Class modules are similar to form modules, except class modules have no visible user interface. You can use class modules to create your own objects, including code for methods and properties.

- Standard Module (.bas)

  Standard modules can contain global declarations of types, constants, variables, external procedures, and public procedures.

- User Control (.ctl) and Property Page Modules (.pag)

  User Control and Property Page modules are similar to forms, but are used to create ActiveX controls and their associated property pages for displaying design-time properties.

- ActiveX Controls (.ocx)

  ActiveX controls are optional controls that you can add to the toolbox and use on forms. When you install Visual Basic, the files containing the controls included with Visual Basic are copied to a common folder (the \Windows\System folder under Windows 95). Additional ActiveX controls are available from a wide variety of sources. You can also create your own controls using the Professional or Enterprise editions of Visual Basic.

- ActiveX Documents (.dob)

  ActiveX documents are similar to forms, but are displayable in an Internet browser such as Microsoft Internet Explorer.

- Active Designer File (.dsr)

  Active Designer files store information about the designers you add to your project. These files cannot be edited and are automatically generated for any designer used in an application.

- Resource File (.res)

  Resource files contain bitmaps, text strings, and other data that you can change without having to reedit or recompile your code. A project can contain no more than one resource file.

For more information about binary data files and project files, read the article "Visual Basic Specifications, Limitations, and File Formats" in Visual Basic Help.

For a complete list of the files in a Visual Basic project, read the article "Project File Formats" in Visual Basic Help.

Choosing a Visual Basic Project Template

Visual Basic offers several project templates designed to support the development of different kinds of applications and components. As you begin developing an application, you first decide what kind of project template to use. A project template contains the basic project objects and environment settings you need to create the type of application or component you want.

You will learn about the following project templates in this course:

◆ Standard EXE

Standard EXE projects contain a form by default. Use this project template to develop a stand-alone application. For more information, see "Creating a Simple Visual Basic Application" on page 3 in this chapter.

◆ Data Project

A Data Project is a Standard EXE project that, in addition to a form, contains a **DataEnvironment** object and a **DataReport** object by default. Use this project template to develop an application that reads or manipulates data from a data source. For more information, see Chapter 2, "Using Visual Data Access Tools" on page 39.

Note Data Project templates contain references to the Microsoft ActiveX Data Objects (ADO) library and several other data-specific components. If you do not need all of the components that are included by default, you can use a Standard EXE project template instead, and set references manually for the components you want. For information about how to set references, see "Using Components" on page 16 in this chapter.

◆ ActiveX EXE/ActiveX DLL

ActiveX EXE and ActiveX DLL projects contain a class module by default. Use these project templates to develop COM components that expose functionality to other applications.

Use an ActiveX EXE project template if your component will both expose functionality programmatically and run as a stand-alone application. Use an ActiveX DLL project template if your component will only be used programmatically by another application. For more information, see Chapter 8, "Building COM Components" on page 267.

◆ ActiveX Control

ActiveX Control projects contain a **UserControl** object by default. Use this project template to create a component designed to be a user interface element in a form or dialog box. For more information, see Chapter 4, "Building ActiveX Controls" on page 113.

◆ ActiveX Document EXE/ActiveX Document DLL

ActiveX Document EXE and ActiveX Document DLL projects contain a **UserDocument** object by default. Use these project templates to create components designed for use in a document object container, such as Internet Explorer. For more information, see Chapter 10, "Building Internet Applications" on page 327.

◆ DHTML Application

DHTML Application projects contain a **DHTMLPage** object and a class module by default. Use this project template to create a component that can be used on the client side of a Web application. For more information, see Chapter 10, "Building Internet Applications" on page 327.

◆ IIS Application

IIS Application projects contain a **WebClass** object by default. Use this project template to create a component that can be used on the server side of a Web application. For more information, see Chapter 10, "Building Internet Applications" on page 327.

▶ **To create a new project**

1. On the **File** menu, click **New Project**.

   The **New Project** dialog box appears.

2. Select the project template you want, and then click **OK**.

Getting Assistance

Visual Basic provides a variety of resources to help you find the information you need when you are working in the development environment.

 To see the demonstration "Getting Assistance," see the accompanying CD-ROM.

Visual Basic Help

Visual Basic provides extensive online Help. You can access Visual Basic Help by clicking **Contents** on the **Help** menu. This starts the Microsoft Developer Network (MSDN) Library that contains Help topics for all of Visual Studio 98.

Note If you have worked with a previous version of Visual Basic, read the article "What's New in Visual Basic 6.0" in Visual Basic Help for a summary of the new features.

Context-Sensitive Help

You can also get context-sensitive help in Visual Basic. To use context-sensitive Help in a code window, type the word for which you want information, and then press F1. For example, if you want information about the **Open** statement, type **Open** and then press F1.

If you receive a run-time error, you can press F1 when the error message is displayed to get Help for that error message.

Code Editor

The Visual Basic code editor automatically provides you with relevant information as you enter code. For example, if you type the name of a control, followed by the dot (.) operator, the code editor displays the properties and methods of that control in a list box, as shown in the following illustration. You can then choose the appropriate property or method to complete the statement.

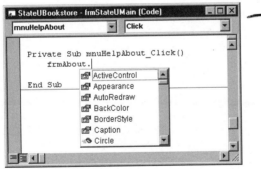

When you enter a function name in the code window, Visual Basic provides you with the syntax of the function, as shown in the following illustration.

```
StateUBookstore - frmStateUMain (Code)
mnuFileExit                    Click

    Private Sub mnuFileExit_Click()
        Unload |
            Unload(object As object)
    End Sub
```

Sample Applications

Visual Basic includes a number of sample applications for you to use. These can be found on the MSDN Library CD in the \Disk1\Samples folder.

Microsoft Visual Basic Web Site

To find the most up-to-date information about Visual Basic, and gain access to a library of technical information, go to the Microsoft Visual Basic Web site at http://msdn.microsoft.com/vbasic/.

To get technical assistance, go to the Microsoft Support Online Web site at http://www.microsoft.com/support/.

To go to other Visual Basic Web sites, on the **Help** menu, click **Microsoft on the Web,** and then click one of the links listed.

Creating an Application

The first step in creating an application in Visual Basic is to design the user interface that will be exposed in the application. After you create the forms and add controls, you add code to implement the functionality of the application.

Users prefer applications that are easy to learn and that help them become productive quickly. Design your forms carefully, and work with users to determine the best design.

For more information about user interface conventions, refer to *The Windows Interface Guidelines for Software Design* available from Microsoft Press.

For information about books from Microsoft Press, go to the Microsoft Press Web site at http://mspress.microsoft.com.

Using Controls

When you build an application in Visual Basic, you begin by creating the user interface.

Using the Toolbox, you draw or place controls on a form to create the visual elements of your application. The Toolbox is available at design time only.

Using the Toolbox

The Toolbox contains intrinsic Visual Basic controls and any ActiveX controls or other insertable objects you have added to the project. If the Toolbox is closed, you can open it by clicking **Toolbox** on the **View** menu. The following illustration shows the Toolbox.

Adding Controls to the Toolbox

You can extend the Toolbox by adding ActiveX controls. The Professional and Enterprise Editions of Visual Basic provide additional ActiveX controls. You can also purchase ActiveX controls from third-party vendors, or create your own using Visual Basic. For more information about creating ActiveX controls, see Chapter 4, "Building ActiveX Controls" on page 113.

▶ **To add an ActiveX control to the Toolbox**

1. On the **Project** menu, click **Components**.

   Visual Basic displays the Components dialog box.

2. On the **Controls** tab, click the control you want to include, and then click **OK**.

   Visual Basic adds the control to the Toolbox.

Note You can add Tabs to the Toolbox by clicking the **Add Tab** command on the right mouse menu for the Toolbox. Use Tabs to group controls in a way that makes sense to you.

There are a number of new controls that ship with Visual Basic 6.0, such as the **DateTimePicker**, and the **DataRepeater** controls. To see a list of the controls and examples of how to use them, read the article "Using the ActiveX Controls" in Visual Basic Help.

Using Controls on Forms

Once you've added a control to the Toolbox you can use it on the forms of your application.

To place a control on a form, you can either double-click the control, or single-click it and draw the control on the form. You can drag to move the control on the form, or use commands on the **Format** menu to align, size, or space the control in relation to other controls on the form.

You can then set properties for the control. Setting the **Name** property of the control is important because it determines how you refer to the control in code. There are some standard naming conventions you should follow when naming a control. For information on naming conventions, read the article "Object-Naming Conventions" in Visual Basic Help.

Setting Properties

When building the user interface of a Visual Basic application, you must set the properties for the objects you create.

To see the demonstration "Adding Controls and Setting Properties," see the accompanying CD-ROM.

Setting Properties at Design Time

Some properties can be set at design time. To set these properties, you can use the Properties window or property pages.

To access the Properties window, right-click an object, and then click **Properties**.

The following illustration shows the Properties window.

You can set properties for multiple controls at the same time. To select multiple controls, click and drag the mouse. The Properties window displays only the properties that are common to all of the selected controls. Any change you make to a property applies to all of the controls.

Setting Properties at Run Time

At run time, you can write code to set or retrieve properties. The following example code sets the **Font** property to bold for a text box named **txtData**:

```
txtData.Font.Bold = True      'Set text to bold.
```

The following example code sets the **Text** property of the text box **txtData**:

```
txtData.Text = "Hello World" 'Set value of text.
```

If you omit the property name, you set the default property of the control. The default property of a text box is the **Text** property. The default property of a label is the **Caption** property.

The following example code sets the default **Text** and **Caption** properties for a text box and a label control:

```
txtData = "Set the Text property of this text box"
lblData = "Set the Caption property of this label"
```

Getting Properties at Run Time

At run time you can assign a property to a variable to retrieve the property. The following example code gets the **Text** property of a text box:

```
Dim sName As String
sName = txtName.Text
```

Writing Procedures

Once you have designed forms and set properties, you are ready to add code to your application.

For information on Visual Basic coding standards, read the article "Visual Basic Coding Conventions" in Visual Basic Help.

Procedures

There are two types of procedures you will create in Visual Basic: event procedures and general procedures.

Event Procedures

Visual Basic automatically calls event procedures in response to keyboard, mouse, or system actions. For example, command buttons have a **Click** event procedure. The code you place in a **Click** event procedure is executed when the user clicks a command button.

To open a code window for an event procedure, double-click the control or form, or click **Code** on the **View** menu. Each control has a fixed set of event procedures. The event procedures for each control are listed in a drop-down list box in the code window.

General Procedures

General procedures are **Sub** or **Function** procedures that you create to perform specific tasks. **Function** procedures can return a value, but **Sub** procedures cannot. To execute a general procedure, you must explicitly invoke it.

The following sample code shows the use of both **Sub** and **Function** procedures. To copy this code for use in your own projects, see "Writing Sub and Function Procedures" on the accompanying CD-ROM.

```
Private Sub cmdProcess_Click()

    ' call the Sub routine to process the student
    ProcessStudent

End Sub

Sub ProcessStudent()

  Dim bResult As Boolean

    ' call CheckID function to validate an ID
  bResult = CheckID(3)

  If bResult = True Then
      MsgBox "Student has been Processed successfully."
  End If

End Sub

Function CheckID(iID As Integer) As Boolean

    ' if ID is less than 0, it is invalid
  If iID < 0 Then

      ' return false
      CheckID = False

  Else

      ' all other IDs are valid
      ' return true
      CheckID = True

  End If

End Function
```

Declaring Arguments for a Procedure

Procedures may require information about the state of the program to perform an action. This information is generally passed to the procedure in the form of a variable, and is called an argument. A procedure may require an argument to be passed by value or by reference.

You use the **ByVal** keyword to declare an argument that is passed by value. In this case a copy of the value is passed to the procedure, and the procedure cannot change the variable itself.

You use the **ByRef** keyword to declare an argument that is passed by reference. In this case a pointer to the variable is passed to the procedure, and the procedure has the ability to change the value of the variable.

If you declare an argument without using either the **ByVal** or **ByRef** keyword, the argument will be passed by reference by default.

Scope of Procedures

Standard code modules are a good place to store code that is global in scope (available to all forms and class modules in the project at all times). Class modules are a good place to store code that you want to share with other applications.

You can create **Public** or **Private** procedures in forms, standard code modules, or class modules.

Private procedures in a form, a standard code module, or a class module can be called only by other procedures located in that form, code module, or class.

Public procedures on a form become methods of the form. The procedure can be called from anywhere in the application by specifying the form and procedure name.

Public procedures in a standard code module are available throughout the application, and can be called by specifying the procedure name.

Public procedures in a class module become methods of the class. The procedure can be called from anywhere in the application by specifying the class and procedure names.

For more information about using class modules, see Chapter 3, "Using Class Modules" on page 73.

For more information about using modules, read the articles "Programming Fundamentals" and "Programming with Objects" in Visual Basic Help.

Control Structures

Visual Basic is a complete programming language that supports programming constructs for looping, decision making, and efficient processing. These constructs include: **For...Next, Do...Loop, Select ...Case, With...End With,** and **If...Then...Else.**

For information on adding control structures to a Visual Basic application, read the article "Introduction to Control Structures" in Visual Basic Help.

Using Variables and Constants

In Visual Basic you can make your code more readable and maintainable by using variables and constants to store values. You use variables to store temporary values in your application. You use constants to store values that remain fixed throughout the execution of your application.

For information about declaring variables and the available data types, read the article "Introduction to Variables, Constants and Data Types" in Visual Basic Help.

Variables

To declare a variable, you use the **Dim, Private, Public,** or **Static** statement.

◆ **Dim**

Variables declared with the **Dim** statement in a module are available to all procedures within the module. Variables declared with the **Dim** statement in a procedure are available only within that procedure.

◆ **Private**

Variables declared with the **Private** statement in a module are available to all procedures within the module.

◆ **Public**

Variables declared with the **Public** statement in a module are available to all procedures in all modules throughout the project.

◆ **Static**

Variables declared with the **Static** statement in a module are available to all procedures within the module. Variables declared with the **Static** statement in a procedure are available only within the procedure, but their values are preserved for the lifetime of the application.

The data type of a variable determines the type of information that a variable can store and the range of possible values. If you do not provide a data type when you declare a variable, the variable is given the **Variant** data type. A **Variant** variable can store null, numeric, date/time, string, or object data. However, the **Variant** data type requires more memory than other data types.

To create concise and fast code, use explicit data types where appropriate. To enforce the use of explicit data types, and to avoid the problem of misnaming variables, you can place an **Option Explicit** statement in the Declarations section of a class, form, or standard module.

Constants

To declare a constant, you use the **Const** statement. A constant can be private or public in scope, similar to a variable.

◆ **Private**

Constants declared with the **Private** statement in a module are available to all procedures within the module.

◆ **Public**

Constants declared with the **Public** statement must be declared in a standard code module, and are available to all procedures in all modules throughout the project.

To declare a constant, use the following syntax:

[Public|Private] **Const** name *[As* type*]* = expression

Using Components

Historically, applications were written as many lines of continuous code. However, designing an application in modular segments of code, or components, benefits both you and your users.

Using components, you can modularize your application, creating objects that contain both data and functionality for a particular application feature. You can create components that are reusable in other applications, and easily maintained and modified.

When you create a component, you create a class, or a blueprint for an object. Then you reuse that modularized code by creating instances of the object wherever you need it. You can set properties and methods for the object, and respond to events generated by the object.

Working with Objects and Classes

An object is a combination of data and functionality that is treated as a unit. An object can be an element of an application, such as a control or a form. It can also be a block of code that does not have a user interface, such as the **Err** object.

A class is a template for an object, just as a blueprint is a template for a house. All objects are created as identical copies or instances of their class. Once they exist as individual objects, the values of their properties can be changed and their methods can be invoked.

For information on creating objects in your application, see Chapter 3, "Using Class Modules" on page 73.

Setting References

In your application development, you can either use objects created within the scope of your application, or you can use objects exposed in other applications or libraries. Before you can use an object external to your application, you must set a reference in your project to that object's type library or application.

▶ **To set a reference to a type library**

1. On the **Project** menu, click **References**.

   Visual Basic displays the **References** dialog box.

2. Click the reference to the type library you want to use, and then click **OK**.

Once you have set a reference to a type library, you can find the specific object you want and information about its methods and properties in the Object Browser. For more information about the Object Browser, see "Using the Object Browser" on page 84 in Chapter 3, "Using Class Modules."

Using an Object's Properties and Methods

All objects have properties and methods. Properties are values you set to determine the object's appearance and behavior. Methods are procedures provided by the object.

For example, a form provides a **Show** method that causes the form to be displayed. An **Employee** object might expose a **Hire** method to use when adding a new employee to a database and a **HireDate** property to hold the value of the employee's date of hire.

The benefit of working with pre-built objects is that objects provide code that you do not have to write. You simply set the object's properties and call the object's methods, and the object performs various functions. For more information about working with pre-built objects, see Chapter 7, "Using COM Component" on page 245.

The benefit of writing your own objects is that you can write the code once and reuse it, specifying different property values for each occurrence of the object rather than writing unique code each time.

Working with Collections

A collection is an object that contains zero or more related objects. Each object in a collection has its own properties, methods, and events. The collection itself also has properties and methods so that the set of objects can be referred to as a unit.

There are some collections created automatically by Visual Basic, such as the **Forms** collection and the **Controls** collection. You can create your own collections in Visual Basic by using the **Collection** object. The **Collection** object has the following properties and methods.

Property or method	Description
Add method	Adds an item to the collection.
Remove method	Deletes an item from the collection.
Item method	Returns an item.
Count property	Returns the number of items in the collection. Read-only.

To loop through a collection and perform the same action to each item in the collection, you can use the **For Each...Next** control structure. The following sample code adds objects to a collection called **colEmployees** and displays employee names in a listbox on a form. To copy this code for use in your own projects, see "Using Collections" on the accompanying CD-ROM.

```
Private Sub cmdUseCollection_Click()

    ' declare and instantiate the collection
    Dim colEmployees As Collection
    Set colEmployees = New Collection

    ' declare and instantiate the employee object
    Dim empCurrent As CEmployee
    Set empCurrent = New CEmployee

    ' create and add an employee
    empCurrent.iID = 1
    empCurrent.dSalary = 30000
    empCurrent.sName = "John Doe"
    colEmployees.Add empCurrent
    Set empCurrent = Nothing

    ' create and add an employee
    Set empCurrent = New CEmployee
    empCurrent.iID = 2
    empCurrent.dSalary = 35000
    empCurrent.sName = "Jane Smith"
    colEmployees.Add empCurrent
    Set empCurrent = Nothing

    ' add all the employees in the collection
    ' to the list box on the form
    For Each empCurrent In colEmployees
        lstEmployees.AddItem empCurrent.sName
    Next empCurrent

End Sub
```

For more information about working with collections, read the article "Collections in Visual Basic" in Visual Basic Help.

Adding a Menu

You can enhance your application with menus. Menus provide users with a convenient way to execute commands.

Using the Menu Editor

The Menu Editor is an interactive tool that enables you to create and modify menus with a minimum of coding. With the Menu Editor, you can add new commands to existing menus, replace existing menu commands with your own, create new menus and menu bars, and change and delete existing menus and menu bars.

The following illustration shows the Menu Editor.

```
Menu Editor                                    [X]
  Caption:   &Save                        |   OK   |
  Name:      mnuFileSave                  | Cancel |
  Index:  [      ]        Shortcut:  [ Ctrl+S      ▼]
  HelpContextID: [ 0 ]    NegotiatePosition: [0 - None ▼]
  ☐ Checked   ☑ Enabled   ☑ Visible   ☐ WindowList
  [←][→][↑][↓]  [ Next ]  [ Insert ]  [ Delete ]
  ┌──────────────────────────────────────────────┐
  │ &File                                         │
  │ ····&Open                                     │
  │ ····&Save                      Ctrl+S         │
  │ ····E&xit                                     │
  │                                               │
  │                                               │
  └──────────────────────────────────────────────┘
```

▶ **To add a menu to a form**

1. On the **Tools** menu, click **Menu Editor.**

   The Menu Editor dialog box appears.

2. In the **Caption** text box, type the menu or command name that you want to appear on the menu bar in your menu.

3. In the **Name** text box, type a name for the item so you can refer to it programmatically.

4. Use the arrow command buttons to move menu items up or down in the command list.

Note To add a separator bar to a menu, enter a menu with a hyphen (-) as the caption.

To see the demonstration "Adding a Menu," see the accompanying CD-ROM.

Modifying the Appearance of Menu Items

At run time, you can dynamically modify the appearance of a menu and add new menu items by setting properties of the menu item. The following table shows a list of properties you can set.

Property	Effect
Checked	Shows or removes a check mark next to the menu item.
Visible	Hides or displays the menu item.
Enabled	Enables or disables (grays out) the menu item.

For more information about dynamically modifying menus, read the article "Creating and Modifying Menus at Run Time" in Visual Basic Help.

Creating Pop-Up Menus

Pop-up menus (also known as context or shortcut menus) are great for providing quick access to common user interface options. Pop-up menus are commonly displayed when the user clicks an object with the right mouse button.

▶ **To create and show a pop-up menu**

1. Create a top-level menu with the menu items you want to display.

2. Make the top-level menu invisible by clearing the **Visible** check box in the Menu Editor.

3. In the **MouseUp** event for the form, determine whether the user clicked the right mouse button and call the **PopupMenu** method of the form, as shown in the following example code:

```
Private Sub frmMain_MouseUp(Button As Integer, Shift As Integer,
X As Single, Y As Single)
  If Button = vbRightButton Then
      frmMain.PopupMenu mnuFilePop
  End If
End Sub
```

For more information about creating and displaying pop-up menus, read the article "Displaying Pop-up Menus" in Visual Basic Help.

Debugging and Error Handling

As you develop Visual Basic applications, it is important to debug code you have written, and to add code to handle any run-time errors that might occur.

Tools for Debugging

Visual Basic provides interactive tools for finding run-time errors and errors in your program's logic. You can access all of the debugging tools by using the **Debug** menu or the **Debug** toolbar.

To see the demonstration "Using the Debugging Tools," see the accompanying CD-ROM.

Visual Basic debugging support includes:

◆ Breakpoints and break expressions

Set a breakpoint to stop a program while it is running. You can set a breakpoint at design time, or at run time while in Break mode.

◆ Watch expressions

Use watch expressions to monitor a particular variable or expression. The value of each watch expression is updated at breakpoints.

◆ Step options

Use the step options to run portions of your code either one statement or one procedure at a time.

◆ Call Stack

Use Call Stack to view all active procedure calls and trace the execution of a series of nested procedures.

◆ Immediate window

In Break mode, you can test an executable statement by typing it in the Immediate window. Visual Basic runs the statement immediately so that you can evaluate your code.

◆ Locals window

This window automatically displays all of the declared variables in the current procedure, along with their values.

Handling Run-Time Errors

No matter how well you design your application, run-time errors will occur. Users forget to put disks in disk drives, systems run low on memory, and files are not located where you expect to find them. By adding effective error-handling code to your application, you create a more robust application.

The Error-Handling Process

The error-handling process involves the following steps:

1. Set an error trap that specifies the location of the error-handling code.

2. Write the error-handling code.

3. Exit the error-handling code.

The **On Error GoTo** statement enables an error trap and specifies where the execution of the application will jump to when an error occurs. If a run-time error occurs, execution jumps to the label indicated in the **On Error GoTo** statement. The error handler runs error-handling code, followed by a **Resume** statement that indicates where processing should continue.

The following example code shows how to use the **On Error GoTo** and **Resume** statements:

```
Private Sub cmdRunApp_Click()
  On Error GoTo CheckError
  Dim AppName as String

  AppName = InputBox("Enter application name")
  Shell AppName
Exit Sub
CheckError:
  'handle error
  ...
  Resume Next
End Sub
```

Resume Options

To specify where your application will continue processing after handling an error, you use the **Resume** statement. The following table lists the three types of **Resume** statements available in Visual Basic.

Statement	Description
Resume	Return to the statement that caused the error. Use **Resume** to repeat an operation after correcting the error.
Resume Next	Return to the statement immediately following the statement that caused the error.
Resume *line* or *label*	Return to a specific line number or label.

If there is no **Resume** statement, the procedure will exit.

The Err Object

In error-handling code, use the properties and methods of the **Err** object to check which error occurred, to clear an error value, or to raise an error.

The **Number** property is an integer that indicates the last error that occurred. To determine which error has occurred, check the value of **Err.Number**. In some cases, you can correct an error and allow processing to continue without interrupting the user. Otherwise, you must notify the user of an error, and take some action based on the user's response.

The **Description** property is a string that contains a description of the error.

The **Source** property contains the name of the object application that generated the error. This is helpful when using components. For example, if you launch Microsoft Excel and it generates an error, Microsoft Excel sets **Err.Number** to the correct error code and sets **Err.Source** to **Excel.Application**.

For more information about the properties and methods of the **Err** object, read the article "Err Object" in Visual Basic Help.

Inline Error Handling

Rather than setting up a separate error handler, you may sometimes want to address an error immediately after it occurs.

Inline error handling involves the following steps:

1. Set the **On Error Resume Next** statement.

2. After each line of code that could generate a run-time error, check the value of **Err.Number**. If **Err.Number** equals 0, no error occurred. If **Err.Number** does not equal 0, an error occurred.

3. Handle the error appropriately.

4. **Err.Number** contains the value of the last error that occurred. If a statement succeeds, it does not change the value of **Err.Number**. Therefore, after you handle an error, use **Err.Clear** to reset the error number.

   The **Clear** method sets the value of **Err.Number** back to zero. You use the **Clear** method primarily when you handle inline errors.

The following sample code handles inline errors. To copy this code for use in your own projects, see "Inline Error Handling" on the accompanying CD-ROM.

```
Sub cmdOpenFile_Click ()
    Dim temperr As Integer
    On Error Resume Next
    Open "c:\AAA.txt" For Input As #1
    Select Case Err.Number
        Case 0:
            'No error. Do nothing.
        Case 53:
            'File not Found
            'Code to prompt for file
        Case 55:
            'File already open
            'Code to correct
        Case Else
            temperr = Err.Number
            On Error GoTo 0
            Err.Raise temperr
    End Select
    Err.Clear      'Reset Err.Number
    Open "c:\BBB.txt" For Input As #2
End Sub
```

Passing Back Errors

Error handling becomes a bit more complicated when your application invokes several procedures. If a called procedure doesn't have an error handler enabled, it passes any error it encounters back to the calling procedure. For example, suppose you have a **ProcessPayroll** procedure that calls a **NewEmployee** function. If an error occurs in **NewEmployee** and **NewEmployee** does not contain an error trap, Visual Basic passes the error back to **ProcessPayroll**. If no error handler is encountered, Visual Basic displays a message box and the application ends.

The **Raise** method causes an error. You use the **Raise** method to pass an error back to a calling procedure, or to test your own error-handling code. The following example code raises the "File not found" error:

```
Err.Raise 53 'File not found error.
```

Error-Handling Options

It can be difficult to debug code that has error handling enabled. Visual Basic may execute error-handling code when you want to enter Break mode and debug the application.

Visual Basic provides options to specify when to break for errors.

▶ **To change how errors are handled**

1. On the **Tools** menu, click **Options**.

2. On the **General** tab, under **Error Trapping**, click the option you want, and then click **OK**.

This table describes the error-handling options that are available under **Error Trapping** on the **General** tab.

Option	Description
Break on All Errors	If you click this option, Visual Basic ignores any **On Error** statements and enters Break mode if any run-time errors occur.
Break in Class Module	Set this option when debugging a COM component. This causes the component to enter Break mode rather than passing the error back to the client application.

table continued on next page

Option	Description
Break on Unhandled Errors	Visual Basic enters Break mode on any error for which you do not supply specific error-handling code.

For more information about choosing an error-trapping option, read the articles "Debugging Class Modules" and "Using Break on Error in Components" in Visual Basic Help.

Compiling an Executable File

Creating an executable file in Visual Basic is a simple process.

▶ **To create an executable file**

1. On the **File** menu, click **Make <Project Name>.exe**.

2. Type the name of the executable file.

3. To add version-specific information:

   a. In the **Make Project** dialog box, click the **Options** button.

   b. On the **Make** tab, type the version numbers and text for the version information, and then click **OK**.

The following illustration shows the **Version Number** options on the **Make** tab.

You can also start Visual Basic from an MS-DOS prompt to create an executable file. This enables code generators to create .exe files without user intervention, and enables developers to start large compile jobs programmatically.

The following example code shows how to compile an application from the command line using the existing settings stored in the project file:

```
vb6 /make projectname
```

Tip To see a list of all the command line options available for vb6.exe, navigate to the Visual Basic folder in an MS-DOS prompt, and use the following syntax:

```
vb6 /?
```

In addition to the executable file, you must provide various DLLs and other files to your users. You should create a Setup program that installs your application onto the user's computer.

The Visual Basic Package and Deployment Wizard makes it easy to create distribution disks or to create a distribution server folder for your application. Users can then run the resulting Setup program on their computers to install and register the appropriate files.

For information about creating a Setup program, see Chapter 9, "Optimizing and Deploying Applications" on page 295.

Overview of the State University Bookstore Application

In the labs for this course, you will create an application for a fictitious State University Bookstore. Through this application, students will be able to buy books for the classes they're enrolled in. They will also be able to look up account information such as their purchase history and balance due. Bookstore staff will use the application to maintain the inventory in the bookstore. Building this application will allow you to use key concepts you learn in each chapter in the course as you complete the corresponding labs.

Purpose of the State University Bookstore Application

Using the State University Bookstore application, students will be able to accomplish the following tasks:

◆ Obtain a list of the books they need to buy based on the classes in which they are enrolled.

◆ Buy a book using their State University credit account.

◆ Generate an account report to see their purchase history and balance due.

The Bookstore staff will use the application to add and remove books from the inventory and generate reports on inventory levels.

Design of the State University Bookstore Application

Throughout the labs in the course, you will build the State University Bookstore application feature by feature. The following illustration shows the components you will build in the State University application.

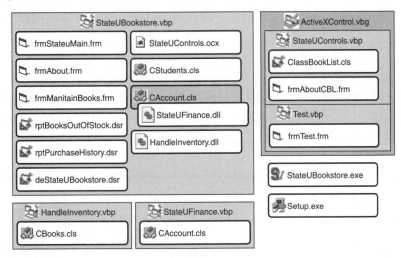

To view the solution application in the final lab of the course, see "Lab 9: Deploying the StateUBookstore Solution" on page 322.

Components	Description
Forms frmStateUMain.frm frmMaintainBooks.frm frmAbout.frm	You will create forms in "Lab 1: Visual Basic Essentials." Students use the StateUMain form to log on, look up their required book lists, and buy books. Bookstore staff uses the MaintainBooks form to maintain the inventory. There is also an About dialog associated with the application.
Data environment deStateUBookstore.dsr	You will use the Visual Basic visual data access tools to create the data environment in "Lab 2: Using Visual Data Access Tools." This data environment connects to the database and provides data to the application's forms.
Reports rptBooksOutOfStock.dsr rptPurchaseHistory.dsr	You will create reports in "Lab 2: Using Visual Data Access Tools." Bookstore staff use the BooksOutOfStock report to plan the bookstore's stocking schedule. Students use the PurchaseHistory report to view their purchase history and balance due.
ActiveX control StateUControls.ocx	You will create an ActiveX control in "Lab 4.1: Building an ActiveX Control." You will use this control in the State University Bookstore application in "Lab 4.2: Data-Binding an ActiveX Control." The StateUControls control is used to display the list of books a student needs to buy, based on the classes that the student is enrolled in.
Class modules CStudents.cls CAccount.cls CBooks.cls	You will create and use classes in "Lab 3: Using Class Modules," "Lab 5: Using ActiveX Data Objects," and "Lab 7: Using COM Components." The CStudents class validates user log in. The CAccount class handles the financial transaction for buying a book. The CBooks class handles the inventory maintenance transaction associated with buying a book.

table continued on next page

Components	Description
COM components StateUFinance.dll HandleInventory.dll	You will create a COM component named StateUFinance.dll from the CAccount class in "Lab 8: Building COM Components." You will use the HandleInventory component that is provided for you in "Lab 7: Using COM Components."
Setup program StateUBookstore.cab Setup.exe	You will create a .cab file and a setup program in "Lab 9: Deploying the StateUBookstore Solution." The setup program extracts all the pieces of the application from the .cab file, and installs the application on the user's computer.

Lab 1: Visual Basic Essentials

In this lab, you will create the user interface for a Visual Basic application. You will create forms and add a menu to a form. You will then compile the application and run it.

To see the demonstration "Lab 1 Solution," see the accompanying CD-ROM.

Estimated time to complete this lab: **45 minutes**

To complete the exercises in this lab, you must have the required software. For detailed information about the labs and setup for the labs, see "Labs" in "About This Course."

Objectives

After completing this lab, you will be able to:

◆ Create forms and add controls to forms.

◆ Add a menu to a form.

◆ Write code in event procedures.

◆ Compile an executable application.

Prerequisites

There are no prerequisites for this lab.

Exercises

The following exercises provide practice working with the concepts and techniques covered in this chapter:

♦ Exercise 1: Creating Forms and Menus

   In this exercise, you will begin to create the user interface for the State University Bookstore application. You will create a main form and add menus to it. You will also create an About form.

♦ Exercise 2: Customizing the User Interface

   In this exercise, you will add code to resize the main form and enable and disable menu items when a student logs on to the application. You will also disable the **Student ID** text box and the **Login** button after a student has logged on, to prevent logging on twice.

♦ Exercise 3: Making an Executable

   In this exercise, you will compile your project into an executable application, and then test the application.

Exercise 1: Creating Forms and Menus

State University has a bookstore where students can purchase books required by the classes they are enrolled in. The State University Bookstore application provides a way for students to find out what books they need to buy, and to purchase them on credit.

In this exercise, you will begin to create the user interface for the State University Bookstore application. You will create a main form and add menus to it. You will also create an About form.

▶ **Create the main form**

1. Start a new Visual Basic Standard EXE project and name it **StateUBookstore**.

2. Rename the default Form1 to **frmStateUMain**.

3. Set the **Caption** property of the form to **State University Bookstore**.

4. Set the **Icon** property of the form to the suicon.ico file located in the *<install folder>*\Labs\Lab01 folder.

5. Add controls to the form, as shown in the following illustration. Name the text box **txtStudentID**. Name the **Login** command button **cmdLogin**, and name the **Buy Book** button **cmdBuyBook**.

Note The total size of the form will accommodate a control you will build in Lab 4. In the next exercise, you will add code to change the form size dynamically.

For more information about adding controls to a form, see "Using Controls" on page 10 in this chapter.

6. Using the Visual Basic Menu Editor, add menus to the form, as shown in the following illustration.

Use the following table to name the menu items:

Caption	Name
File	mnuFile
Exit	mnuExit
Account	mnuAccount

table continued on next page

Caption	Name
Buy Book	mnuBuyBook
Get Purchase History	mnuGetPurchaseHistory
Bookstore	mnuBookstore
Update Inventory	mnuUpdateInventory
Out-of-Stock Report	mnuOutOfStockReport
Refresh	mnuRefresh
Help	mnuHelp
About	mnuAbout

For more information about adding a menu to a form, see "Adding a Menu" on page 19 in this chapter.

▶ **Create the About form**

1. Add a new About form to the project using the About Dialog form template.

2. The picture in the upper-left corner is a **PictureBox** control. Add a second **PictureBox** control to the form. You can add the .gif files located in the *<install folder>*\Labs\Lab01 folder to set the **Picture** property of the **PictureBox** controls on the About form.

▶ **Add code for menu items on frmStateUMain**

1. In the **Click** event for the **Exit** menu item, unload the form.

2. In the **Click** event for the **About** menu item, show the About box as a modal form.

   For information about modal forms, read the article "Show Method" in Visual Basic Help.

   To see an example of how your code should look, see Lab Hint 1.1 in Appendix B.

3. Save the project in the *<install folder>*\Labs\StateULabSolution folder (you will need to create this folder).

▶ **Test the application**

1. Run the State University Bookstore application.

2. Test the **About** and **Exit** menu items.

Exercise 2: Customizing the User Interface

Some students at State University are also employees of the State University Bookstore. These students need to have access to special features of the bookstore application, such as the ability to update the inventory of books.

In this exercise, you will add code to resize the main form and enable and disable menu items when a student logs on to the application. You will also disable the **Student ID** text box and the **Login** button after a student has logged on, to prevent logging on twice.

▶ **Add validation to the main form**

1. Initially disable the **Login** button on frmStateUMain.

2. As a student enters a student ID, enable the **Login** button if the number is numeric, and disable the **Login** button if the student ID is not numeric.

   To see an example of the completed code, see Lab Hint 1.2 in Appendix B.

3. Size the form so that only the **Student ID** text box and **Login** button are initially visible (Height = 1470, Width = 7350).

4. Add code to the **Click** event procedure of the **Login** button that resizes the form to show the **Buy** button (Height = 5350, Width = 7350).

To see an example of the completed code, see Lab Hint 1.3 in Appendix B.

5. Save the project.

▶ **Enable menu items for bookstore employees**

1. Make the menu items on the **Bookstore** and **Account** menus initially disabled.

2. Add code to the **Click** event procedure of the **Login** button that makes the menu items on the **Account** menu enabled for all students.

3. Add code to the **Click** event procedure of the **Login** button that makes the items on the **Bookstore** menu enabled if the student ID is between 1 and 5.

   In Lab 3, you will change the code to see if the entered student ID is a bookstore employee or not.

4. Add code to the **Click** event procedure of the **Login** button that disables the **Student ID** text box and the **Login** command button.

   To see an example of the completed code, see Lab Hint 1.4 in Appendix B.

5. Save your work.

▶ **Test the application**

1. Run the StateUBookstore application.

2. Test the enabling and disabling of the **Login** button.

3. Test the resizing of form **frmStateUMain** when you click the **Login** button.

4. Log on as a bookstore employee (Student IDs from 1 to 5) and as a non-bookstore employee and test the enabling and disabling of the **Account** and **Bookstore** menus.

Exercise 3: Making an Executable

In this exercise, you will compile your project into an executable application, and then test the application.

▶ **Create an executable file**

1. On the **File** menu, click **Make StateUBookstore.exe**.

2. Name the executable **StateUBookstore.exe**, and save it in the *<install folder>*\Labs\StateULabSolution folder.

3. To compile the application, click **OK**.

▶ **Test the executable file**

1. Using Windows Explorer, navigate to the *<install folder>*\Labs\StateULabSolution folder.

2. Run StateUBookstore.exe.

Self-Check Questions

To see the answers to the Self-Check Questions, see Appendix A.

1. **You want to display the message "This is a text box" in a text box named txtMyBox by setting the value of the Text property with the following code:**

```
txtMyBox.Text = "This is a text box"
```

By mistake, you enter the following code:

```
txtMyBox = "This is a text box"
```

What is the result?

A. "This is a text box" is stored in a string variable named txtMyBox.

B. The **Text** property of txtMyBox is set to "This is a text box".

C. The **Name** property of txtMyBox is set to "This is a text box".

D. The **DataField** property of txtMyBox is set to "This is a text box".

2. **When creating a menu, how do you create a menu separation bar?**

A. In the **Caption** text box, enter an ampersand (&).

B. Select the **Menu Separator** check box.

C. In the **Caption** text box, enter a hyphen (-).

D. In the **Caption** text box, enter the text "Separator".

3. **Which line of code will enable an error trap and send code execution to an error handler to handle any run-time errors?**

A. On Error HandleErrors

B. On Error Goto 0

C. On Error Resume Next

D. On Error Goto RunTimeErrorHandler

4. What is the purpose of the .vbg file in a Visual Basic project?

A. The .vbg file contains information about the forms and modules in the current project.

B. The .vbg file contains information about the most recent projects you've worked on.

C. The .vbg file contains information about the projects in the current group.

D. The .vbg file contains a list of the most recent files you've opened.

5. Which Visual Basic debugging tool is used to monitor a particular variable or expression?

A. Watch window

B. Breakpoint

C. Immediate window

D. Call Stack dialog box

6. Why would you want to enter Break mode?

A. You want to step through a section of code line by line.

B. You want to interrogate all of the properties of an object at run time.

C. You want to change the value of a variable to test different scenarios.

D. All of the above.

7. How do you add a pre-built ActiveX control to the Toolbox?

A. On the **Project** menu, click **Add User Control**. In the **Add User Control** dialog, select the control to include, and then click **OK**.

B. Right click the Toolbox, and then click **Add Tab**.

C. On the **Project** menu, click **Components**. In the Components dialog, select the control to include, and then click **OK**.

D. On the **Project** menu, click **References**. In the References dialog, select the control to include, and then click **OK**.

Chapter 2:
Using Visual Data Access Tools

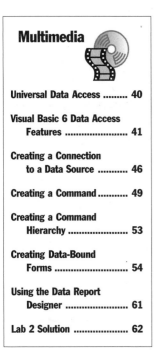

Multimedia

In this chapter, you will learn how to use the visual data access tools that come with Microsoft Visual Basic 6 to create applications that connect to a database. You will also learn how to use the ADO Data control to create an application that reads information from a database, and how to use the Data Report designer to create a report.

For more information about ActiveX Data Objects (ADO) and using code to access data, see Chapter 5, "Using ActiveX Data Objects" on page 163 and Chapter 6, "Advanced Data Access Issues" on page 215.

Objectives

After completing this chapter, you will be able to:

◆ Describe the visual data access tools that come with Visual Basic.

◆ Use the visual data access tools to create a connection to a data source and access data from the connection in an application.

◆ View the structure of a database using the Data Environment designer and the Data View window.

◆ Create database queries using the Query Builder.

◆ Create data-bound forms using the Data Environment designer, the Data Form Wizard, and the ADO Data control.

◆ Create a report using the Data Report designer.

Universal Data Access

In this section, you will learn about the Microsoft strategy for Universal Data Access and the visual data access tools that make it easy for Visual Basic programmers to create data access applications.

To see the expert point-of-view "Universal Data Access," see the accompanying CD-ROM.

Understanding OLE DB

OLE DB is Microsoft's strategic, system-level programming interface to access data across an organization. Whereas Open Database Connectivity (ODBC) is designed to allow access to relational data, OLE DB is an open standard designed to allow access to all kinds of data. Conceptually, OLE DB has three types of components: data providers, data consumers, and service components. The following illustration shows an overview of the OLE DB architecture.

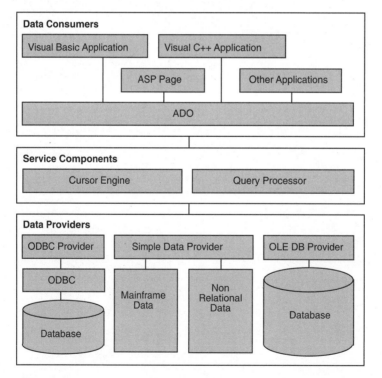

Data Providers

Data providers are applications, such as Microsoft SQL Server or Exchange, or operating system components, such as a file system, that have data that other applications may need to access. These data providers expose OLE DB interfaces that service components or data consumers can access directly. There is also an OLE DB provider for ODBC. This provider makes any ODBC data available to OLE DB data consumers.

Data Consumers

Data consumers are applications that use the data exposed by data providers. ADO is the programmatic interface for using OLE DB data. Any application that uses ADO is an OLE DB data consumer.

Service Components

Service components are components of OLE DB that process and transport data. These components include query processors and cursor engines. Architecturally, OLE DB is separated into components so data providers do not need to have the innate ability to provide data in a way that ADO can understand. These service components give ADO the ability to consume OLE DB data from providers that don't inherently offer handling of result sets or interpretation of SQL queries.

Introduction to Visual Data Access Tools

Visual Basic 6 includes the Data Environment designer and the integrated Visual Database Tools to make it easier for you to create data access applications. To see the expert point-of-view "Visual Basic 6 Data Access Features," see the accompanying CD-ROM.

Data Environment Designer

The Data Environment designer is a design-time tool that lets you create objects that access data. You use the Data Environment designer to:

◆ Add a Data Environment to your project.

◆ Add connections to databases.

◆ Add commands to retrieve and manipulate data.

Data View Window

You use the Data View window to:

◆ List and browse any data source.

◆ View and modify (if permitted) the structure of a database.

Query Builder

You use the Query Builder to create queries that retrieve specific sets of data from a database.

Data Form Wizard

You use the Data Form Wizard to generate Visual Basic forms that display and manage information from database tables and queries.

Data Report Designer

You use the Data Report Designer to create printable reports from a recordset.

Accessing Data from Visual Basic

Although applications that use Data Access Objects (DAO) and Remote Data Objects (RDO) will run correctly in Visual Basic 6, ADO is the data-access method Microsoft recommends for new applications.

Advantages of Using ADO

ADO is an evolution of the RDO and DAO architectures. ADO combines the best features of RDO and DAO, and replaces them with one robust, easy-to-use interface. RDO and DAO limited you to using ODBC and Jet compliant data providers. ADO, however, provides quick, high-performance access to all of the types of data and information that are available through OLE DB, while maintaining a low overhead in terms of memory and disk space.

ADO Overview

For simple applications, you can use the Data Environment designer to add ADO objects to your project at design time. This technique requires little or no code to interact with a data source. In more sophisticated applications, you can add code to work with ADO objects and their properties, methods, and events. For more information about adding ADO code to your applications, see Chapter 5, "Using ActiveX Data Objects" on page 163.

When you work with ADO programmatically, you typically use the following three ADO objects:

◆ Connection

An ADO **Connection** object is used to create a connection to a data source.

◆ Command

An ADO **Command** object is used to return data from a connection. **Command** objects can also manipulate data in a data source or call a SQL Server stored procedure.

◆ Recordset

An ADO **Recordset** object is used to store the result set of a query on the data source.

OLE DB Data Providers

Applications using ADO consume OLE DB data by using the appropriate data provider. For example, you use the OLE DB provider for SQL Server to access data in a SQL Server database. Because there is an OLE DB provider for ODBC, you can write ADO code to access data in your existing ODBC data sources that do not have a native OLE DB provider.

For more information about specifying an OLE DB data provider, see "Setting Connection Properties" on page 46 in this chapter.

 To find the most up-to-date information about ADO and OLE DB, go to the Microsoft Universal Data Access Web site at http://msdn.microsoft.com/data/.

Connecting to a Data Source

In this section, you will learn how to use the Data Environment designer to add a connection to a data source. You will also learn how to use the Data View window to view the structure of a database.

Using the Data Environment Designer

The Data Environment designer is an object you can add to your Visual Basic project that provides an interactive, design-time environment for creating objects that access data.

Adding Connections and Commands

When you create a Data Environment, you add **Connection** and **Command** objects, and set property values for them. The following illustration shows an example of a project that contains a Data Environment with a connection and several commands.

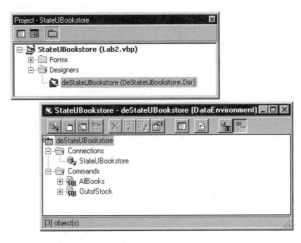

Organizing Data

You can use the Data Environment designer to relate multiple **Command** objects. This relation is called a command hierarchy. Within a hierarchy, you can create aggregate fields whose values are automatically calculated based on the hierarchy. For more information about relating commands, see "Organizing Data" on page 51 in this chapter.

Presenting Data

You can drag and drop objects from the Data Environment to create data-bound forms and reports quickly. For more information about data-bound forms and reports, see "Presenting Data" on page 54 in this chapter.

Data Environment Events

In the code module associated with a Data Environment, you can add code to events generated by the Data Environment or by **Connection** objects and **Command** objects within a Data Environment. For the Data Environment itself, you can write code to its **Initialize** and **Terminate** events. The events generated by connections and commands in a Data Environment are ADO events. For more information about ADO events, see "Using Connection Object Events" on page 173 in Chapter 5, "Using ActiveX Data Objects."

Creating a Connection

When you add a Data Environment to your project, a **Connection** object called Connection1 is included by default. You can also create new connections at any time by choosing **Add Connection** from the Data Environment designer toolbar. For more information about connections, see "Setting Connection Properties" on page 46 in this chapter.

▶ **To create a new Data Environment**

1. If the **Add Data Environment** command is not present on the **Project** menu, then on the **Project** menu, click **Components**.

 Tip If you have several ActiveX designers loaded into your project, you may find the **Add Data Environment** menu item on the **More ActiveX Designers** submenu of the Visual Basic **Project** menu.

2. In the **Components** dialog box, click the **Designers** tab and select the **Data Environment** check box.

3. On the **Project** menu, click **Add Data Environment**.

4. Use the Properties window to set the **Name** property of the Data Environment to something appropriate for your application.

   You will use this name to refer to the Data Environment programmatically.

For more information about opening and closing connections programmatically, read the article "Programmatically Accessing Objects in Your Data Environment Designer" in Visual Basic Help.

Setting Connection Properties

When you create a connection in the Data Environment, you need to specify details about the data source to which you are connecting. The details about this connection are collectively referred to as the data link properties.

Use the **Data Link Properties** dialog box to select the data provider and set the properties for a connection. To display the **Data Link Properties** dialog box, in the Data Environment window, right-click a connection name, and then click **Properties**.

Use the **Provider** tab of the **Data Link Properties** dialog box to select the OLE DB provider you want to use to connect to a data source. Use the **Connection** tab to provide the necessary connection information. The following illustration shows the **Connection** tab in the **Data Link Properties** dialog box for the Microsoft OLE DB provider for SQL Server.

Connection properties vary depending on the data provider you select.

To see the demonstration "Creating a Connection to a Data Source," see the accompanying CD-ROM.

Practice: Connecting to a Data Source

In this practice exercise, you will create a new Visual Basic project and add a Data Environment to it. You will then create an OLE DB connection to the Northwind database.

▶ **Add a Data Environment to a Visual Basic project**

1. Open Visual Basic and create a Standard EXE project named **Practice**.

2. On the **Project** menu, click **Add Data Environment**.

3. In the Data Environment window, right-click **Connection1** and choose **Properties**.

4. On the **Provider** tab of the **Data Link Properties** dialog box, select the Microsoft Jet 3.51 OLE DB Provider from the provider list, and then click **Next**.

5. On the **Connection** tab of the **Data Link Properties** dialog box,

   a. In the **Select or enter a database name** text box, select or type the path *<install location>*\Practices\Chapter02\Connecting to a Data Source\Nwind.mdb.

   b. Accept the default information to log on to the database.

   c. Click the **Test Connection** button to verify the connection to the data source and click **OK**.

6. Click **OK** to save the data link properties.

7. Use the Properties window to change the name of the Data Environment to **dePractice** and to change the name of the connection to **Northwind**.

Using the Data View Window

Once you have added a connection to a data source to a Data Environment in your project, you can use the Data View window to examine database structure. The following illustration shows the structure of the StateUBookstore database in the Data View window.

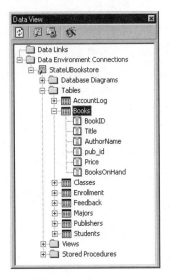

▶ **To view the structure of a database**

1. On the Visual Basic **View** menu, click **Data View Window,** or use the **Data View Window** button on the Visual Basic toolbar.

2. Click to expand the parts of the database structure you want to view.

Tip Some data sources allow you to modify the structure of existing items in a database and create new database items using the Data View window. SQL Server allows modifications; the Microsoft Jet database engine does not.

You can also add a data link to the Data View window to examine the structure of a database that is not associated with a Data Environment currently in your project. To do so, use the **Add a New Data Link** button on the Data View window toolbar.

Getting Data from a Connection

In this section, you will learn how to create commands that perform an action against a database. For example, you will create and set properties of commands that return records. You will also learn how to access the recordset that contains the results of a command.

Creating a Command

You can use a **Command** object to define what data to retrieve from a connection. The command can be based on a table, view, stored procedure, or SQL statement. This chapter focuses on commands that are based upon tables or SQL statements. In Chapter 6, "Advanced Data Access Issues," you will learn how to create commands that use SQL stored procedures.

To see the demonstration "Creating a Command," see the accompanying CD-ROM.

▶ **To add a command**

 ◆ Right-click a connection in the Data Environment window and select **Add Command**.

▶ **To set the properties of a command**

1. In the Data Environment window, right-click the command that you just added, and choose **Properties**.

2. On the **General** tab in the **Command Properties** dialog box,

    a. Type a meaningful name for your command into the **Command Name** text box.

    b. From the **Connection** list box, choose the **Connection** object on which you want to base the command.

    c. In the **Source of Data** group box, click **SQL Statement**, and then click the **SQL Builder** button to open the Query Builder. Visually create a query by dragging and dropping objects from the Data View window to the Query Builder Design window and choose the fields you want returned in the recordset. If you want to create a query that retrieves information from multiple tables, you can drag a field from one table to the related field in another table to create a join. The Query Builder will then generate a SQL statement for use by the **Command** object.

d. Right-click anywhere in the Query Builder Design window and select **Run** to see the results of the command.

The following illustration shows the Query Builder Design window.

For more information about additional command properties, see Chapter 5, "Using ActiveX Data Objects" on page 163.

Accessing the Results of a Command

You can access the records returned by a **Command** object in code by using an ADO **Recordset** object, available through the Data Environment. To access the **Recordset** object for a particular command, use the name of the **Command** object preceded by "rs". The following example code shows how to move to the next record in a recordset returned from a command called **AllBooks** in a Data Environment called **deStateUBookstore**:

```
deStateUBookstore.rsAllBooks.MoveNext
```

Note The **Command** object must be open in order to use the recordset. If the command is bound to a field on a form, it will automatically be opened and available. Otherwise, you'll need to declare an instance of the Data Environment and then execute the appropriate method of the **Command** object, as shown in the previous example code.

For more information about using objects in the Data Environment programmatically, read the article "Programmatically Accessing Objects in Your Data Environment Designer" in Visual Basic Help.

For more information about programmatic access to data objects, see Chapter 5, "Using ActiveX Data Objects" on page 163.

Organizing Data

In this section, you will learn how to group and relate **Command** objects to create rich displays of data using the Microsoft Hierarchical FlexGrid control. You will also learn how to use aggregates to perform an operation, such as count or average, on your data.

Grouping Records

The SQL language provides syntax for grouping similar records. Alternatively, you can use the **Command Properties** dialog box in the Data Environment designer to group records.

Note Grouping only makes sense if there are multiple records in the set with a like value.

▶ **To group records within a Command**

1. In the Data Environment window, right-click the command for which you want to group records and select **Properties**.

2. Select the **Grouping** tab of the **Command Properties** dialog box.

3. Click the **Group Command Object** check box, and choose the fields you want to use for grouping.

The following illustration shows the **Properties** dialog box for the **AllBooks** command. This command will group records on the **pub_id** field.

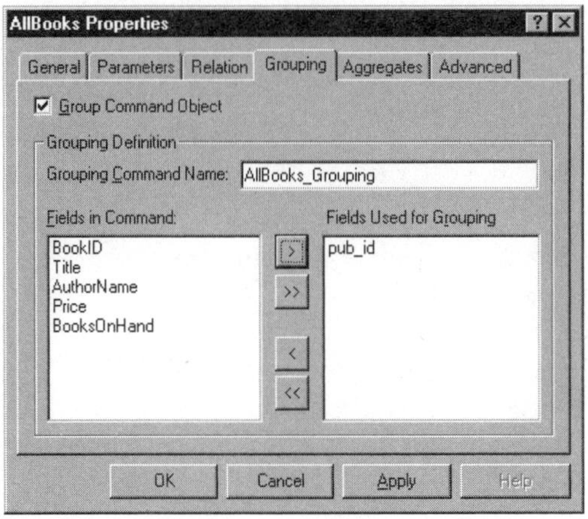

Relating Commands

You can relate several commands to create a hierarchical relationship of data. For example, you can relate commands to create a hierarchical display of all publishers and the books produced by each publisher.

To relate commands, you specify a common field in each recordset. For example, you can relate publishers and books based on the field pub_id.

The following illustration shows a hierarchy displayed in the Microsoft Hierarchical FlexGrid control.

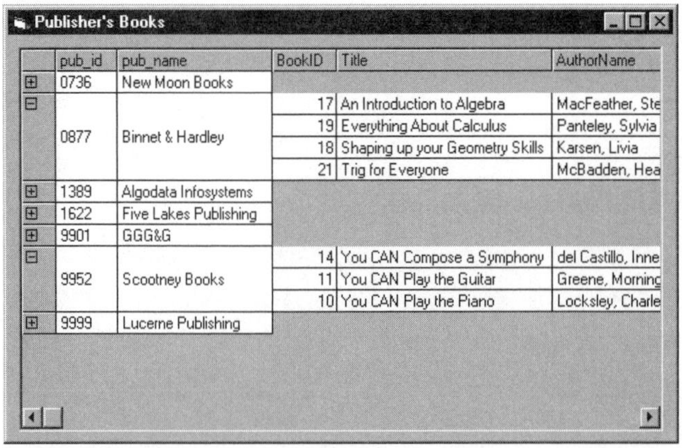

After you relate commands, they form a command hierarchy. The command hierarchy is based upon a parent-child, or one-to-many, relationship in the data. For example, each publisher can publish many books.

To display the data returned by a command hierarchy you can use the Microsoft Hierarchical FlexGrid control.

▶ **To relate two command objects**

1. In the Data Environment window, right-click the child command (the "many" side of the one-to-many relationship) and select **Properties**.

2. On the **Relation** tab of the **Command Properties** dialog box,

    a. Check the **Relate to a Parent Command Object** check box.

    b. Enter the name of the related parent command (the "one" side of the one-to-many relationship) in the **Parent Command** box.

    c. Make sure that the correct parent field and child field are selected in their respective drop down boxes, and click **Add**.

3. Click **OK** in the **Properties** dialog box.

You will see the commands as related in the Data Environment.

The hierarchy created by relating two commands is created by using the SHAPE syntax. To view the SQL syntax, right-click the parent in the command hierarchy and click **Hierarchy Info**.

To see the demonstration "Creating a Command Hierarchy," see the accompanying CD-ROM.

Using Aggregates

You can use aggregates to display data that is calculated from a recordset. For example, if you want to find out how many students are in each class, you can use the aggregate **Count** function to calculate the number of students in each class and display the count in a separate field for each class.

To use aggregate functions, on the **Aggregates** tab in the **Command Properties** dialog box specify the type of calculation you want performed. Choices include calculations such as sum, count, and average. Visual Basic will generate the SQL statement to produce the results.

The following illustration shows the **Aggregates** tab of the **Command Properties** dialog box.

The aggregate in the previous illustration calculates the grand total of the Amount fields for the AccountLog table in the StateUBookstore database.

Presenting Data

In this section, you will learn how to use techniques available in Visual Basic to present data to users.

Creating Bound Forms

To present data from a database to your users, add data-bound controls to a form and bind them to fields in a data source. You can create data-bound forms manually, or you can drag and drop items from a Data Environment onto a form.

To see the demonstration "Creating Data-Bound Forms," see the accompanying CD-ROM.

Binding Controls Manually

You can manually bind a single control to a single field from a command in a Data Environment by setting the following field properties:

Property	Set to...
DataSource	Data Environment name
DataMember	Command name
DataField	Name of the field in the command

Using Drag and Drop to Bind Controls

You can also simply drag a field from a command in the Data Environment window onto a form. Visual Basic will add a control to the form and set the properties correctly. If you drag an entire command onto a form, Visual Basic will add controls to the form for all the columns of the resulting recordset. The following illustration shows an example of a form created by dragging an entire command onto a form.

Adding Navigation Buttons

The form will display one record at a time. To allow users to navigate back and forth in a Recordset, you can add navigation buttons to your form that call the **MoveNext** and **MovePrevious** methods of the Data Environment's recordset. See the following table for example code to use in the **Click** events of the two command buttons.

Button Name	Click Event Name	Navigation Code
cmdPrevious	cmdPrevious_Click	deBookStore.rsBookList.MovePrevious
cmdNext	cmdNext_Click	deBookStore.rsBookList.MoveNext

Using a Data Grid

If you want to display all records within a grid, rather than using navigation buttons, right-click the fields or command in the Data Environment and drag it onto the form. In this case, Visual Basic will add a Data Grid to display the data rather than individual fields. The user can use the grid to scroll through the recordset. The following illustration shows using the Data Grid to display information from the recordset.

Field Mapping

For fields in a data source that require special treatment, map each field to the appropriate type of control. For example, you can map a date field to a calendar control. Map the fields before you drag and drop the fields from the Data Environment onto your form.

▶ **To map a field to a control**

1. In the Data Environment window, expand a command to view the fields, then right-click the field you want to map to a special control and select **Properties**.

2. From the **Control** list, choose the appropriate control.

3. Optionally, in the **Caption** text box, you can enter a customized caption for the label that will appear next to the control on your form.

Using the ADO Data Control

It is possible to upgrade an application that uses forms containing the existing Visual Basic Data control to an application that uses a native OLE DB data connection. Instead of creating a new project using the Data Environment designer and rewriting your application, you can simply upgrade your application's forms to use the Microsoft ADO Data control.

The ADO Data control gives developers the ease of building data-bound forms that include navigation with the power and control of using ADO. The ADO Data control uses Microsoft ActiveX Data Objects (ADO) to quickly create connections between data-bound controls and a data source.

You can also use the ActiveX Data Objects directly in your applications, but the ADO Data control has the advantage of being a graphic control (with **Back** and **Forward** buttons) and an easy-to-use interface that enables you to create database applications with a minimum of code. For more information about accessing data programmatically, see Chapter 5, "Using ActiveX Data Objects" on page 163.

You add an ADO Data control to the toolbox and your form like any other ActiveX control. After you have added an ADO Data control to a form, you must set the data source and the **RecordSource** property for the ADO Data control.

Setting the Data Source

You can use the **Custom Property** page of the ADO Data control to set up the OLE DB data source. Right-click the ADO Data control on your form and select **ADODC Properties**. On the **General** tab of the **Property Pages** dialog box, in the **Source of Connection** group box, select **Use Connection String**, and then click **Build**. Use the **Provider** tab of the **Data Link Properties** dialog box to select the OLE DB provider you want to use to connect to a data source. Use the **Connection** tab to provide the necessary connection information.

Setting the RecordSource Property of the ADO Data Control

Before you can bind other controls to the ADO Data control, you must set its **RecordSource** property to the appropriate SQL query. For example, if you have a connection to a data source that contains a Books table, you can set the value of the **RecordSource** property to the following SQL statement:

```
SELECT * FROM Books
```

Binding Other Controls to the ADO Data Control

The last step is to bind other controls to the ADO Data control. You bind a control to the ADO Data control in the same way you bind a control to any other data source. Set the **DataSource** property for the control that you want to bind to the ADO Data control, and set the **DataField** property to the appropriate value.

Note that not all controls are bindable. For a list of which controls can be bound to a data control, read the article "Data Bound ActiveX Controls" in Visual Basic Help.

For more information about the ADO Data control, read the article "Using the ADO Data Control" in Visual Basic Help.

Using Format Objects

You can use Format objects to format and unformat data passed between a database and a bound control. You can also use the traditional **Format** function to format your data in code, but Format objects offer the following advantages:

◆ You can set formats either through code or at design time. In either case, when you use Format objects you'll write less code.

◆ Format objects give you additional formatting types, such as Boolean, Binary, Object, Picture, and Checkbox, that are not supported by the **Format** function.

◆ Format objects have **Format** and **Unformat** events that allow closer control over data formatting.

Setting Formats at Design Time

After you have created a form with bound controls, you can designate special formatting for the data displayed by a control. Set the **DataFormat** property of the data-bound control to the appropriate format type. The following illustration shows the **Format** property page.

Property Pages

Format

Format Item:

Sample
$12,345.67

Format Type:

General
Number
Currency
Date
Time
Percentage
Scientific
Boolean
Checkbox
Picture
Object
Bytes
Custom

Decimal places: 2

Symbol:
$

Negative numbers:
-123.45
(123.45)

Format$: '$'#,##0.00

OK   Cancel   Apply   Help

Setting Formats at Run Time

To create and use Format objects in your code, first add a reference to the Microsoft Data Formatting Object Library to your project. You can then create a **StdDataFormat** object and use it in your code.

If you declare a **StdDataFormat** object using the **WithEvents** keyword, you can write code to its **Format** and **UnFormat** events. The following illustration shows an overview of data format events.

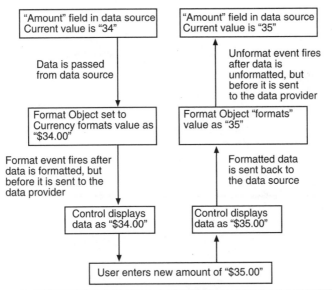

"Amount" field in data source
Current value is "34"

"Amount" field in data source
Current value is "35"

Data is passed
from data source

Unformat event fires
after data is
unformatted, but
before it is sent
to the data provider

Format Object set to
Currency formats value as
"$34.00"

Format Object "formats"
value as "35"

Format event fires after
data is formatted, but
before it is sent to the
data provider

Formatted data
is sent back to
the data source

Control displays
data as "$34.00"

Control displays
data as "$35.00"

User enters new amount of "$35.00"

For more information about Format objects, read the article "Format Objects" in Visual Basic Help.

Using the Data Form Wizard

The Data Form Wizard is a Visual Basic Add-In that automatically generates Visual Basic forms that contain individual bound controls and procedures that manage information derived from database tables and queries. You can use the Data Form Wizard to create either single-query forms to manage the data from a single table or simple query, or a Master/Detail form that is based on hierarchical data.

Use the Data Form Wizard to:

- ◆ Rapidly build forms with controls bound to a data source.

- ◆ Create single record or Master/Detail forms.

- ◆ Rapidly create prototype forms that access data.

The Data Form Wizard can build a form using the ADO Data control, or using ADO code exclusively.

▶ **To use the Data Form Wizard to add a data form to your project**

1. Use the Add-In Manager to add the **DataFormWizard6.Wizard** object to your project.

2. From the **Add-In** menu, click **Data Form Wizard** and respond appropriately to each of the Wizard's steps.

Building Reports with the Data Report Designer

The Microsoft Data Report designer is a versatile data report generator that features the ability to create banded reports. Used in conjunction with a data source, such as a Data Environment, you can create reports from several different tables. In addition to creating printable reports, you can also export the report to a variety of formats, including HTML.

Use the Data Report designer to:

- ◆ Print reports that are richly formatted.

- ◆ Create reports that visually show hierarchies of data.

- ◆ Export hierarchical data to HTML format for instant distribution on the Internet.

To see the demonstration "Using the Data Report Designer," see the accompanying CD-ROM.

Creating the Data Report

Once you have a Data Environment with a command that returns a recordset in your project, you can create a Data Report to display that command's data.

▶ **To create a simple data report**

1. If the Data Report designer is not present in your project, on the **Project** menu, click **Components,** and then in the **Components** dialog box, click the **Designers** tab and select the **Data Report** check box.

2. On the **Project** menu, click **Add Data Report.**

3. Add fields to the report by clicking and dragging from a command in the Data Environment window and dropping the items onto the Data Report.

4. Set the data-binding properties for the report object:

   a. Set the **DataSource** property to the Data Environment that contains the connection to the data source you want to use for the report.

   b. Set the **DataMember** property to the command that returns the recordset with the information the report will display.

Displaying the Data Report as the Startup Object

There are two ways to display the report:

◆ Set the Data Report as the Startup Object

This method causes the report to be displayed automatically when a user runs the application.

◆ Write code to show the Data Report

Use this method when you want more control over when the report is displayed.

▶ **To set the data report as the Startup Object**

1. On the **Project** menu, click *Project Name* **Properties.**

2. In the **Startup Object** box, select the name of the Data Report you wish to use.

3. Run the project.

▶ To write code to show the Data Report

- ◆ Invoke the **Show** method of the report object. The following example code displays the rptOrders report when the user clicks the **Show Report** command button.

```
Sub cmdShowReport()
    rptOrders.Show
End Sub
```

For more information about the Data Report designer, read the article "Creating a Simple Data Report" in Visual Basic Help.

Lab 2: Using Visual Data Access Tools

In this lab, you will add a data connection to the State University Bookstore project. You will create a Data Environment and use it to retrieve records from a database. You will then create a data-bound form.

To see the demonstration "Lab 2 Solution," see the accompanying CD-ROM.

Note The lab solution code throughout this course uses a SQL Server named MSERIES1. To run the lab solution code with a different server name, replace all occurrences of MSERIES1 with the name of your SQL Server.

Estimated time to complete this lab: **60 minutes**

To complete the exercises in this lab, you must have the required software. For detailed information about the labs and setup for the labs, see "Labs" in "About This Course."

Objectives

After completing this lab, you will be able to:

- ◆ Run the labs from a local SQL Server database on your computer.
- ◆ Add a Data Environment to a project.
- ◆ Connect to a data source using a **Connection** object.
- ◆ Use a **Command** object to retrieve records from a data source.
- ◆ Create a data-bound form.

Prerequisites

Before working on this lab, you should be familiar with the following:

◆ The design and use of a relational database.

Exercises

The following exercises provide practice working with the concepts and techniques covered in this chapter:

◆ Exercise 1: Creating the StateUBookstore Database

In this exercise, you will set up the State University Bookstore database using Microsoft SQL Server.

◆ Exercise 2: Connecting to a Data Source

In this exercise, you will connect to a database.

◆ Exercise 3: Creating a Command

In this exercise, you will create a query that looks up all of the books in the State University Bookstore's inventory.

◆ Exercise 4: Creating a Data-Bound Form

In this exercise, you will create a data-bound form. This form will be bound to the Books table in the StateUBookstore database.

◆ Exercise 5 (Optional): Creating a Report

In this exercise, you will add two reports to the StateUBookstore project.

Exercise 1:
Creating the StateUBookstore Database

In this exercise, you will set up the State University Bookstore database using Microsoft SQL Server.

Note The labs for this course were designed to use a Microsoft SQL Server database. If you do not have Microsoft SQL Server, you can use StateUBookstore.mdb, an Access 97 database located in *<install folder>*\Labs\Lab02\StateUBookstore Database, to complete most of the lab exercises. If you use the Access database, you may have to adjust some steps and code accordingly.

▶ Start the SQL Server service

1. On your SQL Server computer, run the SQL Service Manager from the Microsoft SQL Server 6.5 folder on the **Start** menu.

2. In the Services list, select **MSSQLServer**.

3. Double-click **Start/Continue** to start the service, and then close the SQL Service Manager.

▶ Register your SQL Server if necessary

1. Run the SQL Enterprise Manager from the Microsoft SQL Server 6.5 folder on the **Start** menu.

2. If your SQL Server is listed in the SQL Enterprise Manager, open it by clicking the plus sign (**+**) next to the server name.

   – or –

   If your SQL Server is not listed in the SQL Enterprise Manager, you will need to register your server.

   a. On the **Server** menu, click **Register Server**.

   b. In the **Server** box, enter your server name.

   c. Under **Login Information**, enter the login ID **sa** and a blank password.

   d. Click **Register**, and then click **Close**.

▶ Create the State University Bookstore database device

1. In the SQL Enterprise Manager, right-click the Database Devices folder, and then click **New Device**.

2. Name the new device **StateUBookstore**.

3. In the **Size (MB)** box, type **15**.

4. Click **Create Now** to create the StateUBookstore database device.

▶ Create the State University Bookstore database

1. In the SQL Enterprise Manager, right-click the Databases folder, and then click **New Database**.

2. Name the new database **StateUBookstore**.

3. In the **Data Device** list, select the StateUBookstore device.

4. In the **Size (MB)** box, type **15**.

5. Click **Create Now** to create the StateUBookstore database.

▶ **Create the tables and load the data for the State University Bookstore database**

1. In the SQL Enterprise Manager, on the **Tools** menu, click **SQL Query Tool** or click the **SQL Query Tool** toolbar button.

2. Select the StateUBookstore database from the **DB** list.

3. Click the **Load SQL Script** toolbar button.

4. Select StateUBookstore.sql from *<install folder>* \Labs\Lab02\StateUBookstore Database, and then click **Open**.

5. To run the SQL script, click the **Execute Query** toolbar button.

This script creates tables and adds data to the tables. The script is complete when the **Execute Query** toolbar button changes from a black arrow to a green arrow.

▶ **Execute the instcat.sql script**

1. In the SQL Query Tool, click the **Load SQL Script** toolbar button.

2. Select instcat.sql from *<Windows NT folder>*\System32, and then click **Open**.

3. Click the **Execute Query** toolbar button.

The instcat.sql script improves the way Visual Basic uses the OLE DB Provider for SQL Server to communicate with SQL Server. For more details, see the Visual Basic readme file. The script is complete when the **Execute Query** toolbar button changes from a black arrow to a green arrow.

4. Close the Query Tool window and then click **Yes** to confirm that the window should be closed.

Exercise 2: Connecting to a Data Source

In this exercise, you will connect to a database. The lab instructions describe how to connect to a SQL Server database.

▶ **Add a Data Environment**

1. In Visual Basic, open the StateUBookstore project you created in Lab 1. If you did not complete Lab 1, you can open the starting point in the *<install folder>*\Labs\Lab02 directory named StateUBookstore.vbp.

2. On the **Project** menu, click **Add Data Environment**.

   A new connection is automatically created for which you must set data link properties.

3. Change the name of the connection to cnStateUBookstore.

4. In the Data Environment window, right-click cnStateUBookstore and choose **Properties**.

5. On the **Provider** tab of the **Data Link Properties** dialog box, select the Microsoft OLE DB Provider for SQL Server and click **Next**.

6. On the **Connection** tab of the **Data Link Properties** dialog box:

   a. Enter the name of your SQL Server.

   b. Enter the User Name "sa".

   c. Enter the name of the database (StateUBookstore).

   d. Click the **Test Connection** button to see if the connection works, and click **OK** in the **Microsoft Data Link** message box.

   e. Click **OK** to save the new **Connection** object.

7. Name the Data Environment object **deStateUBookstore**.

8. Save your work.

Exercise 3: Creating a Command

In this exercise, you will create a query that looks up all of the books in the State University Bookstore's inventory.

▶ **Explore the database structure**

1. From the **View** menu, chose **Data View Window**.

2. In the Data View window, open the cnStateUBookstore folder.

3. In the cnStateUBookstore folder open the Tables folder.

4. In the Tables folder, open the Books table.

5. Review the Books table schema.

▶ **Create a database command**

1. In the Data Environment window's toolbar, click **Add Command**.

2. Name the command **AllBooks**.

3. In the Data Environment window, right-click the **AllBooks** command and choose **Properties**.

4. Verify that this command is using the cnStateUBookstore connection.

5. Select the option for SQL Statement, and click the **SQL Builder** button.

6. Select the Books table in the Data View window and drag it into the diagram pane of the Design: AllBooks window.

7. Select the Publishers table in the Data View window and drag it into the diagram pane of the Design: AllBooks window.

8. Add the following columns to the query by checking the box next to their name:

Table	Column Name
Books	Title
Books	AuthorName
Publishers	pub_name
Books	Price
Books	BooksOnHand

9. Close the Design: AllBooks window and save your changes.

10. In the Data Environment window, click on the plus to open the **AllBooks** command to see a list of its fields.

11. Right click on the pub_name field and choose **Properties**.

12. Change the Caption to "Publisher Name" and click **OK**.

13. Save your work.

Exercise 4: Creating a Data-Bound Form

In this exercise, you will create a data-bound form. This form will be bound to the Books table in the StateUBookstore database.

▶ **Build a data-bound form**

1. Create a new form in the StateUBookstore project and name it **frmBooks**.

2. In the Data Environment window, select the **AllBooks** command and drag it onto **frmBooks**.

3. Save your work.

▶ **Implement the Update Inventory menu item on the Bookstore menu**

1. In the code module for frmStateUMain, add an event handler for the **Update Inventory** menu item on the **Bookstore** menu.

2. In the event handler, call the **Show** method of the new form **frmBooks**.

3. Run the project and login using a student ID in the range 1 to 5.

4. Select the **Update Inventory** menu item from the **Bookstore** menu.

   The form displays the first record from the **AllBooks** query.

5. Click the **End** button on the Visual Basic toolbar and save your work.

▶ **Add navigation to frmBooks**

1. Add two command buttons to the **frmBooks** form.

   a. Set the name of the first button to **cmdPrevious** and set the Caption to **Move Previous**.

   b. Set the name of the second button to **cmdNext** and set the Caption to **Move Next**.

The following illustration shows what your form should look like.

2. Add code to the **Click** event for the **cmdNext** command button to move to the next record in the recordset:

```
deStateUBookstore.rsAllBooks.MoveNext
```

3. Add code to the **Click** event for the **cmdPrevious** command button to move to the previous record in the recordset:

```
deStateUBookstore.rsAllBooks.MovePrevious
```

4. Save your work and test the project.

Use the **Move Next** and **Move Previous** buttons to navigate between the records.

Exercise 5 (Optional): Creating a Report

In this exercise, you will add two reports to the StateUBookstore project.

▶ **Create the Out of Stock Report**

1. Add a new command to the Data Environment that returns the records from the Books table for those books that are out of stock. These records will have a BooksOnHand value of 0.

2. Add a new Data Report to the StateUBookstore project.

3. Drag the command from the Data Environment on to the Data Report to create fields on the report for each field in the command.

4. Set the **DataSource** property of the Data Report to the data environment.

5. Set the **DataMember** property of the Data Report to the command.

6. Format the report so the fields are displayed in columns in the Detail section of the report.

7. Move the field labels into the report's Page Header to identify each column of data.

8. Add a title to the Report Header section of the report.

9. At design time, your report should resemble the following illustration.

▶ **Implement the Out Of Stock Report menu**

1. In the code module for **frmStateUMain,** add an event handler for the **Out of Stock Report** menu item.

2. In the event handler, call the **Show** method of the new Out of Stock Report.

3. Save your work.

▶ **Create the Purchase History Report**

1. Add a new command to the Data Environment that returns the records from the AccountLog table for the student logged in. The SQL syntax for this query is: "SELECT * FROM AccountLog WHERE StudentID = ?".

2. Add a new Data Report to the StateUBookstore project.

3. Drag the command from the Data Environment on to the Data Report to create fields on the report for each field in the command.

4. Set the **DataSource** property of the Data Report to the data environment.

5. Set the **DataMember** property of the Data Report to the command.

6. Format the report so the fields are displayed in columns in the Detail section of the report.

7. Move the field labels into the report's Page Header to identify each column of data.

8. Add a title to the Report Header section of the report.

▶ **Implement the Get Purchase History menu**

1. In the code module for the **frmStateUMain** form, add an event handler for the **Get Purchase History** menu item.

2. In the event handler, add code to call the command and pass the student ID argument. Your code should resemble the following:

```
deStateUBookstore.PurchaseHistory CInt(txtStudentID.Text)
```

3. In the event handler, call the **Show** method of the new Purchase History report.

▶ **Test the Application**

1. Run the StateUBookstore application.

2. Log in as a bookstore employee.

3. Open the Out Of Stock report.

Self-Check Questions

To see the answers to the Self-Check Questions, see Appendix A.

1. **When using the Data Environment designer, before you create a new command, you must first create:**

   A. A parent command.
   B. An ODBC data source.
   C. A connection to a data source.
   D. A project group.

2. **When using the Query Builder to create a query for a new command, what window do you click and drag tables from?**

   A. The Data Environment Designer window
   B. The Command Properties window
   C. The Database Designer window
   D. The Data View window

3. Which of the following data access methods is an OLE DB Consumer?

   A. ADO

   B. DAO

   C. RDO

   D. Jet

4. With the Data Environment, you can create commands that are related to each other. Which control can you use on a form to display the results of the command?

   A. Microsoft FlexGrid control

   B. Microsoft Hierarchical FlexGrid control

   C. Microsoft ADO Data control

   D. Microsoft DataGrid control

5. Which of the following properties does not need to be set when binding a control to a single field from a command in a Data Environment?

   A. DataSource

   B. DataMember

   C. DataFormat

   D. DataField

6. Which of the following is not an advantage of Format objects?

   A. Format objects will save the data format in the database.

   B. You can set formats either through code or at design time.

   C. Format objects give you additional formatting types that are not supported by the Format function.

   D. Format objects have **Format** and **Unformat** events that allow closer control over data formatting.

Chapter 3:
Using Class Modules

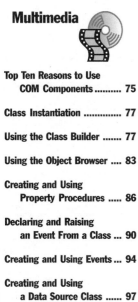

The Component Object Model (COM) enables you to break your application into components. Using components, you can modularize your application, creating objects that contain both code and data for a particular application feature. You can create components that are reusable, and easily maintained and modified.

In this chapter, you will learn how to use class modules in a Visual Basic project to create COM components that are available only within that project. In Chapter 7, "Using COM Components," you will learn how to use external COM components to extend the functionality of your application. In Chapter 8, "Building COM Components," you will learn how to build COM components that can be shared by many applications.

Objectives

After completing this chapter, you will be able to:

◆ Explain the benefits of using class modules in an application.

◆ Use a class module to create a COM component within a Microsoft Visual Basic project.

◆ Create a COM component that exposes properties, methods, and events.

◆ Create and use data-bound class modules.

Designing an Application

With Visual Basic, you can create components that range from code libraries to automation-enabled applications. COM lets you assemble reusable components into applications and services. In this section, you'll learn why breaking your application into separate functional components is good programming practice, and how using components fits in with Microsoft Windows Distributed interNet Applications Architecture (Windows DNA).

Using Objects and Components

COM components are self-contained units of code that provide specific functionality. Using COM, you can build several different components that work together as a single application. Separating your code into components gives you the ability to develop and test small, encapsulated pieces of your application independently. It also enables multiple developers to work on a project together by allowing tasks to be distributed among the members of the development team.

Designing your applications using COM components also enables you to use multiple instances of an object within your application. The following illustration shows how you can create an Employee component, and then, at run time, you can create two instances of that component.

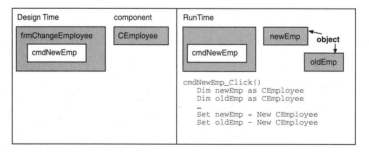

COM components can be either internal components, which are compiled into a project and are available only to that project, or external components, which are compiled into executable files or dynamic-link libraries. External components can be used by any client application that supports COM. You use COM components in exactly the same way, regardless of whether they are internal or external components.

Advantages of Using COM Components

There are many reasons to use COM components in an application:

♦ Reusability

Once you create a COM component, other developers can use it. This enables easy access to your component's features in other applications without requiring developers to write extensive code. A developer can use the Object Browser to get information about the properties, methods, and events exposed by your COM component. For more information, see "Using the Object Browser" on page 82 in this chapter.

♦ Reduced complexity

You can create a COM component to hide programming complexity from other programmers. Other programmers need only know what information to provide to your component, and what information to retrieve.

♦ Easier updating

Components make it easier for you to revise and update your applications. For example, you can create a COM component that encapsulates business rules. If the business rules change, you update just the component, and not all the applications that use the component.

To see the expert point-of-view "Top Ten Reasons to Use COM Components," see the accompanying CD-ROM.

For more information about reusability and other benefits of using COM components as .dll and .exe files external to your application, see Chapter 8, "Building COM Components" on page 267.

Windows Distributed interNet Architecture

Windows Distributed interNet Applications Architecture (Windows DNA) is a development framework for building scalable, distributed applications based on the Windows platform. With Windows DNA, application developers can build and extend solutions that combine the most desirable aspects of personal computer applications, client/server applications, and Internet applications.

You can build these integrated applications and components by writing COM components and by accessing the Windows application services exposed through Microsoft Transaction Server and other enabling technologies.

The following illustration shows the general structure of Windows DNA.

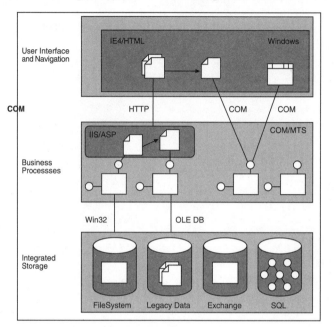

For the most current information about Windows DNA, go to the Windows DNA Web site at www.microsoft.com/dna/default.asp.

What Is a Class Module?

To create a COM component in Visual Basic, you first define a class module within a project. The component can then be used within the Visual Basic project as part of a larger application, or it can be exposed to other applications.

A class module is a type of Visual Basic code module. A class module (.cls file) is similar to a standard code module (.bas file) in that it contains functionality that can be used by other modules within the application. The difference is that a class module provides functionality in the form of an object. Each class module defines one type of object. You may have several class modules in an application.

To use a class module in your application, you create an instance of the class. Then you have access to the properties, methods, and events of the object defined by the class. For example, you might create an **Employee** class that has properties such as **LastName** and **FirstName**, and methods such as **Hire**. Then you can create and use an instance of the **Employee** object whenever you need to process employee information in your application.

To see the animation "Class Instantiation," see the accompanying CD-ROM.

In Chapter 8, "Building COM Components," you will learn how to create an object model for your classes.

Creating Class Modules

In Visual Basic, you create COM components in your application by adding class modules to the project.

This section discusses how to use class modules to define a component, and how to create an instance of a component. It also explains how to use the Visual Basic Class Builder to create a new class.

Using the Class Builder

You can create a class module and add methods, properties, and events to it manually, or you can use the Class Builder Add-In. The Class Builder automates the process of adding properties, methods, and events to a class. With the Class Builder, you can visually define a class and its interface, as shown in the following illustration.

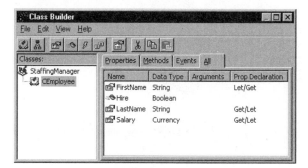

▶ **To add the Class Builder to a project**

1. On the **Add-Ins** menu, click **Add-In Manager**.

2. In the list of available add-ins, select **VB 6 Class Builder Utility**.

3. Under **Load Behavior**, select the **Loaded/Unloaded** check box, and then click **OK**.

To see the demonstration "Using the Class Builder," see the accompanying CD-ROM.

Adding a New Class

To manually add a new class module to a project, click **Add Class Module** on the **Project** menu. However, if you manually add a class module to your project, you will not be able to use all of the features of the Class Builder.

You can add new classes to your project with the Class Builder.

▶ **To use the Class Builder to add a class**

1. On the **Add-Ins** menu, click **Class Builder Utility**.

2. In the Class Builder, on the **File** menu, point to **New**, and then click **Class**.

3. In the **Class Module Builder** dialog box, enter a name for the class.

4. On the **Attributes** tab, enter a description for the class and a Help context ID if there is an associated Help file.

Creating the Class Interface

Once you've created a class, you need to define the properties, methods, and events of the class. Collectively, these are called the interface of the class.

To add properties, methods, and events, select the class in the Class Builder, and then on the **File** menu, point to **New** and click **Property, Method,** or **Event.**

The following illustration shows the **Property Builder** dialog box.

The following illustration shows the **Method Builder** dialog box.

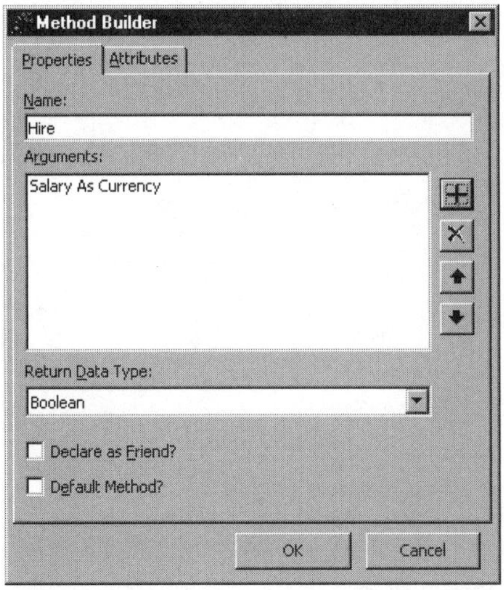

The following illustration shows the **Event Builder** dialog box.

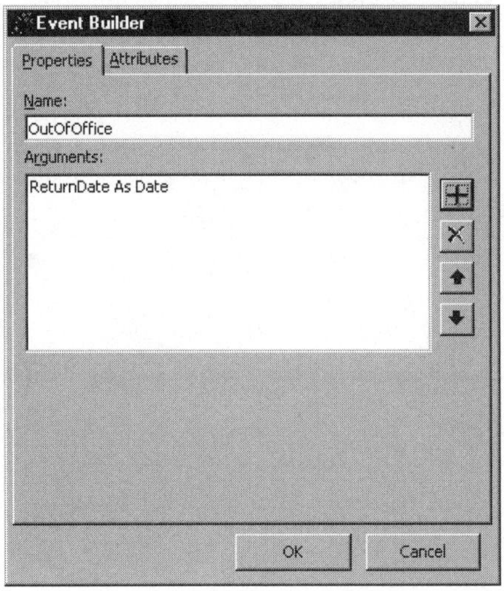

You can also add descriptive text and associate a Help context ID number for each property, method, and event by selecting the **Attributes** tab and typing in the relevant information. The following illustration shows the **Attributes** tab.

![Property Builder dialog showing the Attributes tab with Description field containing "The Last Name of the Employee.", Project Help File field, and Help Context ID field.]

After you've defined all the classes in your project, click **Update Project** on the **File** menu, and then exit the Class Builder.

Note Although you can define the properties, methods, and events for a class by using the Class Builder, you'll still need to write code to add the functionality. For more information, see "Adding Properties, Methods, and Events" on page 84 in this chapter.

Class Module Events

Class modules have two built-in events: **Initialize** and **Terminate**.

To add code to the class module events, open the code window for the class, and click **Class** in the **Object** drop-down list box.

Initialize Event

The **Initialize** event occurs when an instance of a class is created, but before any properties have been set. When you write a class module, you use the **Initialize** event to initialize any data used by the class, as shown in the following example code:

```
Private Sub Class_Initialize()
  'Initialize data.
  iDept = 5
End Sub
```

You can also use the **Initialize** event to load forms used by the class.

Terminate Event

The **Terminate** event occurs when the object variable goes out of scope or is set to **Nothing**. When you write a class module, you use the **Terminate** event to save information, unload forms, or perform tasks that should occur when the class terminates.

```
Private Sub Class_Terminate()
  'Any termination code.
End Sub
```

For information about coding **Initialize** and **Terminate** events, read the article "Adding Code for Initialize and Terminate Events" in Visual Basic Help.

Adding Component Information and Help

To make classes in your code components easier to use, you can add descriptive text and context-sensitive help for each of the properties, methods, and events in a class. This information will then be available as context-sensitive help in the Object Browser for any client application that uses the code component.

To provide this information, you fill in the fields in the **Procedure Attributes** dialog box, as shown in the following illustration.

```
Procedure Attributes                              [×]
Name:  Hire                           ▼        ┌──────────┐
                                               │    OK    │
Description:                                   └──────────┘
┌──────────────────────────────────┐ ▲        ┌──────────┐
│Call this Function to start the hiring│        │  Cancel  │
│routine for a new employee          │ ▼        └──────────┘
└──────────────────────────────────┘          ┌──────────┐
Project Help File:      Help Context ID:       │   Apply  │
┌──────────────┐       ┌──────────┐            └──────────┘
│              │       │ 125      │            ┌──────────┐
└──────────────┘       └──────────┘            │Advanced >>│
                                               └──────────┘
```

▶ **To set help information for a class**

1. Open the project containing the class module.

2. Open the code window for the class module.

3. On the **Tools** menu, click **Procedure Attributes**.

4. Fill in the **Description** and **Help Context ID** fields for each procedure.

Note You cannot set descriptions for properties defined as **Public** variables, but you can set descriptions for properties defined by using property procedures.

The name of your project's help file will be displayed in the **Project Help File** field in the **Procedure Attributes** dialog box. If you have not already done so, you can specify a help file for your project in the **Project Properties** dialog box.

▶ **To specify a help file for your project**

1. On the **Project** menu, click **Project Properties**.

2. Enter a file name in the **Help File Name** field, and then click **OK**.

For information about creating a help file, see "Creating a Help File for an Application" on page 306 in Chapter 9, "Optimizing and Deploying Applications."

Using the Object Browser

To view the properties, methods, and events you've created for a class module, you can use the Object Browser. To run the Object Browser, on the **View** menu, click **Object Browser**. As you select the different properties, methods, and events you've created, the Object Browser will display the help information you added. The

Object Browser displays information about objects in all the type libraries referenced by the project including components intrinsic to the project. For information about setting a reference to a type library, see "Using Components" on page 16 in Chapter 1, "Visual Basic Essentials."

The following illustration shows the properties, methods, and events that are available from a component named **CEmployee**.

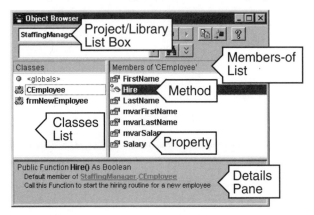

The **Project/Library** list box shows that the Object Browser is viewing the **StaffingManager** project. The **Classes** pane shows that there are two components available in the **StaffingManager** project: **CEmployee** and **frmNewEmployee**. The **Members of** pane shows that **CEmployee** contains three properties (**Salary, FirstName,** and **LastName**) as well as the private member variables for these properties and one method (**Hire**).

To see the demonstration "Using the Object Browser," see the accompanying CD-ROM.

Practice: Using the Class Builder

In this practice exercise, you will use the Class Builder Utility to create an employee component class with one property and one method. You will then use that component in a Visual Basic application.

▶ Create a class module

1. Start a new Standard EXE project.

2. Run the Class Builder Utility Add-In.

    a. Create a new class named **CEmployee**.

    b. Create a public property named **FirstName** that is a **String** data type.

    c. Create a method called **DisplayData** that takes no arguments and does not return a value.

    d. Exit the Class Builder Utility and update the project with the changes.

3. In the code module for the **CEmployee** class, add code to the **DisplayData** method that displays the value of the **FirstName** property:

```
Msgbox "First Name: " & mvarFirstName
```

4. Name the project ClassModulePractice and save your work.

▶ **Add component information**

1. On the **Tools** menu, click **Procedure Attributes**.

2. In the **Procedure Attributes** dialog box, select the procedure name DisplayData.

3. Add description information in the **Description** text box.

▶ **Use the Object Browser**

1. On the **View** menu, click **Object Browser**.

2. In the **Project/Library** box, choose **Project1** or the current project name.

3. Select **CEmployee** from the list of classes.

4. Select the **DisplayData** method in the list of **Members of 'CEmployee'**. The method description should appear in the **Details** pane.

5. Save your work.

Adding Properties, Methods, and Events

You have already seen how to use the Class Builder to add properties, methods, and events. Although Class Builder creates procedure templates, you'll need to write code to create the functionality for your properties, methods, and events.

In this section, you will learn how to add an interface to a class without using the Class Builder.

Creating Properties

Properties define the data or attributes of a class. For example, an **Employee** class may have properties such as **FirstName, LastName,** and **HireDate.**

You can define a property for your class in two ways: You can define public variables, or you can create public property procedures within your class module. Public variables provide a variable to hold a property value. Property procedures enable you to run code when a property is set or retrieved.

Using Public Variables to Create Properties

If you don't need to run any additional code when a property is set or retrieved, you can simply create a **Public** variable to hold the value of the property instead of a **Private** variable.

The following example code defines the string property **FirstName:**

```
Public FirstName As String
```

Users have no way of knowing whether your component uses property procedures or public variables; they get and set properties in the same way. However, with public variables, your component cannot determine when a property is being set or retrieved, nor can it tell what the property is being set to, until it is already set.

Using Property Procedures to Create Properties

Use property procedures if you want to execute code when a property is set or retrieved. With property procedures, you can perform the following tasks:

◆ Run a procedure when a property value is changed or read.

◆ Constrain a property to a set of valid values.

◆ Expose a property that is read-only.

You create property procedures in pairs. For example, you can create a **Set** or **Let** procedure to assign a value to the property, and then create a **Get** procedure to return the value. You give the two procedures the same name, which is also the name of the property. When you read the property, the **Property Get** procedure runs. When you set the property, the **Property Set** or **Property Let** procedure runs.

>To see the demonstration "Creating and Using Property Procedures," see the accompanying CD-ROM.

Define the Property

The first step in defining a property is to define storage for that property in the class module. You can do this by declaring a private variable of some data type. The following example code declares a **String** variable to hold a property:

```
Private mvarFirstName As String
```

Define the Interface

The **Private** variable is only visible to the class module itself, so you need to create a **Public** interface to get and set the value of the variable. Property procedures create this interface. The following example code creates **Property Let** and **Property Get** procedures that assign a string value and return the value for the **FirstName** property.

```
Public Property Let FirstName(passedName As String)
  mvarFirstName = UCase(passedName)
End Property

Public Property Get FirstName() As String
  FirstName = mvarFirstName
End Property
```

To create a property that returns a standard data type, define a **Property Get** procedure and a **Property Let** procedure. To create a property that is an **Object** data type, define a **Property Get** procedure and a **Property Set** procedure. To create a read-only property, define a **Property Get** procedure without a matching **Property Let** or **Property Set** procedure.

> For more information about property procedures, read the article "Programming with Objects" in Visual Basic Help.

Creating a Default Property

You can also create a default property for an object. The default property is the property that is set if the user doesn't provide a property name when working with the object. For example, the **Text** property is the default property for a **TextBox** control. As a user, you can set the default property of a component either explicitly or implicitly, as shown in the following example code:

```
txtEmpFirstName.Text = "Bill"
txtEmpFirstName = "Bill"
```

▶ **To create a default property**

1. Open the class module containing the property.

2. On the **Tools** menu, click **Procedure Attributes**.

3. In the **Procedure Attributes** dialog box, click the **Advanced** button.

4. In the **Name** drop-down list box, select the property you want to set as the default.

5. In the **Procedure ID** drop-down list box, select (**Default**), and then click **OK**.

The following illustration shows a default property set in the **Procedure Attributes** dialog box.

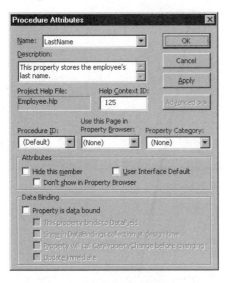

Creating Methods

Methods represent the functionality your class provides. For example, an **Employee** class may have methods such as **Hire** or **PayIncrease**.

To create a method for an object, you create **Public Sub** or **Function** procedures within a class module.

The following example code creates a method that adds an employee record to a database:

```
Public Function Hire() as Boolean
  ' add employee record to database here
  MsgBox "Employee was added to the database"
  ' if successful
  Hire = True
End Sub
```

The following example code creates a method that increases the employee's salary:

```
Public Function PayIncrease(dPercent As Double) As Integer
  mvarSalary = mvarSalary * (1 + dPercent)
End Function
```

Using Named Constants

A named constant is an item that retains a constant value throughout the execution of a program, and can be used in place of literal values. You can use named constants as property values and method arguments, and as return values. By using a named constant, you also make your code easier to read and maintain.

For example, if you want to create a message box that includes **Yes** and **No** buttons, you can use the named constant **vbYesNo** for the argument instead of a literal value of **4**.

Creating Named Constants

To define your own set of named constants, you create an enumeration and define the set of values available in it.

Tip Members of an enumeration do not need to be sequential or contiguous.

The following example code shows how to define an enumeration called **JobLevel** that has three values:

```
Public Enum JobLevel
  jExecutive = 1
  jManagement = 2
  jStaff = 3
End Enum
```

You can make the members of your enumeration available to users of a component by marking the enumeration **Public,** and including it in a class module.

Users of your class can then use the **JobLevel** enumeration with a simple method, as shown in the following example code:

```
Public Sub CheckExecutiveStatus(iLevel as JobLevel)
  If iLevel = jExecutive Then
      MsgBox "Executive Level Status Approved"
  Else
      MsgBox "Executive Status Denied"
  End If
End Sub
```

Visual Basic context-sensitive help will list the values of the enumeration when you are setting a variable of that type. Although the enumeration appears in a module that defines a class, it has global scope in the type library.

Note To avoid enumeration member name conflicts, prefix the member name with lowercase characters that identify the type and the component to which it belongs. For example, the built-in enumeration **VbDayofWeek** contains numeric constants with the names **vbMonday, vbTuesday,** and so on.

Using Enumerations as Property Values

An advantage of using enumerations in your class modules is that you can predefine the set of valid values for the property.

For example, you can define the property **ActiveJobLevel** to only be specific values.

```
Private mvarJobLevel As JobLevel
Public Property Let ActiveJobLevel(jl As JobLevel)
  mvarJobLevel = jl
End Property

Public Property Get ActiveJobLevel() As JobLevel
  ActiveJobLevel= mvarJobLevel
End Property
```

When users of the class attempt to assign a value to the **JobLevel** property, they are given the enumeration values to choose from. And, because the data type of the property is an enumeration, Visual Basic will generate a run-time error if a user tries to assign a value to the property other than one of the values of the enumeration.

Adding Events to a Class

Through the use of events, a class provides notification that some action has occurred. Visual Basic provides two built-in events for class modules by default: the **Initialize** event and the **Terminate** event. For more information about how to write code for these events, see "Class Module Events" on page 80 in this chapter.

You can also declare custom events for your class. You define the event and then write code to cause the event to occur. When a developer works with an object that exposes an event, the developer can write code in an event handler to take action when the event occurs.

For example, if you create an order component called **COrder**, you can raise a **Status** event when the status of the order changes. A developer using an instance of the **COrder** component can write an event handler for the **Status** event that reacts to the new status.

Use the following steps to raise an event from a code component:

1. Declare the event.
2. Raise the event.

To see the demonstration "Declaring and Raising an Event From a Class," see the accompanying CD-ROM.

Declaring an Event

You declare an event in the General Declarations section of a class module by using the **Event** keyword. The following example code shows how to declare an event for a class:

$$\downarrow$$

```
Public Event Status(ByVal StatusText As String)
```

Raising an Event

When you want an event to be raised by the class, you call the **RaiseEvent** statement, and pass the event name and any arguments that the event takes.

The following example code raises the **Status** event to provide status information during a method that takes a long time to process:

```
Public Sub SubmitOrder()
  'code to submit an order goes here
  RaiseEvent Status("Checking credit...")
  'code to check credit goes here
  RaiseEvent Status("Processing Order...")
  'code to process an order goes here
End Sub
```

Communicating with a Component

If a class defines an event that uses **ByRef** arguments, the arguments can be changed when the event is handled. The class can check the arguments after the event has been handled to determine if changes occurred. In this way the class can pass information and get a response using the values of the event's arguments.

In the following example code, a class has an event **LimitChanged** in which it passes a new credit limit by reference. The class can evaluate the new limit value after the event has been handled.

```
Dim iLimit as Integer
iLimit = 400

' raise the event to be handled by the client
RaiseEvent LimitChanged(iLimit)

' now check to see if the client changed the limit
If iLimit <> 400 Then
  'client didn't accept the new limit
End If
```

Raising Errors from a Class

You can create a class module that raises error messages. To pass an error back to the code using your class, you use the **Raise** method of the **Err** object. The code using your class will need to handle the error.

To raise an error, use the following syntax:

ERR.Raise Number, Source, Description, HelpFile, HelpContext

Specify the error number by adding the intrinsic constant **vbObjectError** to the error number you want to raise. This ensures that your error numbers do not conflict with the built-in Visual Basic error numbers. The following example code raises an error that will be handled in the code using this class:

```
Err.Raise vbObjectError + 100, "CEmployee", "Employee could not be
added"
```

Using a Class Module

Class modules are components available within the Visual Basic project that defines them. You can use the classes either in a form, a code module, or another class module. In Chapter 8, "Building COM Components," you will learn how to make these components available to other applications.

In this section, you will learn how to use a class module in a Visual Basic application.

Creating an Instance of a Class

Class modules serve as templates for objects. To use a class module, you must first create an instance of the class module. Then, you can access the properties, methods, and events of that instance.

Class modules differ from standard modules in two ways:

◆ You must explicitly create an instance of a class before you can use it.

◆ You can create multiple instances of a class module.

In the project that contains the class module, you can create an instance of a class with the **Dim, Set,** and **Dim As New** statements, as shown in the following example code:

```
Dim empCurrent As CEmployee
Set empCurrent = New CEmployee
```

You can also use more compact syntax:

```
Dim empCurrent As New CEmployee
```

It is more efficient to use the **Dim** and **Set** statements separately to clearly show where the instance of the class is instantiated. With the **Dim As New** statement, the object is created the first time the object variable is used, but with each subsequent use Visual Basic has to first determine if the object has already been instantiated.

For information about using the **Set** statement, see "Creating Objects for Components" on page 250 in Chapter 7, "Using COM Components."

Releasing the Class

When writing code that uses objects, it is good practice to release the memory used by your objects when you are finished with them. Once you have finished using a class, use the **Set** statement to assign **Nothing** to the variable for the object. The following example code releases the memory for the **empCurrent** object:

```
Set empCurrent = Nothing
```

For information about the differences between class modules and standard modules, read the article "Creating Your Own Classes" in Visual Basic Help.

Using a Class

Once you've created an instance of a class module, you can test the methods and properties of the class. You can use the Object Browser to view the properties, methods, and events that are defined for a class.

For information about using the Object Browser, see "Using the Object Browser" on page 82 in this chapter.

Setting and Retrieving Properties

The following example code creates an instance of the **CEmployee** class, and sets and retrieves the **FirstName** property:

```
Dim empCurrent As CEmployee
Set empCurrent = New CEmployee
empCurrent.FirstName = "Bill" 'Calls Let procedure.
MsgBox empCurrent.FirstName    'Calls Get procedure.
```

Calling Methods

The following example code creates an instance of the **CEmployee** class and calls the **Hire** method:

```
Dim empCurrent As CEmployee
Dim bHired as Boolean

Set empCurrent = New CEmployee

'Call the Hire method
bHired = empCurrent.Hire
If bHired Then
  MsgBox empCurrent.FirstName & " was hired!"
End If
```

Handling Events

Follow these steps to handle an event that is provided by a COM component:

1. Declare an object variable for the class that raises the event using the **WithEvents** keyword.

2. Create an event procedure to handle the event.

   The object variable name will show up in the Object list, and the event for the object will show up in the list of available events for that object.

3. Create an instance of the class so that it can fire the event.

To see the demonstration "Creating and Using Events," see the accompanying CD-ROM.

Declaring a Variable Using WithEvents

When you declare a variable using the **WithEvents** keyword, it contains a reference to the object that will provide the notification events. To do this, you add a standard **Dim** statement and the **WithEvents** keyword, as shown in the following example code:

```
Dim WithEvents ordCurrent As COrder
```

> **Note** You must declare a **WithEvents** variable in the general declarations section. You cannot declare a **WithEvents** variable as a local variable.

After you declare the **WithEvents** variable, it will appear in the code window as an object, along with its associated events, as shown in the following illustration.

```
projBookstore - frmInventory (Code)            _ □ ×
Order ordCurrent            ▼   Status                ▼
(General)                                              ▲
CmdOK
Form
ordCurrent
    Dim WithEvents ordCurrent As Order
```

Writing Event Code

In the event procedures associated with the **WithEvents** variable, you write code to handle the notifications you want, as shown in the following example code:

```
Private Sub Order_Status(ByVal StatusText As String)
    MsgBox StatusText
End Sub
```

Creating an Instance of the Object

When you create an instance of an object that provides events, and store that instance in the variable you dimensioned by using the **WithEvents** keyword, any events fired by the object will automatically be passed to the appropriate event procedure.

The following example code creates an instance of the **Order** object, and calls the **SubmitOrder** method, which then raises an event:

```
Private Sub cmdSubmitOrder_Click()
  Dim ordCurrent As COrder

  Set ordCurrent = New COrder
  ordCurrent.SubmitOrder
End Sub
```

For information about using asynchronous notifications in clients, see "Using Components" on page 253 in Chapter 7, "Using COM Components."

Practice: Using a Class Module

In this practice exercise, you will use the employee component class that you created in "Practice: Using the Class Builder."

▶ **Use the employee component class**

1. Open the project you created in "Practice: Using the Class Builder" called ClassModulePractice.

2. Add a button to the form in the project.

3. In the **Click** event procedure for the button,

   a. Add the following code to create an instance of the **Employee** class:

   ```
   Dim emp as CEmployee
   Set emp = New CEmployee
   ```

   b. Set the **FirstName** property of the **Employee** object:

   ```
   emp.FirstName = "Susan"
   ```

   c. Invoke the method:

   ```
   emp.DisplayData
   ```

4. Save your work and run the application.

   When you click the button on the form, a message box displays the value of the **FirstName** property of the employee object.

Creating Data-Bound Class Modules

Historically data binding was limited to binding data source controls to data consumer controls. Now with Visual Basic, you can create data source classes and data consumer classes that can be bound together using the **BindingCollection** object. You can use this object programmatically to bind all types of data consumers and data sources at run time.

In this section, you will learn how to use class modules to create data sources and data consumers, and you will use the **BindingCollection** object to bind them programmatically at run time. For information about establishing data binding at design time, see "Creating a Data-Bound Control" on page 148 in Chapter 4, "Building ActiveX Controls."

Creating a Data Source Class

You can build a class module that is a data source. Your application can then bind to this data source without requiring a user interface for it. Creating a data source class module is similar to creating a data source control except you don't have to implement the user interface. For information about creating a data source control, see "Creating a Data Source Control" on page 153 in Chapter 4, "Building ActiveX Controls."

To see the demonstration "Creating and Using a Data Source Class," see the accompanying CD-ROM.

Creating a Data Source Class

Creating a data source class requires writing some ADO code. For more information about writing ADO code, see Chapter 5, "Using ActiveX Data Objects" on page 163.

▶ **To create a data source class**

1. Set the **DataSourceBehavior** property of your class module to **vbDataSource**.
   This creates an event procedure called **GetDataMember**.

2. In the **Initialize** event procedure of your class module, establish the data your source will provide.

The following sample code establishes a connection to a database and fills a recordset with data. To copy this code for use in your own projects, see "Establishing Data in a Data Source Class" on the accompanying CD-ROM.

```
Private rBooks As Recordset
Private cStateUBookstore As Connection

Private Sub Class_Initialize()

    Dim sConnect As String

    ' define the OLE DB connection string
    sConnect = "Provider=SQLOLEDB;" & _
               "Data Source=MSERIES1;" & _
               "Initial Catalog=StateUBookstore"

    ' create the ADO objects
    Set cStateUBookstore = New Connection
    Set rBooks = New Recordset

    ' open the database connection
    cStateUBookstore.Open sConnect, "sa", ""

    ' create a recordset from the Books table
    rBooks.Open "Select * from Books", cStateUBookstore, adOpenStatic

End Sub
```

3. Write code in the **GetDataMember** event procedure to return a data object.

   The **GetDataMember** event procedure has two parameters: DataMember and Data. The DataMember parameter is an optional parameter that specifies the name of the data member used if your class provides multiple data members. The Data parameter is a data object that the procedure returns to the data consumer.

Tip A data source can return a data object in the form of an ADO **Recordset** object, or any object that implements the same interfaces as the **OLEDBSimpleProvider** class. For more information about how to create a custom OLE DB provider object, read the article "Data Binding Tools in Visual Basic" in Visual Basic Help.

The following example code returns data from a recordset called **rsBooks**:

```
Private Sub Class_GetDataMember _
                    (DataMember As String, Data As Object)
  ' return the data to the consumer
  Set Data = rsBooks
End Sub
```

4. Add any functionality you want your data source class to provide.

   For example, you may want to include navigation methods that you can call from your data consumer.

   The following example code enables navigation using two methods:

```
Private Sub NextBook()
  rsBooks.MoveNext
End Sub

Private Sub PrevBook()
  rsBooks.MovePrevious
End Sub
```

When a data consumer requests a new data source, the **GetDataMember** event is invoked. Your class then uses the DataMember parameter if appropriate to identify the specific data member the consumer requires, and returns data back to the consumer in the form of a **Recordset** object.

For more information about writing data source classes, read the article "Creating Data-Aware Classes" in Visual Basic Help.

Using a Data Source Class

You can bind any standard data consumer, such a text box, or even a non-standard consumer, such as the caption of a form, to your data source class. When your data source is a control, you generally bind a consumer to the data source at design time using the control's user interface. When your data source is a class, you bind the consumer to the data source in code at run time using the **BindingCollection** object.

▶ **To bind a data consumer control to a data source class at run time**

1. Set a reference in your project to the Microsoft Data Binding Collection.

2. In the procedure in which you want binding to occur, create an instance of the **BindingCollection** object.

3. Set the **DataSource** property of the **BindingCollection** object that you just created.

4. Set the **DataMember** property of the data source if necessary.

   If the data source class returns multiple data members, you set the **DataMember** property to a specific data member. If the data source returns only a single data member, you don't set the **DataMember** property.

5. Establish a relationship between the data consumer and a particular field from the data source by adding a new **Binding** object to the **BindingCollection**.

   To add an object to the **BindingCollection**, use the **Add** method and specify the data consumer object name, the property of the data consumer that you want the field to bind to, and the data field from the data source. You can also specify some optional parameters such as the format of the data.

You can write code to bind a field from a data source class to a data consumer wherever it is appropriate in your application. The following sample code places binding code in the **Click** event of a button. To copy this code for use in your own projects, see "Binding a Control to a Data Source Class" on the accompanying CD-ROM.

```
Private bc As BindingCollection

' declare the data source class
Private dsBookStore as CBookStore

Private Sub cmdEstablishBinding_Click()

   ' create the Binding Collection object
   Set bc = New BindingCollection

   ' create an instance of the data source class
   Set dsBookstore = New CBookStore

   ' establish data source object
   Set bc.DataSource = dsBookStore

   ' identify data member to use if source provides more than one
   bc.DataMember = "Books"

   ' bind a field from the data member to
   '    a text box on this form
   bc.Add txtTitle, "Text", "Title"

End Sub
```

Creating a Data Consumer Class

A data consumer is any control or class that uses data binding to retrieve information from a data provider. In Chapter 4, "Building ActiveX Controls," you will learn how to create a control that acts as a data consumer. In addition to creating a control that is a data consumer, you can create a class that is a data consumer. The difference is that the class does not have a user interface.

To see the demonstration "Creating and Using a Data Consumer Class," see the accompanying CD-ROM.

Creating a Data Consumer Class

Creating a data consumer class requires writing some ADO code. For more information about writing ADO code, see Chapter 5, "Using ActiveX Data Objects" on page 163.

▶ **To create a data consumer class**

1. Set the **DataBindingBehavior** property of your class module to **vbSimpleBound**. This enables the OLE DB functionality that is required to accomplish data binding.

> **Note** You can also set the **DataBindingBehavior** property to **vbComplexBound**. This option gives your data consumer direct access to the **Recordset** object provided by the data source. For more information about how to create complex bound data consumers, read the article "Creating Data-Aware Classes" in Visual Basic Help.

2. Implement the properties that will have binding capability and the methods that use this data. For more information, see "Adding Properties, Methods, and Events" on page 84 in this chapter.

For more information about writing data consumer classes, read the article "Creating Data-Aware Classes" in Visual Basic Help.

Using a Data Consumer Class

You use the **BindingCollection** object to bind a data consumer class to either a data source control or a data source class.

▶ **To bind a property of a data consumer class to a data source at run time**

1. Set a reference in your project to the Microsoft Data Binding Collection.

2. In the procedure in which you want binding to occur, create an instance of the **BindingCollection** object.

3. Set the **DataSource** property of the **BindingCollection** object that you just created.

4. Set the **DataMember** property of the data source if necessary.

   If the data source class returns multiple data members, you set the **DataMember** property to a specific data member. If the data source returns only a single data member, you don't set the **DataMember** property.

5. Establish a relationship between the data consumer and a particular field from the data source by adding a new **Binding** object to the **BindingCollection**.

   To add an object to the **BindingCollection**, use the **Add** method and specify the data consumer object name, the property of the data consumer that you want the field to bind to, and the data field from the data source. You can also specify some optional parameters such as the format of the data.

The following sample code creates an instance of a data consumer class and then binds it to a data source class. To copy this code for use in your own projects, see "Binding a Class to a Data Source Class" on the accompanying CD-ROM.

```
Private bc As BindingCollection

' declare the data source class
Private dsBookStore as CBookStore

' declare the data consumer class
Private dcBookList as CBookList

Private Sub EstablishBinding()

  ' create the Binding Collection object
  Set bc = New BindingCollection

  ' create an instance of the data source class
  Set dsBookstore = New CBookStore

  ' establish data source object
  Set bc.DataSource = dsBookStore

  ' identify data member to use if source provides more than one
  bc.DataMember = "BookList"

  ' bind a field from the data member to
  '   the data consumer object's Title property
  bc.Add dcBookList, "Title", "Title"

End Sub
```

Lab 3: Using Class Modules

In this lab, you will create a class module with properties and methods that will validate a student ID of State University. You will call the method of this component when the user clicks the **Login** button on the main form.

To see the demonstration "Lab 3 Solution," see the accompanying CD-ROM.

Estimated time to complete this lab: **60 minutes**

To complete the exercises in this lab, you must have the required software. For detailed information about the labs and setup for the labs, see "Labs" in "About This Course."

Objectives

After completing this lab, you will be able to:

◆ Create a class module.

◆ Declare methods and properties within a COM component.

◆ Raise a custom error from a COM component.

◆ Add descriptive information and context-sensitive Help for the properties and methods of a COM component.

◆ Test the component.

Prerequisites

Before working on this lab, you should be familiar with the following:

◆ Raising an error and creating an error handler.

Exercises

The following exercises provide practice working with the concepts and techniques covered in this chapter.

◆ Exercise 1: Creating a Class Module

In this exercise, you will create a class module named **CStudent** that will simulate the validation of a student ID entered into the main form.

◆ Exercise 2: Using a Class Module

In this exercise, you will create an instance of the class module and use it to determine the validity of the student ID entered in the main form.

◆ Exercise 3: Debugging and Error Handling

In this exercise, you will raise a custom error from the **Validate** method of the **CStudent** object if the student ID is invalid.

◆ Exercise 4: Adding Component Information and Help

In this exercise, you will define procedure attributes that provide descriptive information and context-sensitive Help for the properties and methods of the **Student** object.

Exercise 1: Creating a Class Module

In this exercise, you will create a class module named **CStudent** that will simulate the validation of a student ID entered into the main form.

The following table shows the method and property you will implement.

Name	Type	Purpose
StudentID	Property	Holds the student ID of the current user.
Validate	Method	Looks up the student ID and determines if it is a valid ID and if the student is a bookstore employee.

▶ **Create the class module**

1. Open the State University Bookstore project.
2. Run the Class Builder Add-In.

   For information about using the Class Builder utility, see "Using the Class Builder" on page 77 in this chapter.

3. Create a new class named **CStudent**.
4. Add the **StudentID** property as a Public Property. Set the data type to **Integer**.
5. Add the **Validate** method. Set the return type to **Integer**.
6. On the Class Builder's **File** menu, click **Update Project** to write changes into the StateUBookstore project.
7. Exit the Class Builder and save your changes.
8. Locate the Property Let and Property Get procedures for the **StudentID** property.

   How is this property stored in the class module?

   For more information about property procedures, see "Creating Properties" on page 85 in this chapter.

9. Locate the **Validate** method.

   What does this method do by default?

   For information about creating methods, see "Creating Methods" on page 87 in this chapter.

▶ **Implement the Validate method**

◆ In the **Validate** method, add code to simulate looking up a student in the StateUBookstore database. The return value from the function will determine whether the student ID is valid, and whether the student is an employee of the bookstore.

For this exercise, use the following logic to validate the student ID.

If...	Then...	Return Value
Student ID is between 1 and 5	Student is valid and a bookstore employee	2
Student ID is between 6 and 51	Student is valid, but not a bookstore employee	1
Student ID is less than 1 or greater than 51	Student is not valid	0

Exercise 2: Using a Class Module

The Student component is used to log students on to the State University Bookstore application. In this exercise, you will create an instance of the class module and use it to determine the validity of the student ID entered in the main form.

▶ **Use the Student component**

1. In the form frmStateUMain, add code to the **cmdLogin_Click** event procedure:

   a. Declare and create a new instance of the **CStudent** class.

   b. Declare an integer variable to hold the return value of the **Validate** method.

   c. Set the **StudentID** property of the **CStudent** class to the student ID entered in the text box.

   d. Call the **Validate** method of the **CStudent** class.

e. Take one of the following actions based on the return value of the **Validate** method.

Validate return value	Action
2	Enable the **Bookstore** menu items.
1	Disable the **Bookstore** menu items.
0	Post an error message, set focus back to txtStudentID, exit the procedure.

To see an example of how your code should look, see Lab Hint 3.1 in Appendix B.

▶ **Test the Validate method**

◆ Run the StateUBookstore application and test that the **Login** button works correctly with different student IDs.

Exercise 3: Debugging and Error Handling

In Exercise 2, you used the return value of the **Validate** method to determine whether the student ID was valid. In this exercise, you will raise a custom error from the **Validate** method of the **CStudent** object if the student ID is invalid.

▶ **Raise a run-time error**

1. Open the **CStudent** class module.

2. Add code to the **Validate** method, so that if the student ID the user has entered is zero or negative, a run-time error is raised with the following arguments.

Argument	Value
Number	vbObjectError + 1000
Source	CStudent
Description	Student ID must be positive.

For more information about generating errors, see "Raising Errors from a Class" on page 92 in this chapter.

3. Add code to the **Validate** method, so that if the student ID the user has entered is greater than 51, a run-time error is raised with the following arguments.

Argument	Value
Number	vbObjectError + 1001
Source	CStudent
Description	Student ID is too large.

4. Remove the code in the **Validate** method so it does not return a value of zero.

5. Save your work.

▶ Test the CStudent error

1. In the **Tools** menu, click **Options**. In the **General** tab of the **Options** dialog box, set the **Error Trapping** option to **Break in Class Module**.

2. Run the application, enter a negative number as the student ID, and click **Login**.

3. Click **Debug** in the **Microsoft Visual Basic** dialog box that reports the run-time error.

   The run-time error pauses in the class module.

4. In the **Tools** menu, click **Options**. In the **General** tab of the **Options** dialog box, set the **Error Trapping** option to **Break on Unhandled Errors**.

5. Run the application, enter a negative number as the student ID, and click **Login**.

6. Click **Debug** in the **Microsoft Visual Basic** dialog box that reports the run-time error.

   This time, the run-time error pauses in the client application.

▶ Add a run-time error handler

1. Add an error handler to the **cmdLogin_Click** event procedure.

2. In the error handler, test for the error generated in the class module.

3. If an error is found, display a message box telling the user that the student ID must be greater than zero.

For more information about handling errors, see "Debugging and Error Handling" on page 22 in Chapter 1, "Visual Basic Essentials."

To see an example of the error handler procedure, see Lab Hint 3.2 in Appendix B.

Exercise 4:
Adding Component Information and Help

In this exercise, you will define procedure attributes that provide descriptive information and context-sensitive Help for the properties and methods of the **Student** object.

▶ **Set procedure attributes**

1. In the **Project Properties** dialog box, set **Help File Name** to StateUBookstore.hlp.

   The file StateUBookstore.hlp is located in the *<install folder>*\Labs\Lab03 folder. It is a Help file with two sample topics.

2. Open the **CStudent** class module.

3. On the **Tools** menu, click **Procedure Attributes**. In the **Procedure Attributes** dialog box, add a description for the **Validate** method and **StudentID** property.

4. In the **Procedure Attributes** dialog box, set **Help Context ID** for the **Validate** method to 2 and the **Help Context ID** for the **StudentID** property to 1.

5. In the **Procedure Attributes** dialog box, add descriptions for the **Validate** method and the **StudentID** property.

6. Save your work.

▶ **Test the help file**

1. Run the **Object Browser**, and select the **StateUBookstore** application.

2. Select the **CStudent** class.

3. Test the Help information for the **Validate** method and **StudentID** property.

Self-Check Questions

To see the answers to the Self-Check Questions, see Appendix A.

1. How can you create a read-only property for a class?

A. Define a **Property Get** procedure and define a **Property Let** procedure with no arguments.

B. Define a **Property Get** procedure and a **Property Let** procedure.

C. Define a **Property Get** procedure without a **Property Set** or **Property Let** procedure.

D. Define a **Property Set** or **Property Let** procedure without a **Property Get** procedure.

2. How can you make a property that is an Object data type writeable?

A. Define a **Property Get** procedure and a **Property Let** procedure.

B. Define a **Property Set** procedure and a **Property Let** procedure.

C. Define a **Property Get** procedure without a matching **Property Set** or **Property Let** procedure.

D. Define a **Property Get** procedure and a **Property Set** procedure.

3. Which of the following statements is true of class modules?

A. Only one class module can exist in a project.

B. Class modules provide functionality in the form of objects, and each class module defines one type of object.

C. Class modules contain methods that can be called only from other class modules.

D. You have access only to the methods of an object defined by a class module.

4. The following example code declares an event procedure that passes parameters to a client by value and by reference:

```
Public Event LimitChanged(ByVal iID As Integer, ByRef iLimit As
Integer)
```

What is the result if these parameters are changed when the event is handled?

A. If the **iLimit** argument is changed, the component will see the change.

B. If the **iLimit** argument is changed, the component will not see the change.

C. If the **iID** argument is changed, the component will see the change.

D. If the **iID** and **iLimit** arguments are both changed, the component will see both changes.

5. Why should you use COM components in your application?

A. COM components can be reused.

B. COM components hide programming complexity from other programmers.

C. COM components make it easier for you to revise and update your applications.

D. All of the above.

Student Notes:

Chapter 4:
Building ActiveX Controls

In this chapter, you will learn how to create ActiveX controls. ActiveX controls created in Microsoft Visual Basic can be used in many different container applications, such as other Visual Basic applications, Microsoft Office documents, and Web pages viewed with Microsoft Internet Explorer.

Objectives

After completing this chapter, you will be able to:

◆ Describe the benefits of using ActiveX controls.

◆ Create an ActiveX control that exposes properties, methods, and events.

◆ Use control events to save and load persistent properties.

◆ Test and debug an ActiveX control.

◆ Create and enable property pages for an ActiveX control.

◆ Enable the data-binding capabilities of an ActiveX control.

◆ Create an ActiveX control that is a data source.

Creating an ActiveX Control

In this section, you will be introduced to using ActiveX controls. You will also learn how to create the user interface for a control.

Creating the user interface for an ActiveX control is similar to creating a standard Visual Basic form. You draw controls, and then provide the code that defines the behavior of those controls.

When you design a control, you take advantage of the functionality of existing controls while adding your own custom functionality. As the control developer, you have the ability to choose which pieces of functionality from the existing controls to expose to the user of your custom control.

Introduction to Controls

Controls are reusable objects that include visual elements and code. With Visual Basic, you can use controls to quickly create forms and dialog boxes. Visual Basic ships with built-in controls that are visible on the Control Toolbox when you start Visual Basic, and ActiveX controls that you can add to the Toolbox. Beginning with Visual Basic version 5.0, you have been able to create your own ActiveX controls. Controls must be placed in some type of container, such as a form or an application.

Control Classes

A control you create in Visual Basic is known as a control class, which acts as a template for that control. The control class is compiled into an .ocx file. To use the control in an application, you place the control on a form, which creates a design-time instance of that control. When a user runs the application containing the control, the user gets a run-time instance of the control.

The following illustration shows the evolution of the control and related files as it is created by a control developer, used by an application developer in a standard application, and then used by the user of the completed application.

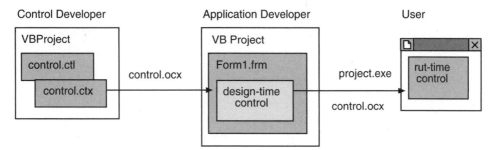

Project Files

The source code and property values for a control class are stored in a text file with a .ctl extension. A .ctl file is equivalent to the Visual Basic .frm file that is used to store this information for a form.

Graphical elements, which cannot be stored as text, are stored in a file with a .ctx extension. A .ctx file is equivalent to a Visual Basic .frx file that is used to store graphical elements in forms.

A Visual Basic ActiveX control project can contain one or more .ctl files, each of which defines a separate control class. When you compile a control project, one .ocx file is created that contains all of the controls in the project, as shown in the following illustration.

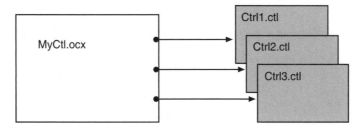

Steps for Creating an ActiveX Control

To see the demonstration "Building an ActiveX Control," see the accompanying CD-ROM.

To build an ActiveX control, you perform the following steps:

1. Create an ActiveX Control project.
2. Create the user interface for the control.

   ActiveX controls are typically made up of constituent controls. A constituent control is any existing control, such as a control that ships with Visual Basic (for example, a text box or command button), or a control that you've purchased.

3. Create the properties and methods of the control.
4. Create event procedures for the constituent controls on your control.
5. Expose events from the control.
6. Create property pages for the control.
7. Debug and test the control.

Adding Constituent Controls

An ActiveX control includes a **UserControl** object and constituent controls.

The UserControl Object

The **UserControl** object is the foundation for building controls. Every ActiveX control that you create with Visual Basic contains a **UserControl** object.

UserControl objects contain code modules and visual designers. When you open a **UserControl** in design mode, the object is displayed in a visual designer window. You can use the visual designer to place constituent controls on the **UserControl** object just as you would on a Visual Basic form.

The following illustration shows the **UserControl** visual designer with a code window in the background.

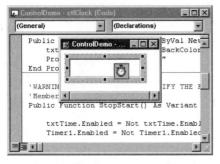

Constituent Controls

A constituent control is an instance of a control that you place on a **UserControl** object. When you place an ActiveX control on a form, an instance of the **UserControl** object is created, along with instances of any constituent controls you placed on the **UserControl** object.

The following illustration shows a **UserControl** object on which several constituent controls have been placed.

You can use any standard Visual Basic control on the **UserControl** object except the OLE Container control. You add constituent controls to a **UserControl** object in the same way you add controls to a standard Visual Basic form.

If you want to use controls that are not built into Visual Basic, you can include those controls on the **UserControl** object, but you must have the appropriate license to distribute the controls.

For information about distributing controls, see "Deploying an ActiveX Control" on page 313 in Chapter 9, "Optimizing and Deploying Applications."

UserControl Events

An ActiveX control is a client that runs in a form or in some other type of container. Therefore, its events behave somewhat differently than control events on a standard .exe project form.

When you create a control, the **UserControl** object acts as the blueprint to place the control on a form or in another container. You use this blueprint to create an instance of the control. When a control is created, a series of control events occurs.

The specific events and the order in which they occur depend on the particular user or system actions that take place during the lifetime of the control instance.

The following table summarizes how controls are created in response to a user's actions, and which events occur when the control is created.

User action	Type of control instance	Events
Places the control on a form.	Design-time instance is created.	**Initialize** **InitProperties** **Resize** **Paint**
Runs an application containing the control at design time.	Design-time instance is destroyed, and run-time instance is created.	**WriteProperties** (if needed) **Terminate** **Initialize** **Resize** **ReadProperties** **Paint**
Exits an application containing the control; returns to design mode.	Run-time instance is destroyed, and design-time instance is created.	**Terminate** **Initialize** **Resize** **ReadProperties** **Paint**
Closes the form containing the control.	Design-time instance is destroyed.	**WriteProperties** (if needed) **Terminate**
Runs the compiled application.	Run-time instance is created.	**Initialize** **ReadProperties** **Resize** **Paint**

For more information about **UserControl** events, read the article "Understanding Control Lifetime and Key Events" in Visual Basic Help.

Interacting with a Container Application

As the author of a control, you cannot always predict which container will be used for your control or what size your control will be in its container. Therefore, you should design your control so that it can function appropriately in a variety of containers and is sized appropriately. To ensure consistency between your control and its container, you can use the container's ambient properties. To ensure that your control is sized correctly, you can add code to the **Resize** event.

Using Ambient Properties

Containers provide ambient properties to suggest behavior to controls that is appropriate for the container. Ambient properties ensure that the user of a control is provided with the expected visual appearance and behavior, regardless of the container.

For example, **BackColor** is one of the standard ambient properties of a Visual Basic form. The container suggests the background color for the control so that it matches the color of the container.

The AmbientChanged Event

The **AmbientChanged** event occurs when an ambient property changes. To enable a control to respond to any changes made to the ambient properties of the container at design time, you place code in the **AmbientChanged** event. This event has one argument, **PropertyName**, that identifies which property has changed.

The Ambient Object

The **Ambient** object lets you read the values of the various ambient properties.

For example, the following example code shows how to use the **Ambient** object in the **AmbientChanged** event:

```
Private Sub UserControl_AmbientChanged(PropertyName As String)
    If PropertyName = "BackColor" Then
        UserControl.BackColor = Ambient.BackColor
    End If
End Sub
```

If the developer who uses your control changes the **BackColor** property of the container, the background color of the control instance will match that of the container.

Supporting the Enabled Property

The **Enabled** property is another ambient property you should consider when designing your control. To correctly support the **Enabled** property of your control, you must write **Get** and **Let** procedures for the **Enabled** property that delegate the enabling of your control to the **UserControl** object, as shown in the following example code:

```
Public Property Get Enabled() As Boolean
  Enabled = UserControl.Enabled
End Property

Public Property Let Enabled(ByVal NewValue As Boolean)
  UserControl.Enabled = NewValue
  PropertyChanged "Enabled"
End Property
```

For more information about using property procedures to expose properties, see "Adding Properties" on page 125 in this chapter.

Because the container is responsible for enabling and disabling controls, you must also assign the **Enabled** property to the **Enabled** procedure ID.

▶ **To assign the Enabled property to the Enabled procedure ID**

1. On the **Tools** menu, click **Procedure Attributes**.

2. In the **Name** box, select your **Enabled** procedure.

3. Click **Advanced** to expand the **Procedure Attributes** dialog box.

4. In the **Procedure ID** box, select **Enabled** to give the property the correct identifier.

For more information on exposing the **Enabled** property of your control, read the article "Allowing Your Control to be Enabled and Disabled" in Visual Basic Help.

Setting Display Characteristics of Your Control

Visual Basic provides several properties and an event that you can use to manage the appearance of your control.

Making Your Control Transparent

If you want to allow whatever is behind your control to show through, in between the constituent controls on your control's surface, you can set the **BackStyle** property of the **UserControl** object to Transparent.

However, setting **BackStyle** to Transparent may affect the performance of your control. Visual Basic must do a great deal of clipping to make the background show through correctly if your control uses:

◆ A large number of constituent controls.

◆ A complex bitmap.

◆ A **Label** control with a transparent background, a TrueType font, and a large amount of text.

Invisible Controls

Most of the controls you create will have a visible user interface. However, you can create a control that is invisible at run time, such as the **Timer** control. To create an invisible control, set the **InvisibleAtRuntime** property of the **UserControl** object.

For more information on creating invisible controls, read the article "Making Your Control Invisible at Run Time" in Visual Basic Help.

Sizing a Control

The factors that determine how a control is displayed include the amount of available screen space, user preference, and the container used to display the control.

At design time, a developer adds your control to a container application and sizes it to fit in the container. At run time, a user can resize the entire application, which in turn might resize your control to better fit the new container size. In both these scenarios, the control needs to respond to the **Resize** event in order to work with the container application.

For example, assume your control consists of a command button, several text boxes, and a list box. When your control is resized to be smaller, unless you have added the appropriate code to the **Resize** event, the text boxes and list box may not be completely visible.

> **Note** Container controls cannot handle errors when the **Resize** event occurs, and will cause the application using the control to fail. Therefore, you should provide error handling in **Resize** event procedures.

Using the Resize Event

You can use the **Resize** event to handle the resizing of controls and adjust the appearance of controls. The sizing of constituent controls is adjusted according to the current property settings for the **UserControl** object.

The following example code adjusts the width of a text box when the **UserControl** object is resized:

```
Private Sub UserControl_Resize()
    Const MinWide = 2000
    If UserControl.ScaleWidth < MinWide Then
        Text1.Width = 1000
    Else
        'Scale textbox to size of the UserControl.
        Text1.Width = UserControl.ScaleWidth - Text1.Left
    End If
End Sub
```

Customizing Your Control for the Visual Basic Environment

There are several features you can add to your ActiveX control to make it easier for developers to interact with your control at design time. You can:

◆ Create an About box for your control.

◆ Create a bitmap to be displayed in the Visual Basic toolbox.

Adding an About Box

ActiveX controls can have an **About** property at the top of the **Properties** window, as shown in the following illustration.

When the user selects this property, an About box appears. The About box can be used to advertise your company or provide copyright information for your control.

▶ **To add an About box to your control**

1. Add an About Dialog form to the project.

2. Create a public procedure in the control class to display the form. The following example code displays the About Dialog form for your control:

```
Public Sub ShowAbout()
    frmAbout.Show vbModal
    Unload frmAbout
    Set frmAbout = Nothing
End Sub
```

3. Assign the public procedure to the **AboutBox** procedure attribute of your control class.

   a. On the **Tools** menu, select **Procedure Attributes**.

   b. In the **Procedure Attributes** dialog box, select the procedure that displays the About box, and click **Advanced**.

   c. In the **Procedure ID** listbox, select **AboutBox**, and click **OK**.

Specifying a Toolbox Bitmap

You can specify a custom bitmap to appear in the Visual Basic Control Toolbox, as shown in the following illustration.

Toolbox bitmaps are 16 by 15 pixels in size. If you specify a bitmap of a different size, it will be scaled to 16 by 15 pixels, which will usually distort the image.

To specify a Toolbox bitmap, set the **ToolboxBitmap** property of the **UserControl** object to the bitmap you want displayed for the control.

Exposing Properties, Methods, and Events

As with any standard control in a Visual Basic application, an ActiveX control provides functionality by exposing its properties, methods, and events.

You can use the ActiveX Control Interface Wizard to create properties, methods, and events.

This section also includes information about how to create properties, methods, and events manually, without the ActiveX Control Interface Wizard. You will learn how to use property procedures to create properties, map properties to multiple controls, and store and retrieve the values of properties. This section also shows how to add methods and raise events.

Using the ActiveX Control Interface Wizard

Visual Basic includes the ActiveX Control Interface Wizard, which simplifies the task of creating a control. This wizard lets you determine which properties, methods, and events will constitute the interface definition of your control.

The ActiveX Control Interface Wizard maps functionality from your control to the functionality of the **UserControl** object or constituent controls. You can change the default mappings later in the process.

In addition, this wizard generates the underlying interface code, including:

◆ Property procedure code to implement procedures.

◆ **Sub** and **Function** procedures to implement methods.

◆ Code to raise the events you have selected.

The wizard generates the correct arguments and data types for standard events and event forwarding code for all your event mappings.

To see the demonstration "Using the ActiveX Control Interface Wizard," see the accompanying CD-ROM.

Adding Properties

The container for an ActiveX control supplies a number of default properties, so you should decide which additional properties you need for the control.

Creating a Property

To create a property for a control, you need to define storage for the property and then create property procedures to set and retrieve the property value. You must also let Visual Basic know when a property value changes. To indicate that a property value has changed, you use the **PropertyChanged** method of the **UserControl** object within a property procedure.

Calling the **PropertyChanged** method notifies Visual Basic that a property of your control changed. This is important so that Visual Basic can mark your control as needing to be saved in the project where it is being used. Also, calling **PropertyChanged** notifies Visual Basic to update the property value in the **Properties** window and in any property pages for your control.

For more information about property pages, see "Creating Property Pages" on page 143 in this chapter.

Using Property Procedures

You create property procedures for a read-write property in pairs. You can create a **Set** or **Let** procedure to assign a value to the property, and then create a **Get** procedure to return the value. You give the two procedures the same name, which is also the name of the property.

When a user reads the property, the **Property Get** procedure runs. When a user sets the property, the **Property Let** or **Property Set** procedure runs.

To see the demonstration "Creating and Using Properties," see the accompanying CD-ROM.

The following example code shows property procedures that define the **UpperCase** property of a control:

```
Private m_UpperCase as Boolean
Public Property Get UpperCase()As Boolean
  UpperCase = m_UpperCase
End Property

Public Property Let UpperCase(ByVal New_UpperCase As Boolean)
  m_UpperCase = New_UpperCase
  PropertyChanged "UpperCase"
End Property
```

To create a read-write property that returns a standard data type, define a **Property Get** procedure and a **Property Let** procedure. To create a read-write property that is an **Object** data type, define a **Property Get** procedure and a **Property Set** procedure.

To create a read-only property, define a **Property Get** procedure without a matching **Property Let** or **Property Set** procedure.

For information about adding properties, read the article "Adding Properties to Controls" in Visual Basic Help.

Exposing Constituent Control Properties

In addition to creating custom properties for an ActiveX control, you can expose properties of the constituent controls in your ActiveX control.

Exposing the Property of a Constituent Control

When a user works with your control, the properties of the **UserControl** object and of any constituent controls are not available by default. You can, however, make the properties available through existing properties of the **UserControl** object or of any constituent controls you have placed on the object.

For example, if you create a control that contains a **Label** control and a **TextBox** control, you can expose the properties of either the **UserControl** object or the constituent controls by using property procedures.

The following sample code shows how to expose the **Caption** property of a **Label** control, which is a constituent control on a **UserControl** object. To copy this code for use in your own projects, see "Exposing the Caption Property of a Constituent Control" on the accompanying CD-ROM.

```
Public Property Get Caption()As String
  Caption = lblName.Caption
End Property

Public Property Let Caption(ByVal NewCaption As String)
  lblName.Caption = NewCaption
  PropertyChanged "Caption"
End Property
```

When an instance of the **UserControl** object is placed on the form, the **Caption** property becomes available in the **Properties** window for that instance. A developer who uses your control can then set the value of the text that will appear in the label.

Resolving Ambiguities in UserControl and Constituent Control Property Names

If you want to expose a property of a constituent control that has the same name as a property of the **UserControl** object, such as **Width,** you must resolve the ambiguity by creating a new property for your control with a unique name.

The following sample code shows how to add a property **LastNameWidth** that maps to the **Width** property of a constituent control **txtLastName**. To copy this code for use in your own projects, see "Resolving Ambiguities in UserControl and Constituent Control Property Names" on the accompanying CD-ROM.

```
Public Property Get LastNameWidth()As Integer
  LastNameWidth = txtLastName.Width
End Property

Public Property Let LastNameWidth(ByVal NewLastNameWidth As Inte-
ger)
  txtLastName.Width = NewLastNameWidth
  PropertyChanged "LastNameWidth"
End Property
```

Mapping a Property to Multiple Controls

You can map more than one constituent control property to a property of your control through delegation.

For example, if you expose the **ForeColor** property of the **UserControl** object, you can match this color in constituent controls. The following sample code shows how to map the **ForeColor** property of multiple constituent controls through delegation. To copy this code for use in your own projects, see "Mapping Multiple Constituent Control Properties to a UserControl Property" on the accompanying CD-ROM.

```
Public Property Get ForeColor() As OLE_COLOR
  ForeColor = UserControl.ForeColor
End Property

Public Property Let ForeColor(ByVal New_ForeColor As OLE_COLOR)
  Dim ctl As Object
  UserControl.ForeColor = New_ForeColor
  For Each ctl In Controls
      If(TypeOf ctl Is Label) _
      Or (TypeOf ctl Is CheckBox) Then
          ctl.ForeColor = New_ForeColor
      End If
  Next
  PropertyChanged "ForeColor"
End Property
```

When a user changes the **ForeColor** property of your control, the **ForeColor** properties of the constituent controls are also changed.

Adding Methods

A method is a **Sub** or **Function** procedure exposed by an object. You can implement custom methods or delegate to existing methods of constituent controls, just as you can with properties.

Creating a Method

You create methods for controls by declaring **Public Sub** or **Function** procedures. For more information about creating a method, see "Creating Methods" on page 87 in Chapter 3, "Using Class Modules."

The following example code creates a method that displays the date:

```
Public Sub ShowDate()
  MsgBox "Date is: " & Now()
End Sub
```

To see the demonstration "Implementing a Custom Method for an ActiveX Control," see the accompanying CD-ROM.

Exposing Methods of Constituent Controls

You can also expose methods of any constituent controls that are part of your control.

The following example code creates the method **IDFocus**, which in turn calls the **SetFocus** method of the constituent text box control:

```
Public Sub IDFocus()
    txtEmpID.SetFocus
End Sub
```

In the example code, the **TextBox** control txtEmpID is a constituent control of the **UserControl** object. When the method is called from a form, focus is set to the txtEmpID control on the **UserControl** object.

In this way, you can expose methods of your constituent controls and enhance them with your own code as well.

Storing and Retrieving Property Values

Instances of controls are continually created and destroyed, so you must ensure that the property values are preserved. When you create a control, you must include code that saves and retrieves property values of the control.

To store and retrieve information each time an object is created or destroyed, you use the **ReadProperty** and **WriteProperty** methods of the **PropertyBag** object.

To see the demonstration "Saving and Retrieving Properties," see the accompanying CD-ROM.

Saving Property Values

You save property values in the **WriteProperties** event of the **UserControl** object. This event is called when the design-time control is destroyed.

The **WriteProperty** method takes three arguments: a string indicating the property to save, a value for the property, and a default value if the developer did not set an initial property.

The following example code shows how to save current property values with the **WriteProperty** method of the **PropertyBag** object:

```
Private Sub UserControl_WriteProperties(PropBag As PropertyBag)
  PropBag.WriteProperty "UpperCase", mvarUpperCase, vbUpperCase
  PropBag.WriteProperty "Caption", Label1.Caption, "Username"
End Sub
```

Reading Property Values

You retrieve property values in the **ReadProperties** event of the **UserControl** object. This event is called when either the design-time or run-time control is created.

The **ReadProperty** method takes two arguments: a string designating the property name and a default value. If a property value has been saved, the **ReadProperty** method returns the value. If a property value has not been saved, the method returns the default value.

The following example code shows how to use the **ReadProperty** method to return the saved value of the **Caption** property:

```
Private Sub UserControl_ReadProperties(PropBag As PropertyBag)
  'Trap for invalid property values
  On Error Resume Next
  Label1.Caption = PropBag.ReadProperty("Caption", "Username")
End Sub
```

Default Property Values

When you read and write property values, it is important to provide default values. Visual Basic writes a line of code in the source file (.frm, .dob, .pag, or .ctl) of the control's container only if the property value differs from the default value you have provided. As a result of providing a default value, the file size is reduced and application performance is improved.

Initializing Property Values in the InitProperties Event

The first time an instance of a control is placed on a container, it receives the **InitProperties** event. Thereafter, only the **ReadProperties** event occurs.

In the **InitProperties** event, you set the initial value for a property using the same default value that you provide with the **WriteProperty** and **ReadProperty** methods to save and retrieve the property value.

Since mapped properties are already initialized by the constituent control, you only need to initialize properties that don't map to properties of constituent controls. The following example code shows how to initialize the **UpperCase** property of an ActiveX control:

```
'set up storage for the property
Dim mvarUpperCase as Boolean
..
'Use that default value in the InitProperties event
Private Sub UserControl_InitProperties()
  mvarUpperCase = vbUpperCase
End Sub
```

Exposing Named Constants

You can use enumerations to provide named constants for a component. Enumerations provide a convenient way to group a set of related named constants and associate them with constant values. To display constants, you can use enumerations to write code for a control so it appears in the **Auto List Members** drop-down list box.

You make the members of an enumeration available to users of your control by declaring the enumeration as **Public**. Include the enumeration in any public module that defines a class, such as a class module, **UserControl**, or **UserDocument**.

The following example code defines an enumeration that contains named constants representing the Celsius boiling temperatures of various substances:

```
Public Enum TempBoilCelsius
  mtempWater = 100
  mtempIron = 2750
  mtempNitrogen = -195.8
  mtempGold = 2807
End Enum
```

You can use this enumeration as the data type of the property **BoilingPoint**, as shown in the following illustration.

Raising Control Events

An event is the way a control communicates with a container application. When a user interacts with the constituent controls on your control, your control receives those events and can react to them. However, the container of your control will not receive these same events unless your control specifically raises them to the container.

You use the following steps to raise an event from an ActiveX control:

1. Declare the event.

2. Raise the event.

To see the demonstration "Adding an Event to an ActiveX Control," see the accompanying CD-ROM.

Declaring an Event

You declare an event in the General Declarations section of a **UserControl** by using the **Event** keyword. This makes the event visible to client applications that use your control. The following example code declares an event named **StatusChanged**:

```
Public Event StatusChanged(status as Integer)
```

Raising an Event

When you want an event to be raised to the client application, you call the **RaiseEvent** statement, and pass the event name and any arguments that the event takes. You can raise an event at any time from your control: from an event procedure of one of your constituent controls, or from a method of your control.

The following example code raises the **StatusChanged** event when the user clicks the **cmdPlaceOrder** constituent control:

```
Private Sub cmdPlaceOrder_Click()
  Dim iStatus as Integer
  'set iStatus and raise the event
  iStatus = 3
  RaiseEvent StatusChanged(iStatus)
End Sub
```

Receiving an Event

There is an important distinction between the events received by your control, or by its constituent controls, and the events your control raises. The control developer uses the events a control receives to add functionality to that control. A developer who uses the control uses the events the control raises to add functionality to the application containing the control.

When developers use your control, they will trap the events raised by your control just like handling any other event from any other control. In the following example code, a form uses your control and handles the **StatusChanged** event:

```
Private Sub ctlOrder_StatusChanged(iStatus as Integer)
  Msgbox "Status of the order is now: " & iStatus
End Sub
```

Events raised by an ActiveX Control are handled in the container application using the control. For more information on how to handle events from a control, see "Testing the Control Programmatically," on page 136 in this chapter.

Exposing Constituent Control Events

Unlike exposing properties and methods by delegation, you expose an event of a constituent control by raising your own event.

▶ **To expose the events of a constituent control**

1. Declare a new event in the **UserControl** object.

2. In the constituent control's event, raise your own event.

In the following example code, the **KeyPress** event from a **TextBox** control is exposed through an event of the control named **UserNameKeyPress**:

```
Public Event UserNameKeyPress(KeyAscii As Integer)

Private Sub txtUserName_KeyPress(KeyAscii As Integer)
    RaiseEvent UserNameKeyPress(KeyAscii)
End Sub
```

Notice that arguments to the event are passed to the client.

Testing a Control

When you test your ActiveX control, you must test the control's design-time as well as run-time functionality.

An ActiveX control will behave differently, depending on how the control is instantiated. Understanding this behavior will help you test your controls properly.

Testing the Control's User Interface

Because an ActiveX control cannot run by itself, you test the control by running it inside a container.

Testing the Control in Internet Explorer

If you open an ActiveX Control project and select **Run** from the Visual Basic menu, Visual Basic will run the control in Internet Explorer. This allows you to test the user interface of the control from a Web page.

Testing the Control on a Form

Visual Basic allows you to load two or more projects into a project group, which is saved with the extension .vbg. While you have your control project open, add a standard EXE project to your project group and place an instance of your control on a form in this new test project. Use this technique when you want to run and test the control on a form. You can test the design-time and run-time behavior of the control.

▶ **To add a test project to a project group**

1. On the **File** menu, click **Add Project**.

2. In the **Add Project** dialog box, double-click the Standard EXE icon to add an .exe project to your project group.

You can now see both projects in the Project window. The title of the Project window indicates the project group name, as shown in the following illustration.

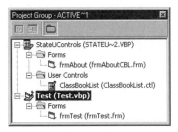

To test the design-time features of your control, you must close the control's visual designer. This causes Visual Basic to display the icon for the control in the Control Toolbox, so you can place instances of the control on a container form.

Debugging

Once you have created a test project for your ActiveX control, you can test and debug the control by placing breakpoints in the control's procedures and stepping through the code. However, a unique trait of debugging ActiveX controls is that the control can run when the client is in Design mode as well as when the client is running.

There are several situations in which the control runs in Design mode:

♦ When a developer sets the properties of your control.

♦ When property values are read and saved.

♦ When the control is initially displayed.

In these cases, your breakpoints can be reached before the client is run.

Testing the Control Programmatically

Using controls is an integral part of building a standard application. In general, using a custom ActiveX control is no different than using a control that ships with Visual Basic. However there are a few things to keep in mind about ActiveX controls at design time.

Using Properties

You can set and retrieve properties of the ActiveX control at either design time or run time. Be aware that property procedures run in both cases.

♦ Design time

   When you use the Properties window at design time to set property values of your control, Visual Basic invokes your control's **Property Let** or **Property Set** procedures. This means that your control is running even though the application using the control is not. Therefore you must close any design windows of the control before you can test it in a container application.

♦ Run time

   There are no special considerations to keep in mind about getting and setting properties of an ActiveX control at run time. Behavior is the same as for any other control.

Handling Events

When you place a custom ActiveX control on a form, it gets added to the list of objects in the Code window and any events you've exposed for the control are listed in the Procedure list for the control. This makes it easy for you to add event procedures for the control in the same way you add event procedures for standard controls. The following illustration shows an example of using the Procedure list to open the Code window for a custom control's event procedure.

For example, this is the event procedure for the control's **UserNameKeyPress** event:

```
Private Sub ctlNewEmployee_UserNameKeyPress(KeyAscii As Integer)
    'Convert the character to uppercase.
    'Since KeyAscii is passed ByRef it can be changed
    'in the client.
    KeyAscii = Asc(UCase(Chr(KeyAscii)))
End Sub
```

Lab 4.1: Building an ActiveX Control

In this lab, you will create an ActiveX control that displays the classes a student is enrolled in, and the books required by those classes.

To see the demonstration "Lab 4.1 Solution," see the accompanying CD-ROM.

Estimated time to complete this lab: **45 minutes**

To complete the exercises in this lab, you must have the required software. For detailed information about the labs and setup for the labs, see "Labs" in "About This Course."

Objectives

After completing this lab, you will be able to:

◆ Create a basic ActiveX control with Visual Basic.

◆ Add properties and methods to the control.

◆ Raise an event from the control.

Prerequisites

Before working on this lab, you should be familiar with the following:

◆ Placing controls on forms.

◆ Creating an About box form.

Exercises

The following exercises provide practice working with the concepts and techniques covered in this chapter:

◆ Exercise 1: Creating a Control

In this exercise, you will create an ActiveX control consisting of three constituent controls. You will also add a timer control to the control for testing purposes.

◆ Exercise 2: Adding the Interface

In this exercise, you will create the **ClassName, BookName,** and **Price** properties, and the **DblClick** event for the **ClassBookList** control.

Exercise 1: Creating a Control

The StateUBookstore solution will display a list of books that a student will need to purchase for class. This book list will be displayed on the main form of the application. To facilitate displaying the book information, you will build an ActiveX control that will be hosted in another ActiveX control called the **DataRepeater** control. By the end of Lab 4.2 you will be able to see the book list; however, you must first build a control to hold book information.

In this exercise, you will create an ActiveX control consisting of three constituent controls. You will also add a timer control to the control for testing purposes.

▶ **Create the ActiveX control**

1. Create a new ActiveX Control project.

2. Name the project StateUControls.

3. Name the **UserControl** object **ClassBookList**. This control will be used in Lab 4.2 to contain the class name, book title, and price information for books that a student will need to purchase.

4. Save the **UserControl** object and project files as ClassBookList.ctl and StateUControls.vbp, respectively.

5. Add three **TextBox** controls, and one **Timer** control to the user control, and size it as shown in the following illustration.

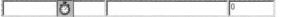

> **Note** The timer is only for testing, and you will delete it in Lab 4.2, Exercise 1.

6. Set the names of the controls to: **txtClass, txtBook, txtPrice,** and **Timer1.**

7. Set the **DataFormat** property of the **txtPrice** text box to Currency.

8. Set the **Timer** control's **Interval** property to 1000.

9. In the **Timer** control's **Timer** event, add the following code:

```
txtBook.Text = Time
```

10. Save your work.

▶ **Add a toolbox icon**

1. Set the **ToolboxBitmap** property of your control to \Labs\Lab04.1\ClassBookList.bmp.

2. Close the control window to see the icon in the Toolbox.

3. Save your work.

▶ **Add an About box**

1. Add an **About Box** form to the StateUControls project. Save the form file as frmAboutCBL.frm.

2. Fill in the description and warning labels on the **About** box with information about your control.

3. Close the form.

4. Create a method of the **ClassBookList** control named **ShowAbout**.

   a. The method doesn't take any parameters.

   b. Display the **About** box as a modal form, then unload it.

   To see an example of the method, see Lab Hint 4.1 in Appendix B.

5. Make the **ShowAbout** method the AboutBox procedure of your control.

   a. On the **Tools** menu, click **Procedure Attributes**.

   b. In the **Procedure Attributes** dialog box, select the **ShowAbout** method, and click **Advanced**.

   c. In the **Procedure ID** list box, select **AboutBox**, and click **OK**.

   You will test the control's About form after you place the control on a test form.

▶ **Test the ActiveX control**

1. Add a new Standard EXE project to the project group.

2. Right click the Standard EXE project and chose Set as Startup.

3. Save the new form and project as frmTest.frm and Test.vbp, respectively.

4. Save the project group as ActiveXControl.vbg.

5. Add a **ClassBookList** control to the form frmTest.

   If the toolbox icon for the **ClassBookList** is disabled, make sure all of the windows associated with the StateU project are closed.

   Notice that when the control is placed on the form, the time is displayed in the **txtBook** text box at both design time and run time.

6. Select the **About** property of the control.

   The **About** form displays.

7. Run the Test project.

Exercise 2: Adding the Interface

In this exercise, you will create the **ClassName**, **BookName**, and **Price** properties, and the **DblClick** event for the **ClassBookList** control.

▶ **Create properties**

1. Using property procedures, add the following properties to the **ClassBookList** control.

Name	Type	Value
ClassName	String	txtClass.Text
BookName	String	txtBook.Text
Price	Double	txtPrice.Text

If you are unsure of the syntax of the procedures, see Lab Hint 4.2 in Appendix B.

2. Open the code module for the user control.

3. The **Price** Property Get property procedure will return the value in the **txtPrice** text box. If this text box is empty, an error may occur. Change the code of the **Price** Property Get procedure to use the **Val** function to avoid getting an error for no value. Your solution code should resemble the following:

```
Price = CDbl(Val(txtPrice.Text))
```

▶ **Raise an event**

1. Declare the event **CBLDblClick** with no arguments.

2. In the **DblClick** event of each of the text box constituent controls, raise the **CBLDblClick** event of the user control.

3. Save your work.

▶ **Test the control**

1. Close all of the windows associated with the **ClassBookList** control.

2. Open the **Test** form.

3. Add a text box and three command buttons to the **Test** form, as shown in the following illustration.

```
Form1                                            _ □ ×
┌──────────────────────────┬─────────────┬──────┐
│                          │ 12:39:23 PM │ 0    │
└──────────────────────────┴─────────────┴──────┘

┌──────────────────────────┐
│ txtTestClassName         │
└──────────────────────────┘

     ┌─────────────┐       ┌──────────────┐ ┌────────────┐
     │ Set ClassName│      │ Show ClassName│ │ Show About │
     └─────────────┘       └──────────────┘ └────────────┘
```

4. Add code to the command buttons, to set the **ClassName** property to the value of the text box, display the **ClassName** property in a message box, and call the **ShowAbout** method of the **ClassBookList** control.

To see an example of the solution code, see Lab Hint 4.3 in Appendix B.

5. Add code to the **CBLDblClick** event of the **ClassBookList** control that displays a message box.

To see an example of the event procedure, see Lab Hint 4.4 in Appendix B.

6. Run the Test project.

   a. Test each of the command buttons.

   b. Test the **DblClick** event by double-clicking the control.

Creating Property Pages

In this section, you will learn how to add property pages to an ActiveX control.

Property pages provide an alternative to organizing ActiveX control properties. With property pages, a user can view related properties in a tabbed dialog box.

For example, if you create a **Font** property that has several different values, you can create a property page for each of them instead of displaying the values in a drop-down list box in the Properties window.

Using the Property Page Wizard

Property pages enable you to define a custom interface for setting properties of an ActiveX control. This gives you more flexibility than using the Properties window. Users can identify a property that is associated with a property page by the ellipsis (...) button next to the property in the Properties window. When the user clicks this button, Visual Basic opens the property page for the associated property.

Furthermore, if more than one of your properties can be set with property pages, you can create a tabbed property page dialog box and add a **Custom** property to your control to access this dialog box. In this way, users can set many properties of your control at once.

The following illustration shows a tabbed **Property Pages** dialog box.

Creating Property Pages

To add a property page for your control, you perform the following main steps:

♦ Create the user interface for the property page.

♦ Add code to synchronize the property page with the current state of the control.

♦ Set up the appropriate property page relationships: associate properties with a property page, and associate a tabbed **Property Page** dialog box with your control.

Using the Property Page Wizard

Visual Basic provides a Property Page Wizard that you can use to carry out these steps. To see the demonstration "Using the Property Page Wizard," see the accompanying CD-ROM.

▶ **To run the Property Page Wizard**

1. On the **Add-Ins** menu, click **Add-In Manager**.

2. In the **Add-In Manager** dialog box, select **VB Property Page Wizard** and click **OK**.

3. On the **Add-Ins** menu, click **Property Page Wizard.**

4. Add a new property page for each grouping of properties in your control.

   If you have a property that is a standard data type (like color or font) the wizard will automatically add the standard property page to the list of property pages for your control.

5. Add the properties of your control to the property pages you've created.

6. Click **Finish.**

Creating the Property Page Interface Manually

The Property Page Wizard adds a **PropertyPage** object to your project and creates a standard user interface for the properties of your control. If you want to change the look of the property page, edit the property page manually. The following illustration shows a sample property page with some controls drawn on it.

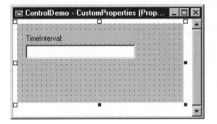

You can also add property pages to your control project manually.

▶ **To add a property page to your control project**

1. On the **Project** menu, click **Add Property Page.**

2. On the **New** tab of the **Add Property Page** dialog box, double-click the Property Page icon.

   A visual designer appears.

3. Add a control for each property, just as you would on a standard form.

Implementing Property Page Behavior

When you use the Property Page Wizard to add property pages to your control, it adds the necessary code to synchronize them with the current state of the control.

When a user opens a property page for your control, the **SelectionChanged** event procedure sets the values of the controls on the property page to the current property values of the control. When the user closes the property page, or clicks the **Apply** button, the **ApplyChanges** event procedure updates the appearance of the control with the new property values.

To see the demonstration "Implementing Property Page Behavior," see the accompanying CD-ROM.

SelectedControls Collection

Users can select multiple instances of your control on a form and set properties for all of the controls at once. The **SelectedControls** collection contains all controls in a container that are currently selected.

To determine whether multiple controls have been selected, you use the **Count** property of the **SelectedControls** collection. If the **Count** property is greater than 1, then multiple controls are currently selected in the container.

In the **SelectionChanged** event you need to either set the value of the controls on the property page to the common state of the controls or leave the value blank. In the **ApplyChanges** event, you need to update the state of all controls to the new property values by looping through the **SelectedControls** collection.

SelectionChanged Event

The **SelectionChanged** event occurs whenever a property page is opened and when the list of currently selected controls changes. You use this event to set the values of the controls on the property page.

The following example code assigns the value of a **Timer** control's **Interval** property to a text box on the property page:

```
Private Sub PropertyPage_SelectionChanged()
  txtTimeInterval.Text = SelectedControls(0).Interval
End Sub
```

Changed Property

To notify Visual Basic of changes to properties on a property page, you set the **Changed** property of the **PropertyPage** object to **True**. This also enables the **Apply** button in the **Property Pages** dialog box.

The following example code notifies Visual Basic that the value of the **Interval** property displayed in a text box has been changed on the property page:

```
Private Sub txtTimeInterval_Change()
  PropertyPage.Changed = True
End Sub
```

ApplyChanges Event

To write any changed property values back to the currently selected controls, you use the **ApplyChanges** event.

The **ApplyChanges** event occurs in the following situations:

◆ The **OK** button is clicked to dismiss the **Property Pages** dialog box.

◆ The **Apply** button is clicked.

◆ Another tab in the **Property Pages** dialog box is selected.

The following example code applies changes to the **Interval** property of all currently selected controls:

```
Private Sub PropertyPage_ApplyChanges()

  Dim objControl As Object
  For Each objControl In SelectedControls
      ' this code assumes all controls have an Interval property
      '  you should write code to handle different control types
      objControl.Interval = txtTimeInterval.Text
  Next

End Sub
```

Establishing Property Page Relationships

If you have specified more than one property page for your control, the tabs are automatically added. Also, the **OK**, **Cancel**, and **Apply** buttons in the **Property Pages** dialog box are created for you.

When you use the Property Page Wizard to add property pages to your control, it also sets up the appropriate relationships between the properties of your control and the property pages. The wizard adds the ellipsis (...) buttons to the properties that can be set by property pages, and it adds the **Custom** property, which displays the tabbed **Property Pages** dialog box showing all the property pages used by your control.

To see the demonstration "Establishing Property Page Relationships," see the accompanying CD-ROM.

Assigning Property Pages to a Control

Assigning property pages to your control makes it possible for users to set multiple properties of your control at once using the **Custom** property of your control in the Properties window, or the **Properties** menu item on the context menu.

To assign one or more property pages to a control, you use the **Connect Property Pages** dialog box. To display the **Connect Property Pages** dialog box, set the **PropertyPages** property of the **UserControl** object. The **Connect Property Pages** dialog box also allows you to add standard property pages (**StandardColor**, **StandardFont**, and **StandardPicture**) to your control.

The following illustration shows how to gain access to the **Connect Property Pages** dialog box from the Properties window.

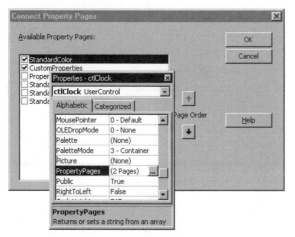

Associating a Property Page with a Property

Associating a property page with a given property allows users of your control to use the property page to set that property by clicking the ellipsis (...) button in the property window.

▶ **To associate a property page with a property**

1. On the **Tools** menu, click **Procedure Attributes**, and then click **Advanced**.

   This opens the **Procedure Attributes** dialog box to display additional options.

2. In the **Name** box, select the property you want to associate with a property page.

3. In the list **Use this Page in Property Browser**, select the property page, and then click the **Apply** button or **OK**.

Using Standard Property Pages

Standard property pages let you provide a familiar user interface to set properties of your ActiveX controls.

Visual Basic provides the following standard property pages:

- ◆ StandardFont
- ◆ StandardColor
- ◆ StandardPicture

When you create properties of type **Font**, OLE_COLOR, or **Picture**, Visual Basic automatically associates these properties with the appropriate standard property page. In the **Properties** window, an ellipsis (...) button next to any one of these properties indicates that a standard property page will be displayed when a user clicks the button.

Creating a Data-Bound Control

You can create ActiveX controls that can bind to the ADO Data control. You simply add data-aware constituent controls to your new ActiveX control and then use them to access data.

For more information about using the ADO Data control, see "Using the ADO Data Control," on page 57 in Chapter 2, "Using Visual Database Tools."

You can also use your ActiveX control with the **DataRepeater** control. The **DataRepeater** control allows you to display multiple records from a data source at one time.

Making a Control Bindable

Each data-bound ActiveX control can have many data-bound properties, and each property can bind to a different field in the database. The collection of data-aware properties along with the data fields they bind to is called the **DataBindings** collection. The default data-bound property is specified as the **DataField** property of that control.

Setting the DataField Property

The **DataField** property is used to identify one property of your control as the default data-bound field. To identify this property as the **DataField** property, use the **Procedure Attributes** dialog box. In the dialog box, you can select only one property to bind to **DataField**.

The following illustration shows how to set the data-binding options in the **Procedure Attributes** dialog box.

Setting the DataBindings Collection

Although your ActiveX control can only expose one **DataField** property, you can designate many properties of an ActiveX control as bindable by using the **Procedure Attributes** dialog box. Each property that you mark as bindable is added to the **DataBindings** collection.

▶ **To add properties to the DataBindings collection**

1. On the **Tools** menu, click **Procedure Attributes**.

2. In the **Procedure Attributes** dialog box, click the **Advanced** button.

3. For the one property you want exposed as the **DataField** property,

    a. Select the property in the **Name** list box.

    b. Check the **Property is data bound** check box, and then check the **This property binds to DataField** check box along with the other appropriate fields.

4. For all the other properties you want to mark as bindable,

  a. Select the property in the **Name** list box.

  b. Check the **Property is data bound** check box, and then select the appropriate fields except the This property binds to DataField field.

Marking additional properties as bindable lets developers place an instance of your control on a client, and bind the additional properties to a data source.

Updating Bound Properties

You can enable developers who use your control to bind the properties of your control to a data source by marking the properties as bindable. However, binding the properties to a new data source will not enable users to update the data source.

In addition to marking properties as bindable, you must also add code so that users will be able to update the database through those bound properties.

Using Constituent Controls

If you are binding to a constituent control, you delegate to that control in the associated property's **Property Get** and **Property Let** procedures.

For example, if you have a **LastName** property that applies to a text box on an **Address** control, you would map the **LastName** property to the **Text** property of the text box control.

CanPropertyChange Method

A constituent data-bound control should always call the **CanPropertyChange** method before changing the value of a property. In Visual Basic, the value this method returns depends on the data provider.

PropertyChanged Method

In addition to calling the **CanPropertyChange** method, you must also call the **PropertyChanged** method in the constituent control's **Change** event. This will ensure that your control is bound for updating, and the data is written to the database.

The following code shows how the **LastName** property delegates to the **txtLastName** text box control, calls the **CanPropertyChange** method in the **Prop-**

erty **Let** statement, and then calls the **PropertyChanged** method in the text box control's **Change** event:

```
Public Property Get LastName() As String
  LastName = txtLastName.Text
End Property

Public Property Let LastName(ByVal  NewLastName As String)
  If CanPropertyChange("LastName") Then
      txtLastName.Text = NewLastName
  End if
End Property

Private Sub txtLastName_Change()
  PropertyChanged "LastName"
End Sub
```

Using the DataRepeater Control

The **DataRepeater** control functions as a data-bound container of any user control you create. For example, you might create a user control that contains three **TextBox** controls designed to show one record of an employee database—displaying name, birth date, and employee number.

After compiling your control into an .ocx file, you can create a form that contains the **DataRepeater** control. Set the **DataRepeater** control's **RepeatedControlName** property to the name of your control. You then bind the **DataRepeater** control to a data source, such as the ADO Data control, which sets up a connection between the repeated control and the data source. At run time, the **DataRepeater** control displays several instances of your control, each in its own row, and each bound to a different record in the data source. The user of your application sees something similar to the following illustration.

To see the demonstration "Using the DataRepeater Control," see the accompanying CD-ROM.

▶ **To use the DataRepeater control**

1. Create a data-bound ActiveX control.

2. Create a new project with a form to hold the **DataRepeater** control.

3. Add the **DataRepeater** control and ADO Data control to the Toolbox.

4. Draw a **DataRepeater** control on the form.

5. Draw an ADO Data control on the form.

   a. Set the **DataSourceName** property of the ADO Data control to access the appropriate database.

   b. Set the **Source** property of the ADO Data control to a SQL string that will display the data you want.

6. Set the **DataSource** property of the **DataRepeater** control to the ADO Data control.

7. Set the **RepeatedControlName** property of the **DataRepeater** control to the name of your data-bound ActiveX control.

8. Bind the data-bound properties of the ActiveX control to fields in the record source.

   a. Select the **Custom** property of the **DataRepeater** control.

   b. On the **RepeaterBindings** tab of the **Property Pages** dialog box, select the PropertyNames and corresponding Data Fields, and click **Add** to add the pairs of property and data fields to the **RepeaterBindings** collection.

For information about the **DataRepeater** control's events, read the article "Exposing User Control Events of the RepeatedControl" in Visual Basic Help.

Testing Data-Bound Controls

To test a data-bound control you can use either the ADO Data control or the DataRepeater control.

Using ADO Data Control

With the ADO Data control you can test both the **DataField** property of your control and the **DataBindings** collection.

▶ **To test the DataField property**

1. Place the ADO Data control on a form, and then set the **DataSourceName** and **Source** properties to retrieve a recordset from your database.

2. Place your ActiveX control on the form, and then set the **DataSource** and **DataField** properties.

3. Run the test project and move through the recordset. The field you've designated as the **DataField** property of your control should display a field from the database.

▶ **To test the DataBindings collection**

1. Set the remainder of the data-bound properties by clicking the ellipsis (...) button for the **DataBindings** property.

2. Run the form and scroll through records with the ADO Data control.

For more information about using the ADO Data control, see "Using the ADO Data Control," on page 57 in Chapter 2, "Using Visual Database Tools."

Creating a Data Source Control

The ADO Data control is a data source control that provides data to other controls. It is a general data access solution and is sufficient for most applications. However, if you have data that is not easily accessible through the ADO Data control, such as your computer's file system or a proprietary data file, you can build your own data source as an ActiveX control. Your custom data source control can then be reused, and data-bound controls can bind to it in a standard way.

Creating a data source control requires writing some ADO code. For more information about writing ADO code, see Chapter 5, "Using ActiveX Data Objects" on page 163.

To see the demonstration "Creating a Data Source Control," see the accompanying CD-ROM.

▶ **To create a data source control**

1. Set the **DataSourceBehavior** property of your control to **vbDataSource**.

   This creates an event procedure called **GetDataMember**.

2. In the **Initialize** event procedure of your control, establish the data your source will provide.

   The following sample code establishes a connection to a database and fills a recordset with data. To copy this code for use in your own projects, see "Establishing Data in a Data Source Control" on the accompanying CD-ROM.

```
Private rsBooks As Recordset
Private cnStateUBookstore As Connection

Private Sub UserControl_Initialize()

  Dim sConnect As String

  ' define the OLE DB connection string
  sConnect = "Provider=SQLOLEDB;" & _
             "Data Source=MSERIES1;" & _
             "Initial Catalog=StateUBookstore"

  ' create the ADO objects
  Set cnStateUBookstore = New Connection
  Set rsBooks = New Recordset

  ' open the database connection
    cnStateUBookstore.Open sConnect, "sa", ""

  ' create a recordset from the Books table
    rsBooks.Open "Select * from Books", cnStateUBookstore,
adOpenStatic

End Sub
```

3. Write code in the **GetDataMember** event procedure to return a data object.

   The **GetDataMember** event procedure has two parameters: DataMember and Data. The DataMember parameter is an optional parameter that specifies the name of the data member used if your control provides multiple data members. The Data parameter is the data object that the procedure returns to the data consumer.

Tip A data source can return a data object in the form of an ADO **Recordset** object, or any object that implements the same interfaces as the **OLEDBSimpleProvider** class. For more information about how to create a custom OLE DB provider object, read the article "Data Binding Tools in Visual Basic" in Visual Basic Help.

The following example code returns data from a recordset called **rsBooks**:

```
Private Sub UserControl_GetDataMember _
                (DataMember As String, Data As Object)
  ' return the data to the consumer
  Set Data = rsBooks
End Sub
```

4. Add any additional functionality you want your data source control to contain.

For example, you may want to include features to navigate through records or display the current record. The following sample code enables navigation using two command buttons. To copy this code for use in your own projects, see "Enabling Recordset Navigation Using Command Buttons" on the accompanying CD-ROM.

```
Private Sub cmdMoveNext_Click()

  rsStudents.MoveNext

End Sub

Private Sub cmdMovePrev_Click()

  rsStudents.MovePrevious

End Sub
```

Once you have created your data source control, you can place it on a form and add controls that bind to it. The **GetDataMember** event is invoked when a data consumer requests a new data source. Your control then uses the DataMember parameter if appropriate to identify the specific data member the consumer requires, and returns data back to the consumer in the form of a **Recordset** object.

Lab 4.2: Data-Binding an ActiveX Control

In this lab, you will make the **ClassBookList** control bindable, and place this control, along with the ADO Data control and the **DataRepeater** control, on the **Login** form.

To see the demonstration "Lab 4.2 Solution," see the accompanying CD-ROM.

Estimated time to complete this lab: **45 minutes**

To complete the exercises in this lab, you must have the required software. For detailed information about the labs and setup for the labs, see "Labs" in "About This Course."

Objectives

After completing this lab, you will be able to:

◆ Create a data-bound control.

◆ Use a custom control with the **DataRepeater** control.

◆ Save and load control properties.

◆ Create a property page for a control.

Prerequisites

Before working on this lab, you should be familiar with the following:

◆ Creating and using an ActiveX control.

◆ Using the ADO Data control.

Exercises

The following exercises provide practice working with the concepts and techniques covered in this chapter:

◆ Exercise 1: Creating a Data-Bound Control

In this exercise, you will bind the **ClassBookList** control to the StateUBookstore database.

◆ Exercise 2 (Optional): Persisting Property Values

In this exercise, you will add code to save and restore a property of the **ClassBookList** control.

Exercise 1: Creating a Data-Bound Control

In this exercise, you will bind the **ClassBookList** control to the StateUBookstore database.

▶ **Delete the Timer control**

◆ The timer control was used for testing only, so delete it and the **Timer1_Timer** event procedure.

▶ **Make the control properties bindable**

1. Select the control and on the **Tools** menu, click **Procedure Attributes**.

2. In the **Procedure Attributes** dialog box, click **Advanced**.

3. For each property of the control, **ClassName**, **BookName**, and **Price**, check the **Property is data bound** and the **Show in DataBindings collection at design time** check boxes.

4. For the **BookName** property, check the **This Property binds to DataField** check box.

▶ **Test the ClassBookList control's data bindings**

1. Open the test project's **frmTest** form.

2. Add the Microsoft ADO Data Control to the control toolbox.

3. Draw an ADO Data Control on the form.

4. With the ADO Data Control:

   a. Set the **ConnectionString** property of the data control to the following:

   ```
   Provider=SQLOLEDB;User ID=sa;Initial Catalog=StateUBookstore;
   Data Source=MSERIES1;
   ```

   b. Set the **RecordSource** property of the data control to the following:

   ```
   SELECT * FROM Books
   ```

5. With the **ClassBookList** control:

   a. Select the **DataBindings** property and click the build button.

   b. Bind the three fields from the data source to the **ClassBookList** control.

   The fields that you choose are only to test the data-binding feature of the control.

6. Run the Test project. Does the **ClassBookList** control display the data?

▶ **Build StateUControls.ocx**

1. Select the StateUControls project.

2. From the **File** menu, choose **Make StateUControls.ocx**.

3. Close the ClassBookList and Test projects.

▶ **Add the control to the StateUBookstore project**

1. Open the StateUBookstore project.

2. Add the Microsoft **DataRepeater** control to the **frmStateUMain** form. Name it **drClassBookList**.

3. Set the **RepeatedControlName** property of the **DataRepeater** control to the **StateUControls.ClassBookList** control.

4. Set the **Caption** property of the **DataRepeater** control to "Class Name - Book Title - Price."

5. Set the **CaptionStyle** property of the **DataRepeater** control to drpCentered.

▶ **Add a command to the data environment**

◆ In the Data Environment, add a new command called **ClassesPerStudent**. It takes the following properties.

Property	Value
Connection	cnStateUBookstore
SQL Statement	"SELECT Enrollment.StudentID, Classes.Title AS ClassName, Books.Title AS BookName, Books.Price FROM Enrollment
	INNER JOIN Students ON Enrollment.StudentID = Students.StudentID
	INNER JOIN Books ON Classes.BookID = Books.BookID
	INNER JOIN Classes ON Enrollment.ClassID = Classes.ClassID
	WHERE Enrollment.StudentID = ?"

The SQL Statement uses a parameter (the ?) to retrieve the classes in which the student is enrolled, the book required for the classes, and the price of the book.

▶ **Set up the Data Bindings**

1. Add a new Sub procedure called **SetUpDataRepeater** to the main form code module.

2. In the **SetUpDataRepeater** procedure, call the **ClassesPerStudent** command specifying the **Text** property of txtStudentID as the parameter value.

3. Set the **DataSource** property of the **DataRepeater** control equal to the recordset for the **ClassesPerStudent** command.

4. Call the **Add** method of the **RepeaterBindings** collection of the **DataRepeater** control to set up the bindings between the three fields in the recordset and the three data-bound fields in the **ClassBookList** control.

To see how your completed **SetUpDataRepeater** procedure should look, see Lab Hint 4.5 in Appendix B.

5. Call the **SetUpDataRepeater** procedure from the **Login** button's click event.

6. Save your work and test the login form.

Exercise 2 (Optional): Persisting Property Values

In this exercise, you will add code to save and restore a property of the **ClassBookList** control.

▶ **Create a Font property**

1. Open the StateUControls project.

2. Select the **ClassBookList** control and run the ActiveX Control Interface Wizard.

   a. Select the **Font** property to add to the interface for your control.

   This property will be used to set the font for all of the constituent controls on the **ClassBookList** control.

   b. Map the **Font** property to the **Font** property of the **UserControl** object, then click **Finish**.

3. In the **Property Set** procedure, assign the passed in **Font** value to the **Font** property for all of the constituent controls on the **ClassBookList** control.

To see sample code for the **Property Set** procedure, see Lab Hint 4.6 in Appendix B.

▶ **Save and load property values**

1. Look at the **WriteProperties** event procedure created by the ActiveX Control Interface Wizard. What code saves the **Font** property?

2. Look at the **ReadProperties** event procedure created by the ActiveX Control Interface Wizard. What code retrieves the value of the **Font** property?

3. In the **ReadProperties** event procedure, add code to set the **Font** properties of the three constituent text boxes to the saved **Font** value.

   For more information about saving and loading properties, see "Storing and Retrieving Property Values" on page 130 in this chapter.

4. Save the project.

▶ **Test property save and load functionality**

1. Close all of the windows associated with the **ClassBookList** control.

2. Open the **Test** form and select the **ClassBookList** control.

3. Set the **Font** property to **Bold**.

   Because this is a **Font** type property, it is automatically set up to use the **StandardFont** property page.

4. Run the project.

   The **Font** property should maintain its value.

▶ **Enable the property page for the Font property**

1. Click the ellipsis (...) button to set the **PropertyPages** property of the **ClassBookList** control.

2. In the **Connect Property Pages** dialog box, select the **StandardFont** property page, and click **OK**.

   This will let you set the **Font** property from the **Properties** dialog box of the control.

3. Save the project.

▶ **Test the property page**

1. Close all of the windows associated with the **ClassBookList** control.

2. Open the **Test** form.

3. Right-click the **ClassBookList** control, and then click **Properties**.

4. In the **Property Pages** dialog box, click the **Font** tab.

   The font information should match the value of the **Font** property.

5. Change the font, and then click **OK**.

6. In the **Properties** window, click the ellipsis (**...**) button next to the **Font** property.

   Clicking this button will also display the **Property Pages** dialog box.

Self-Check Questions

To see the answers to the Self-Check Questions, see Appendix A.

1. Which action will create a design-time instance of an ActiveX control?

A. Running an application containing the control

B. Closing a form containing the control

C. Ending an application containing the control

D. Running a compiled application containing the control

2. How do you set up a property to be data-bound?

A. In the **Procedure Attributes** dialog box, check the **Property is data bound** check box for the data-bound property.

B. Add the ADO Data control to your **UserControl** object.

C. In the **Initialize** event of your control, connect to a known data source.

D. Declare the data-bound property with the keyword **Data**.

3. What is the function of the following code shown?

```
Public Event UserNameKeyPress(KeyAscii As Integer)

Private Sub txtUserName_KeyPress(KeyAscii As Integer)
    RaiseEvent UserNameKeyPress(KeyAscii)
End Sub
```

A. It handles the **KeyPress** event for the **txtUserName** text box.

B. It raises a **KeyPress** event whenever a user types in the **txtUserName** text box on the **UserControl**.

C. It raises a custom event, **UserNameKeyPress**, when a user types in the **txtUserName** text box.

D. It declares and raises an event for the **txtUserName** text box.

4. How do you notify Visual Basic that properties on a property page have changed?

A. Use the **Count** property of the **SelectedControls** collection to determine if the returned value is greater than one.

B. Set the **Changed** property of the **PropertyPage** object to **True**.

C. Add code to the **SelectionChanged** event.

D. Use the **WriteProperties** method of the **PropertyBag** object.

5. When a user closes a property page, how do you write changed property values back to the currently selected controls?

A. Add code to the **ApplyChanges** event.

B. Use the Connect Property Pages dialog box.

C. Set the **PropertyPage** object's **Changed** property to **True**.

D. Add code to the **SelectionChanged** event.

6. How do you make a UserControl object a Data Source control?

A. Set the **DataSource** property of the control to the data source object.

B. Write a function in the **UserControl** object called **GetDataMember**.

C. Drag the **UserControl** object into the Data Environment.

D. Set the **DataSourceBehavior** property of the control to **vbDataSource**.

Chapter 5:
Using ActiveX Data Objects

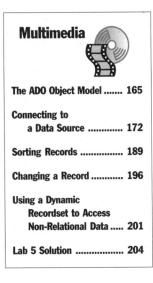
In Chapter 2, "Using Visual Data Access Tools," you learned how to use the visual data access tools to create solutions that access data without writing much code yourself. In this chapter, you will learn how to write code that uses ActiveX Data Objects (ADO) to connect to a data source, retrieve and manipulate data, and disconnect from a data source. You will also learn how to build and manage disconnected recordsets.

Objectives

After completing this chapter, you will be able to:

◆ List the major components of the ADO object model.

◆ Explain how to handle errors using ADO.

◆ Connect to a data source using ADO.

◆ Use an ADO **Recordset** object to retrieve and manipulate data.

◆ Describe and use a disconnected recordset.

◆ Use an ADO **Recordset** object to store non-database data.

Overview of ADO

In this section, you will learn about the relationship between ADO and other development tools. You will also learn about the ADO object model.

Introduction to ADO

ADO allows you to access and manipulate data from a data source. It also provides a universal data access interface. Writing code to ADO provides access to object properties, methods, and events, allowing for more flexibility than that provided by the visual data access tools. In addition, ADO is supported by a variety of development platforms.

Development Platforms and ADO

Many development platforms support ADO. For example, using ADO, you can add code to Active Server Pages to return data from a database to a Web page. Using the same code, you can also return those records to a Microsoft Visual Basic program.

The following development platforms can implement solutions using ADO:

◆ Microsoft Visual Basic

◆ Microsoft Visual InterDev

◆ Microsoft Visual C++

◆ Microsoft Visual J++

◆ Microsoft Visual FoxPro

◆ Microsoft VBScript

◆ Microsoft Visual Basic for Applications

Understanding the ADO Object Model

ADO objects provide you with fast and easy access to all types of data. The ADO object model has three main components: the **Connection** object, the **Command** object, and the **Recordset** object. The following illustration shows how the ADO objects relate to one another.

ADO 2.0 Object Model

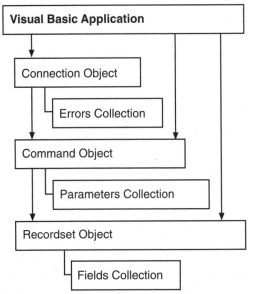

The ADO object model differs from the RDO and DAO object models in that many of the objects can be created independently of one another. For example, you can create a **Recordset** object without first explicitly creating a **Connection** object. ADO implicitly creates the required **Connection** object for you.

To see the animation "The ADO Object Model," see the accompanying CD-ROM.

ADO Objects

The three main components of the ADO object model are the **Connection** object, the **Command** object, and the **Recordset** object.

Connection Object

The **Connection** object is the highest-level object in the ADO object model. It is used to make a connection between your application and an external data source, such as Microsoft SQL Server.

Command Object

The **Command** object is used to build queries, including user-specific parameters, to access records from a data source. Typically, these records are returned in a **Recordset** object.

Recordset Object

The **Recordset** object is used to access records returned from a SQL query. Using this object, you can navigate returned records, modify existing records, add new records, or delete specific records.

ADO Collections

ADO supports three collections: the **Errors** collection, the **Parameters** collection, and the **Fields** collection. While these collections can provide additional functionality to an application, they are not required to build ADO solutions.

Errors Collection

The **Errors** collection is used to return detailed information about run-time errors or other messages returned from a data source.

Parameters Collection

The **Parameters** collection is used to pass specific data to a parameterized query or stored procedures in a SQL Server database.

Fields Collection

The **Fields** collection is used to access specific fields in an existing **Recordset** object.

Handling Data Access Errors

Trapping ADO errors is similar to trapping errors in most Visual Basic applications. You enable an error trap and write error-handling code to contend with errors that may occur. When you use error trapping the **Err** object is cleared for you. If you use inline error handling to handle errors without an error trap, you should use the **Clear** method to remove any existing error information before proceeding with code execution.

However, unlike other Visual Basic applications where you only rely on the **Err** object for error information, when you write ADO code you also need to use the ADO **Errors** collection to get more detailed information about an error or a group of errors from the data source.

When an error occurs or the data source returns a message, an **Error** object is created and added to the **Errors** collection. Error traps or inline code can interrogate the **Errors** collection and each specific **Error** object for more detailed information.

Note Some data sources return non-critical information to the ADO **Errors** collection in the form of a message.

The following sample code creates an error trap to support errors that may be returned while connecting to an external data source. To copy this code for use in your own projects, see "Creating a Connection Error Handler" on the accompanying CD-ROM.

```
Sub StartConnection()
    ' Declare a connection and error object
    Dim cnStateUBookstore As Connection
    Dim adoErr As Error

    Set cnStateUBookstore = New Connection

    ' Enable the error trap
    On Error Goto StartConnection_Handler

    ' Establish a connection to the data source
    With cnStateUBookstore
        .Provider = "SQLOLEDB"
        .ConnectionString = "User ID=sa;" & _
                            "Data Source=MSERIES1;" & _
                            "Initial Catalog=StateUBookstore"

        .Open
    End With

    ' If the connection succeeds, exit the procedure
    Exit Sub

StartConnection_Handler:
    ' If an error occurs, loop through the collection
    ' There can be more than one error code for a single
    ' Run time error
    For Each adoErr in cnStateUBookstore.Errors
        ' Show each error description to the user
        MsgBox adoErr.Description
    Next
End Sub
```

Note For the previous sample code to work correctly, the developer must have set a reference in the project to the Microsoft ActiveX Data Objects 2.0 Library. For information about setting a reference to ADO, see "Introduction to the Connection Object" on page 169 in this chapter.

Connecting to a Data Source

In this section, you will learn how to use the ADO **Connection** object to establish a connection to a data source. Connecting and disconnecting from a data source and connection management will also be discussed.

Introduction to the Connection Object

The **Connection** object establishes a connection to a data source. It allows your application to pass client information, such as username and password, to the database for validation.

▶ **To use ADO to establish a connection to a database**

1. Set a reference to the ADO Object Library.

2. Declare a **Connection** object.

3. Specify an OLE DB data provider.

4. Pass connection information.

Once you have completed these steps, you will be ready to establish a connection using the **Open** method.

Setting a Reference to ADO

Before you can use ADO in your Visual Basic application, you must first set a reference to the Microsoft ActiveX Data Objects 2.0 Library.

▶ **To create a reference to the ADO Object Library**

1. On the **Project** menu, click **References**.

2. Select **Microsoft ActiveX Data Objects 2.0 Library,** and then click **OK**.

Declaring a Connection Object

Once you have made a reference to the ADO object library, you can declare a **Connection** object in your application. Using the **Connection** object, you can then create a **Command** object or **Recordset** object.

Note Unless you are using both ADO and DAO in the same application, you do not need to use the prefix "ADODB" before ADO data types.

The following example code declares and instantiates a new **Connection** object:

```
Dim cnStateUBookstore As Connection
Set cnStateUBookstore = New Connection
```

Specifying a Data Provider

Once you have instantiated a **Connection** object, you must specify an OLE DB data source provider. You do this by setting the **Provider** property.

The following example code specifies the Microsoft SQL Server OLE DB data provider:

```
cnStateUBookstore.Provider = "SQLOLEDB"
```

 Note For a complete listing of ADO Connection Object properties, read the article "Connection Object (ADO)" in ADO Help.

Passing Connection Information

The final step before establishing a connection to a data source is to specify the connection information. You do this by setting the **Connection** object's **ConnectionString** property. Connection string arguments are provider specific, are passed directly to the provider, and are not processed by ADO.

For more information about connection string syntax, read the article "ConnectionString Property (ADO)" in ADO Help.

The following connection string arguments are used with the SQL Server OLE DB provider.

Connection argument	Description
User ID	Valid user name
Password	Valid user password
Data Source	Name of the remote server
Initial Catalog	Database name in the external data source

The following example code specifies a Microsoft SQL Server data provider and supplies connection information in the **ConnectionString** property:

```
With cnStateUBookstore
  .Provider = "SQLOLEDB"
  .ConnectionString = "User ID=sa;Password=;" & _
                      "Data Source=MSERIES1;" & _
                      "Initial Catalog=StateUBookstore"
End With
```

Note In the previous example code, the connection string argument Password=; used to signify a blank password is redundant since this is the default value for this argument.

The following table describes some of the OLE DB providers currently available.

OLE DB data provider	Description
SQLOLEDB	OLE DB provider for Microsoft SQL Server
MSDASQL	OLE DB provider for ODBC
Microsoft.Jet.OLEDB.3.51	OLE DB provider for Microsoft Jet
MSIDXS	OLE DB provider for Microsoft Index Server
ADSDSOObject	OLE DB provider for Microsoft Active Directory Service
MSDAORA	OLE DB provider for Oracle

For more information about specific OLE DB data providers, read the article "Using OLE DB Providers with ADO and RDS" in Platform SDK Help.

Connecting to and Disconnecting from a Data Source

Proper connection management is critical for efficient use of both client and server resources. Although ADO will disconnect automatically when an object goes out of scope, it is proper coding technique to explicitly close the connections your application opens. This also ensures that any server-side resources are released.

To see the demonstration "Connecting to a Data Source," see the accompanying CD-ROM.

Connecting to a Data Source

Once you have specified an OLE DB data provider and have passed the **ConnectionString** information, you use the **Open** method to establish a connection to the data source.

The following example code creates a connection to a Microsoft SQL Server database called StateUBookstore on the server called MSERIES1 using the SQL Server OLE DB data provider:

```
Sub cmdConnect_Click()
  ' The connection object variable cnStateUBookstore
  ' was declared at Module level
  ' Instantiate the connection object variable
  Set cnStateUBookstore = New Connection

  ' Establish a connection
  With cnStateUBookstore
      .Provider = "SQLOLEDB"
      .ConnectionString = "User ID=sa;" & _
                          "Data Source=MSERIES1;" & _
                          "Initial Catalog=StateUBookstore"
      ' Open the connection
      .Open
  End With
End Sub
```

Disconnecting from a Data Source

Once you have finished with the connection, you use the **Close** method to disconnect from a data source. In the case of a SQL Server, any server-side resources that were in use under this active connection will be released. It is proper coding technique for all open connections to be closed before the application is terminated.

The following example code closes an active connection to a data source and releases the **Connection** object variable:

```
Sub cmdClose_Click()
  cnStateUBookstore.Close
  Set cnStateUBookstore = Nothing
End Sub
```

Using Connection Object Events

The **Connection** object supports a number of events that allow your application to execute custom code. These events are associated with connecting to a data source, executing SQL commands, and managing transactions at the connection level.

The following table describes the events associated with the **Connection** Object.

Event	Description
AbortTransaction	Fires after the **RollbackTrans** method is called.
BeginTransaction	Fires after the **BeginTrans** method is called.
CommitTransaction	Fires after the **CommitTrans** method is called.
ConnectComplete	Fires when a connection attempt has completed successfully, failed, or timed out.
Disconnect	Fires when an active connection is closed.
ExecuteComplete	Fires after the **Execute** method is called.
InfoMessage	Fires when a message is returned from OLE DB or the data source.
WillConnect	Fires after the **Open** method is called, but before the connection is established.
WillExecute	Fires after the **Execute** method is called, but before the command is completed.

Enabling ADO Events

When you declare an ADO object, you can use the **WithEvents** keyword to expose the object's events to your application. If you declare a **Connection** object with its events exposed, the **Connection** object appears in the Visual Basic **Object** box list and all the available events for the object appear in the **Procedures/Events** box list.

The following example code declares a **Connection** object and exposes its events:

```
Public WithEvents cnStateUBookstore As Connection
```

You can now use the **Connection** object to execute statements or create **Command** objects or **Recordset** objects.

Adding Code to Connection Object Events

When you declare a **Connection** object using the **WithEvents** keyword, code is added to any of its associated events. The following example code displays a message box to the user when a connection attempt has successfully completed:

```
Sub cnStateUBookstore_ConnectComplete(ByVal pError As ADODB.Error, _
  adStatus As ADODB.EventStatusEnum, _
  ByVal pConnection As ADODB.Connection)

  If adStatus = adStatusOK Then
      MsgBox "The connection has been established with the data
source."
  End If

End Sub
```

Note There are additional values that can be returned in the **EventStatusEnum** object.

Using Multiple Connections on a Database

While it is possible to open multiple active connections to the same data source, it is not advised. Each active connection consumes resources on both the client and the server. For example, if your application opens two active connections to a SQL Server, the server treats each connection as a separate request, even though they originated from the same application. Therefore, each connection is given equal access to the server resources. One reason that your application might open more than one connection to the same data source is that you need to use separate transaction spaces.

For more information on transactions, see "Using Database Transactions" on page 226 in Chapter 6, "Advanced Data Access Issues."

For more information on the effects of a connection on a server, see "Understanding Performance Considerations" on page 203 in this chapter.

If your application requires multiple recordsets built against the same data source, ADO supports the creation of independent recordsets from the same active connection.

The following illustration shows the relationship of **Recordset** objects to **Connection** objects.

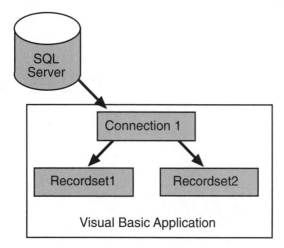

For information about creating **Recordset** objects, see "Using the Recordset Object" on page 179 in this chapter.

Connecting to Multiple Data Sources

If your application needs to access data concurrently from different data sources, you must open multiple **Connection** objects.

The following illustration shows the relationship of **Connection** objects to data sources.

Connecting to Multiple Data Sources

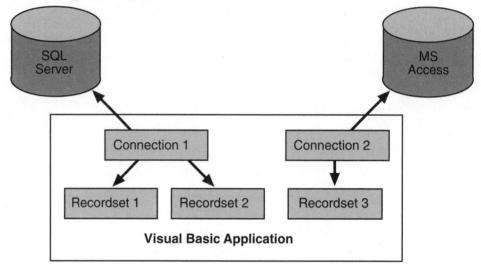

Once independent connections have been established, you can execute SQL statements or build recordsets from each of the **Connection** objects.

Retrieving Data from a Data Source

In this section, you will learn how to return data from a data source using a **Recordset** object. You will also learn techniques for building recordsets and commands. Presenting data to the user and navigating records will also be discussed.

Using the Command Object

The ADO **Command** object accesses and builds queries that are executed against a data source. You can also use **Command** objects to access stored procedures in an external database.

For more information about using SQL Server stored procedures, see "Executing Statements on a Database" on page 233 in Chapter 6, "Advanced Data Access Issues."

Using ADO, you don't have to create a **Connection** object before using the **Command** object. However, if you do not associate the new **Command** object with an active connection, a new implicit **Connection** object will be created automatically, using additional server resources.

Command Object Properties

The following table describes commonly used properties of the **Command** object. For a complete listing of **Command** object properties, read the article "Command Object (ADO)" in ADO Help.

Property	Description
ActiveConnection	Sets or returns the active connection used by the object.
CommandText	SQL command, stored procedure name, or table name that will be used by the object.
CommandType	Indicates if the **CommandText** property is an SQL command, stored procedure, or a table name.
Prepared	Indicates whether the SQL command should be created as a temporary stored procedure.
State	Indicates whether the command is currently opened, closed, or executing.

If you do not use an active connection when you create the **Command** object, you must pass the required connection string to the **ActiveConnection** property.

Command Object Methods

The following table describes methods of the **Command** object.

Method	Description
Cancel	Cancels the currently executing command.
CreateParameter	Creates a parameter object (for use with stored procedures).
Execute	Executes a SQL command.

Creating a Command from a Connection

Although an existing active connection is not required, it is more efficient to create **Command** objects from established connections. Once the **Command** object has been created, it can be used to execute the specified command or build a recordset.

The following example code uses a **Connection** object and a **Command** object to increase the book price for all records in the Books table by 10 percent:

```
Dim comPriceUpdate As Command
Set comPriceUpdate = New Command
With comPriceUpdate
  ' An existing Connection Object is referenced
  .ActiveConnection = cnStateUBookstore
  .CommandText = "UPDATE Books SET Price = Price * 1.1"

  ' call the Execute method to update the prices
  .Execute
End With
```

Creating a Stand-Alone Command Object

Since ADO provides a flat object model, you do not have to explicitly create a **Connection** object. Instead, you can pass the required connection information to the **ActiveConnection** property of the **Command** object. Then, when you use the **Execute** method to run the SQL command, a connection is established for you. However, using this technique, you cannot access the **Connection** object from your Visual Basic code.

The following example code uses a **Command** object to increase the book price for all records in the Books table by 10 percent:

```
Dim comPriceUpdate As Command
Set comPriceUpdate = New Command
With comPriceUpdate
  ' No connection object is used
  .ActiveConnection = "Provider=SQLOLEDB;" & _
                      "User ID=sa;" & _
                      "Data Source=MSERIES1;" & _
                      "Initial Catalog=StateUBookstore"
  .CommandText = "UPDATE Books SET Price = Price * 1.1"

  ' call the Execute method to update the prices
  .Execute
End With
```

Using the Recordset Object

The **Recordset** object allows your application to access data returned from a SQL query. This query can be created by the application, or it can reside on the server as a stored procedure. Using the **Recordset** object, you can navigate the records that have been returned, or edit their values.

Recordset Object Properties

The following table describes properties of the **Recordset** object that are commonly used to create a **Recordset**. For a complete listing of **Recordset** object properties, read the article "Recordset Object (ADO)" in ADO Help.

Property	Description
ActiveCommand	Returns the active command for the recordset.
ActiveConnection	Sets or returns the active connection for the recordset.
CursorLocation	Sets or returns the location of the cursor. The default is adUseServer.
CursorType	Sets or returns the cursor type. The default is adOpenForward.
LockType	Sets or returns the type of record locking. The default is adLockReadOnly.
MaxRecords	Sets or returns the maximum number of records to return.
PersistFormat	Determines the format in which the recordset data is saved when calling the **Save** method.
RecordCount	Returns the number of records in the recordset.
State	Returns the current state of the recordset.

Tip The only available value for the **PersistFormat** property in ADO 2.0 is adPersistADTG, but ADO may support other formats in future releases.

Recordset Object Methods

The following table describes methods of the **Recordset** object that are commonly used to create a recordset. For a complete listing of **Recordset** object methods, read the article "Recordset Object (ADO)" in ADO Help.

Method	Description
Open	Executes a SQL command and opens a cursor.
Close	Closes the recordset.
Requery	Re-executes a SQL command and rebuilds the recordset.
Resync	Refreshes cached records in a recordset.
Save	Saves an open recordset to a file that can be re-opened later.

Creating a Recordset

You can build a **Recordset** object based on an active connection to a data source. This limits the number of connections and can reduce the amount of client and server resources used by your application. Depending on the needs of the recordset, you may need to build an explicit **Connection** object or **Command** object first. If you do not explicitly use a **Connection** object or a **Command** object, a stand-alone recordset is automatically created.

The functionality of the recordset you create is determined by the values specified for the **CursorLocation** and **CursorType** properties. For information about cursors, see "Using Cursors" on page 218 in Chapter 6, "Advanced Data Access Issues."

Using a Connection Object and a Command Object

You can create a new recordset from an existing **Command** object. Open the connection and create the **Command** object. Then use the **Command** object's **Execute** method to build the recordset.

The following sample code uses an existing **Command** object to build a recordset. To copy this code for use in your own projects, see "Creating a Recordset from a Connection and Command Object" on the accompanying CD-ROM.

```
Sub cmdConnect_Click()
  ' Declare the object variables
  Dim cnStateUBookstore As Connection
  Dim comPriceUpdate As Command
  Dim rsStudents As Recordset

  ' Instantiate the variables
  Set cnStateUBookstore = New Connection
  Set comPriceUpdate = New Command
  Set rsStudents = New Recordset

  ' Establish a connection
  With cnStateUBookstore
      .Provider = "SQLOLEDB"
      .ConnectionString = "User ID=sa;" & _
                          "Data Source=MSERIES1;" & _
                          "Initial Catalog=StateUBookstore"
      .Open
  End With

  ' Create a Command object
  With comPriceUpdate
      .ActiveConnection = cnStateUBookstore
      .CommandText = "SELECT StudentID FROM Students"
  End With

  ' Build the recordset
  Set rsStudents = comPriceUpdate.Execute
End Sub
```

Using the Open Method

You can create a new recordset directly from an existing active connection. Open the connection normally, and pass the **Connection** object to the recordset using the **Open** method.

The following sample code creates a recordset from an existing **Connection** object. To copy this code for use in your own projects, see "Creating a Recordset with the Open Method" on the accompanying CD-ROM.

```
Sub cmdOpenRecordset_Click()
  ' Declare and instantiate the object variables
  Dim cnStateUBookstore As Connection
  Dim rsStudents As Recordset
  Set cnStateUBookstore = New Connection
  Set rsStudents = New Recordset

  ' Establish a connection
  With cnStateUBookstore
      .Provider = "SQLOLEDB"
      .ConnectionString = "User ID=sa;" & _
                          "Data Source=MSERIES1;" & _
                          "Initial Catalog=StateUBookstore"
      .Open
  End With

  ' Open a recordset using the Connection object variable
  rsStudents.Open "SELECT StudentID FROM Students",
cnStateUBookstore
End Sub
```

Using the Execute Method

You can also create a recordset using the **Execute** method of the **Connection** object. The **Execute** method does not support the same arguments as the **Open** method and therefore your recordset assumes the properties set originally on the **Connection** object. Using this technique, you are limited in the features that can be associated with the recordset.

The following sample code creates a **Recordset** object against an existing active connection. To copy this code for use in your own projects, see "Creating a Recordset Using the Execute Method" on the accompanying CD-ROM.

```
Sub cmdConnect_Click()
    ' Declare and instantiate the object variables
    Dim cnStateUBookstore As Connection
    Dim rsStudents As Recordset
    Set cnStateUBookstore = New Connection
    Set rsStudents = New Recordset

    ' Establish a connection
    With cnStateUBookstore
        .Provider = "SQLOLEDB"
        .ConnectionString = "User ID=sa;" & _
                            "Data Source=MSERIES1;" & _
                            "Initial Catalog=StateUBookstore"
        .Open
    End With

    ' Open a recordset using the Execute method
    Set rsStudents = cnStateUBookstore.Execute("SELECT StudentID FROM
Students")
End Sub
```

Creating a Stand-Alone Recordset

When you create a stand-alone **Recordset** object, a **Connection** object does not have to already exist. A **Connection** object will be created automatically, but it cannot be accessed from Visual Basic. When the **Open** method is used, the required connection information must be passed to ADO.

The following example code shows how to create a **Recordset** object as a stand-alone object:

```
Dim rsStudents As Recordset
Set rsStudents = New Recordset

rsStudents.Open "SELECT StudentID FROM Students", _
                "Provider=SQLOLEDB;" & _
                "User ID=sa;" & _
                "Data Source=MSERIES1;Initial
Catalog=StateUBookstore"
```

Presenting Data to the User

There are two ways to present data to the user. You can manually place the contents of the current record's fields in appropriate controls, such as a text box, or you can bind the controls to the **Recordset** object.

Referencing Fields in a Recordset

In order to show a record's value to the user, you must reference the fields of the recordset. The most efficient technique is to reference the field name directly. You can use the **Fields** collection, which is more explicit code, but it is less efficient. The following example code directly references the First_Name field of a recordset:

```
' most efficient
txtFirstName.Text = rsStudents!First_Name

' explicit, but less efficient
txtFirstName.Text = rsStudents.Fields("First_Name").Value
```

Note Some databases such as Microsoft Access allow spaces in field names. Visual Basic supports this syntax, but square brackets must be placed around field names that contain a space.

Manually Populating Controls

After a recordset has been created, you can manually reference fields of the recordset in order to present its values to the user. For example, if the Visual Basic form you are using has two text boxes, one to display the student's first name and a second to display the student's last name, you can manually populate the text boxes. This process must occur each time the user navigates to a new record. The following example code populates the text boxes on a form:

```
Sub FillControls()
  txtFirstName.Text = rsStudents!First_Name
  txtLastName.Text = rsStudents!Last_Name
End Sub
```

Binding Controls to a Recordset

New to Visual Basic is the ability to bind controls to objects. This is similar to the technique that you use to bind controls to an ActiveX Data control. Using the **Recordset** object, you can bind any data-aware control to any field in a recordset. As the user navigates from record to record, the text box automatically shows the record's values.

The following example code binds a text box to a field of an existing **Recordset** object:

```
Set txtFirstName.DataSource = rsStudents
txtFirstName.DataField = "First_Name"

Set txtLastName.DataSource = rsStudents
txtLastName.DataField = "Last_Name"
```

Note Use the binding technique as an alternative to writing a general procedure that manually populates controls on a form.

Navigating Through a Recordset

Of the ADO objects, only the **Recordset** object allows users to navigate through a group of records. Only one record within a recordset can be current at a given time. Therefore, the **Recordset** object supports a number of properties and methods that allow users to navigate through the recordset.

Recordset Navigation Properties

The following table describes properties of the **Recordset** object that are used to navigate a recordset. For a complete listing of **Recordset** object properties, read the article "Recordset Object (ADO)" in ADO Help.

Property	Description
AbsolutePage	Sets or returns the absolute page in which the current record exists.
AbsolutePosition	Sets or returns the absolute position of the current record (this can be affected by record additions or deletions).

table continued on next page

Property	Description
BOF	Indicates if the pointer has moved before the first record.
Bookmark	Returns a unique identifier for the current record. This property can also be used to move the pointer to a specified record.
EOF	Indicates if the pointer has moved past the last record.

Recordset Navigation Methods

The following table describes methods of the **Recordset** object that are used to navigate through a recordset. For a complete listing of **Recordset** object methods, read the article "Recordset Object (ADO)" in ADO Help.

Method	Description
Move	Moves a specified number of records forward or backward.
MoveFirst	Moves to the first record.
MoveLast	Moves to the last record.
MoveNext	Moves to the next record.
MovePrevious	Moves to the previous record.

Note You can only use the **MoveNext** method if the cursor type of the recordset is adForwardOnly. For information about cursors, see "Choosing a Cursor Type" on page 218 in Chapter 6, "Advanced Data Access Issues."

The following sample code shows the **Click** events for various navigation buttons. To copy this code for use in your own projects, see "Navigating a Recordset" on the accompanying CD-ROM.

```
Sub cmdFirst_click()
  rsStudents.MoveFirst
End Sub


Sub cmdLast_Click()
  rsStudents.MoveLast
End Sub


Sub cmdPrevious_Click()
  rsStudents.MovePrevious
  ' Check to see if tried to move prior to the first record
  If rsStudents.BOF then
      ' Moved prior to the first record
      ' Set the user back to the first
      rsStudents.MoveFirst
  End If
End Sub


Sub cmdNext_Click()
  rsStudents.MoveNext
  ' Check to see if tried to move beyond the last record
  If rsStudents.EOF then
      ' Moved beyond the last record
      ' Set the user back to the last
      rsStudents.MoveLast
  End If
End Sub
```

Practice: Creating a Recordset

In this practice, you will add ADO code to an existing project to connect to a Microsoft SQL Server database and create a recordset.

▶ **Create a connection to a SQL Server database**

1. Start Visual Basic and open the **Publishers.vbp** project located in the \<*install folder*>\Practices\Chapter05\Creating a Recordset folder.

2. Open the code window for the **cmdConnect** click event.

3. Review the code that already appears in this event procedure.

4. Add the following code inside the **With** statement to connect to the database:

```
.Provider = "SQLOLEDB"
.ConnectionString = "Data Source=MSERIES1;" & _
                    "Initial Catalog=StateUBookstore;" & _
                    "User ID=sa"
.Open
```

Note In the connection string, change the data source name of MSERIES1 to that of your SQL Server.

▶ **Create a recordset**

♦ Add the following code to create a default recordset:

```
rsPublishers.Open "SELECT pub_id, pub_name, city, state FROM Pub-
lishers", cnStateUBookstore
```

▶ **Bind a control to the recordset**

1. Add the following lines of code to bind the **Recordset** object to the **State** text box control:

```
Set txtPubState.DataSource = rsPublishers
txtPubState.DataField = "state"
```

2. Run the application and test your work. Since you used the default recordset, you will only be able to navigate using the **Next** command button.

Sorting and Searching Data

In this section, you will learn how to sort, filter, and search for records in an existing recordset without returning to the data source.

Sorting Records

Using the **Sort** property of a recordset, you can specify the order in which the records appear in an existing recordset. This eliminates the need to return to the data source, perhaps over a network, to get a new recordset of sorted data. Depending on the client's computer and size of the recordset, this may be more efficient than re-creating the recordset.

> **Note** To use the **Sort** property with SQL Server you must use a client-side cursor. This is because, depending on the provider, a server-side cursor may or may not support sorting and SQL server does not.

To see the demonstration "Sorting Records," see the accompanying CD-ROM.

When applying a sort, you can choose between the **ASC** and **DESC** keyword. To sort the records in ascending order, use **ASC**. To sort the records in descending order, use **DESC**.

The following example code sorts an existing recordset based on the LastName field of a recordset in ascending order:

```
rsStudents.Sort = "LastName ASC"
```

Disabling a Sort

In order to return a recordset to its original order, set the **Sort** property to an empty string. The following example code disables a sort:

```
rsStudents.Sort = ""
```

Filtering Records

Using the **Filter** property, you can limit the records that are presented. The original records are still available in memory, but only those that meet the filter's requirements will be displayed as part of the recordset.

The following example code shows only students that have an account balance greater than $1,000:

```
rsStudents.Filter = "AccountBalance > 1000"
```

Disabling a Filter

In order to return a recordset to its original contents, set the **Filter** property to the adFilterNone constant. The following example code disables a filter, making all original records available:

```
rsStudents.Filter = adFilterNone
```

Searching Records

Although the **Filter** property can be used to return a group of specific records from a recordset, you can also search for a specific record. Use the **Find** method to search on a record that matches your criteria.

The following example code moves the recordset pointer to the first record that has "Gray" as a last name:

```
rsStudents.Find "Last_Name = 'Gray'"
```

Note When specifying a string value, use single quotes around the text. When specifying a date, use the # symbol around the value.

The following table describes the parameters supported by the **Find** method.

Parameter	Description
Criteria	Expression stating the field to search and the value to find.
SkipRows	Number indicating how many rows to skip when starting the search. Set this value to zero (default) to include the current row in the search. Set it to 1 to skip the current row.
Direction	Specifies which direction from the current record the search should progress (adSearchForward or adSearchBackward). The default is adSearchForward.
Start	Bookmark to use as the starting position.

The following table describes the search clauses to use when specifying criteria.

Clause	Description
FieldName	Name of the field being searched
Operator	=, <, >, "like"
Value	Date, String, Number

Note You can use the **Find** method together with the **Sort** and **Filter** properties to refine your search.

Updating Data

In this section, you will learn how to update data in a data source using different ADO techniques. You will also learn about using the **Execute** method and recordsets.

Using the Execute Method

When your application needs to update data in an external data source, you can either execute direct SQL statements or use a **Recordset** object (and its various methods for modifying data). Using SQL statements works best when a large number of records need to be updated. Using SQL statements is also more efficient for both the client and the server.

You can use either a **Connection** object or a **Command** object to execute SQL statements directly. It is preferable to use a **Connection** object when the SQL command will be issued only once. If your application needs to send the same SQL command to the data source more than once, it is more efficient to use a **Command** object. Both objects use the **Execute** method to send the SQL command to the data source.

For more information on the Structured Query Language (SQL) syntax, read the article "Creating Basic Queries" in Platform SDK Help.

Inserting New Records

You can use the SQL **Insert** statement to issue a command that will add a new record (or group of records) in a data source.

The following sample code executes an **Insert** statement using a **Connection** object. To copy this code for use in your own projects, see "Inserting a Record Using a Connection Object" on the accompanying CD-ROM.

```
Sub cmdAddRecord_Click()
    ' Declare and instantiate the object variable
    Dim cnStateUBookstore As Connection
    Dim sSQL As String
    Set cnStateUBookstore = New Connection

    ' Establish a connection
    With cnStateUBookstore
        .Provider = "SQLOLEDB"
        .ConnectionString = "User ID=sa;" & _
                            "Data Source=MSERIES1;" & _
                            "Initial Catalog=StateUBookstore"
        .Open
    End With

    ' Build the SQL command
    sSQL = "INSERT INTO Students(First_Name, Last_Name) " & _
        "VALUES ('Lani', 'Ota')"

    ' Execute the SQL command
    cnStateUBookstore.Execute sSQL
End Sub
```

Updating Records

You can use the SQL **Update** statement to issue a command that changes a record or group of records.

The following sample code executes an **Update** statement using a **Connection** object to change a student's major, or area of specialization. To copy this code for use in your own projects, see "Updating a Record Using a Connection Object" on the accompanying CD-ROM.

```
Sub cmdUpdateRecord_Click()
    ' Declare and instantiate the object variable
    Dim cnStateUBookstore As Connection
    Dim sSQL As String
    Set cnStateUBookstore = New Connection

    ' Establish a connection
    With cnStateUBookstore
        .Provider = "SQLOLEDB"
        .ConnectionString = "User ID=sa;" & _
                            "Data Source=MSERIES1;" & _
                            "Initial Catalog=StateUBookstore"
        .Open
    End With

    ' Build the SQL command
    sSQL = "UPDATE Students SET MajorID = 4 WHERE StudentID = 3"

    ' Execute the SQL command
    cnStateUBookstore.Execute sSQL
End Sub
```

Deleting Records

You can use the SQL **Delete** statement to issue a command that deletes a record or group of records in a data source.

The following sample code executes a **Delete** statement using a **Connection** object to remove a record from the **Books** table. To copy this code for use in your own projects, see "Deleting a Record Using a Connection Object" on the accompanying CD-ROM.

```
Sub cmdDeleteRecord_Click()
  ' Declare and instantiate the object variable
  Dim cnStateUBookstore As Connection
  Dim sSQL As String
  Set cnStateUBookstore = New Connection

  ' Establish a connection
  With cnStateUBookstore
      .Provider = "SQLOLEDB"
      .ConnectionString = "User ID=sa;" & _
                          "Data Source=MSERIES1;" & _
                          "Initial Catalog=StateUBookstore"
      .Open
  End With

  ' Build the SQL command
  sSQL = "DELETE FROM Books WHERE BookID = 3"

  ' Execute the SQL command
  cnStateUBookstore.Execute sSQL
End Sub
```

Using a Recordset

If your application has already opened a recordset, you can modify data using the recordset's methods. Modifying records with a **Recordset** object is limited to a single addition, deletion, or update at a time. Consider using the **Connection** object's **Execute** method for performing multiple updates at once.

Adding a New Record

Adding a new record to a recordset is a two-step process. Your application must first create a new record to be added, and then it must use the **Update** method to send the change to the data source. To create a new record entry, use the **AddNew** method.

The following example code creates a recordset and adds a new customer record:

```
Dim rsStudents As Recordset
Set rsStudents = New Recordset

' open a recordset
rsStudents.CursorType = adOpenKeyset
rsStudents.LockType = adLockOptimistic
rsStudents.Open "SELECT First_Name, Last_Name FROM Students",
cnStateUBookstore

' add a new record
rsStudents.AddNew
```

Once the user has entered the new record's information, you must use the **Update** method to send the changes to the data source. The changes will then be made permanent. New records will be added to the end of the current **Recordset** object, regardless of the original SQL command used to create the recordset. The following example code updates a recordset:

```
rsStudents.Update
```

Deleting a Record

To delete the current record from the recordset and the data source, use the **Delete** method. Unlike adding or changing a record, there is only one step to cause a deletion; you do not need to use the **Update** method.

The following example code deletes the current record from the recordset:

```
rsStudents.Delete
```

After deleting a record, you should add code to ensure that there will be no attempts to reference data belonging to a record that has been deleted and is, therefore, invalid. The following example code shows one technique for setting the current record to one that is valid.

```
rsStudents.MoveNext
If rsStudents.EOF Then
  rsStudents.MoveLast
End If
```

Changing a Record

To edit records in an ADO recordset, specify the field to change and the new value. Then use the **Update** method as you would to add a new record to save the changes to the data source. These changes are reflected in the current recordset without refreshing.

To see the demonstration "Changing a Record," see the accompanying CD-ROM.

> **Note** Unlike DAO and RDO, there is no **Edit** method in ADO.

The following example code creates a new **Recordset** object. The application navigates to the last record and changes the student's major:

```
Dim rsStudents as Recordset
Set rsStudents = New Recordset

rsStudents.Open "SELECT MajorID FROM Students"
rsStudents.MoveLast
rsStudents!MajorID = 2
rsStudents.Update
```

Using Disconnected Data

In this section, you will learn how to create a disconnected recordset and manage user changes. A disconnected recordset allows your application to close its live connection to the data source and allow the user to navigate and make changes offline. You can then reconnect to the data source and save all cached changes.

Creating a Disconnected Recordset Object

Using disconnected recordsets, ADO allows your application to create a recordset, disconnect from the data source, and let the user view and edit the recordset offline.

When the user has made the desired changes, your application can reconnect to the data source and update the database.

To support a disconnected recordset, you must specify that the recordset will be built on the client.

For more information on client-side and server-side recordsets, see Chapter 6, "Advanced Data Access Issues" on page 215.

Creating a Client-Side Recordset

To specify that the recordset should be built on the client, use the adUseClient parameter with the **Recordset** object's **Open** method.

The following sample code creates a new recordset that will be built on the client. To copy this code for use in your own projects, see "Creating a Client-Side Recordset" on the accompanying CD-ROM.

```
Sub cmdConnect_Click()
    ' Declare and instantiate object variables
    Dim cnStateUBookstore As Connection
    Dim rsStudents As Recordset

    Set cnStateUBookstore = New Connection
    Set rsStudents = New Recordset

    ' Establish a connection
    With cnStateUBookstore
        .Provider = "SQLOLEDB"
        .ConnectionString = "User ID=sa;" & _
                            "Data Source=MSERIES1;" & _
                            "Initial Catalog=StateUBookstore"
        .Open
    End With

    ' Build a recordset
    With rsStudents
        ' Specify the cursor's location
        .CursorLocation = adUseClient
        .LockType = adLockBatchOptimistic
        .Open "SELECT First_Name, Last_Name FROM Students", _
              cnStateUBookstore
    End With
End Sub
```

Disconnecting from the Data Source

Setting the recordset's **ActiveConnection** property to **Nothing** disconnects the recordset from the active connection. Your application can then close the active **Connection** object using the **Close** method. If the adUseClient parameter was used with the **Open** method, the client will have a copy of the recordset data and can begin navigating or updating the records. The following example code closes the connection and disconnects from the data source:

```
Set rsStudents.ActiveConnection = Nothing
cnStateUBookstore.Close
```

Making Offline Changes

Once a recordset has been disconnected from the data source, your application can use any of the data update and navigation techniques. For more information, see "Retrieving Data from a Data Source" on page 176 in this chapter. New records can be added using the **AddNew** method, records can be deleted using the **Delete** method, and existing records can be changed using the **Update** method. However, all changes are cached on the client until the connection is re-established.

Note   Offline changes made to the same record by more than one user will cause a conflict when the data is saved back to the data source.

Persisting a Recordset

Using the **Save** method, a recordset's contents can be saved to a file. This process is called persisting data. This is particularly useful if the user wishes to close the application and return to it later without reconnecting to the data source.

Persisting data is also useful for a disconnected recordset, since the connection and the application can be closed while the recordset is still available on the client computer.

Saving Data to a File

To save the contents of the current recordset to a file, use the **Save** method. The **Save** method allows you to specify the format of the data and whether an existing file should be overwritten. By default, the **Save** method fails if a file with the same name already exists.

Note If a filter is currently active, only the records that are visible through the filter will be saved to the file.

The following example code saves the recordset's contents to a file on the local computer:

```
rsStudents.Save "c:\studentinfo.dat", adPersistADTG
```

Note Once a recordset has been saved, it is static. Any additional changes made to the recordset after calling the **Save** method will not be reflected in the persisted data when it is retrieved.

Retrieving Persisted Data

To rebuild the recordset from data that was saved, use the **Open** method and refer to the file name. The following example code reopens a persisted recordset:

```
rsStudents.Open "c:\studentinfo.dat"
```

Reconnecting to a Data Source

After a connection has been closed, it can be reopened and any changes the user made offline can be saved to the data source. The original connection information, such as the data source provider, is retained as long as the **Connection** object was disconnected using the **Close** method. If the **Connection** object is set to **Nothing**, all connection information must be re-established.

The following example code reconnects to a data source and associates the **Recordset** object with the connection:

```
Sub cmdReconnect_Click()
  cnStateUBookstore.Open
  rsStudents.ActiveConnection = cnStateUBookstore
End Sub
```

Submitting Changes to a Data Source

One use of a disconnected recordset is to provide offline updating. A client can spend as much time as needed reviewing and editing data while disconnected from the data source.

Sending Batched Changes to the Data Source

Using the **Update** method, all changes to a disconnected recordset are cached on the client. Once reconnected, use the **UpdateBatch** method to send the changes to the data source.

The following example code sends all cached changes to the data source:

```
Sub cmdUpdateAll_Click()
  rsStudents.UpdateBatch
End Sub
```

Conflict Management Issues

When updating records after reconnecting to the data source, you should consider the possibility that conflicts may arise due to concurrent activity by other users of the data source. ADO will report conflicts and retrieve information about conflicts when asked. However, it is your responsibility to specify what types of conflicts ADO should report, request details about the conflicts, and supply code to handle the different types of conflicts in a manner that is appropriate for your application.

After you call the **UpdateBatch** method, you will need to determine if conflicts did occur and then supply the appropriate code to resolve each type of conflict in a way that makes sense for your application. It is advisable to wrap your batch updates and associated conflict resolution in a transaction to ensure that additional changes to the data source do not occur between the time you identify and then handle the conflicts.

For more information about managing conflicts, read the article "UpdateBatch Method (ADO)" in Platform SDK Help.

Canceling a Batch Update

Before the **UpdateBatch** method is used, your application can cancel all the changes that are in the client's cache. Use the **CancelBatch** method to reset the recordset to its original state.

The following example code prompts the user to submit all batched changes:

```
Sub cmdUpdateAll_Click()
  If MsgBox("Submit all changes?", vbYesNo) = vbYes Then
      rsStudents.UpdateBatch
  Else
      rsStudents.CancelBatch
  End If
End Sub
```

Creating Dynamic Recordsets

When you use ADO, you do not have to create recordsets from external data sources. Instead, your application can build dynamic recordsets to manage data internal to your application.

To create a dynamic recordset, declare and instantiate a normal **Recordset** object variable. However, since there is no data source, you will not specify connection information or use the **Open** method.

To see the demonstration "Using a Dynamic Recordset to Access Non-Relational Data," see the accompanying CD-ROM.

Adding Fields to the Recordset

Use the **Fields** collection and the **Append** method to create new fields on the recordset. When you create a field, you must specify a name and a data type for the field. In addition, if you specify a string data type, you must also pass the length of the string. For more information about the ADO data type constants that are supported, read the article "Type Property (ADO)" in ADO Help.

The following example code creates a dynamic recordset and adds two fields:

```
Dim rsFileInfo As Recordset
Set rsFileInfo = New Recordset
rsFileInfo.Fields.Append "ID", adInteger
rsFileInfo.Fields.Append "FileName", adBSTR, 255
```

Using a Dynamic Recordset

Once the fields have been added to the recordset, you can add records, delete records, and change values of the recordset. Dynamic recordsets also support saving and opening persisted data. The following sample code reads file names from a hard drive and saves the information in a recordset. To copy this code for use in your own projects, see "Using a Dynamic Recordset" on the accompanying CD-ROM.

```vb
Dim rsFileInfo As Recordset

Sub cmdLoadFiles_Click()

  Dim sFileDir As String
  Dim Idx As Integer

  Set rsFileInfo = New Recordset

  ' add new fields to the recordset
  rsFileInfo.Fields.Append "ID", adInteger
  rsFileInfo.Fields.Append "FileName", adBSTR, 255

  ' open the recordset
  rsFileInfo.Open

  ' use the Dir command to return the files in the C:\ directory
  sFileDir = Dir("C:\")

  ' if there is a valid file name
  Do While sFileDir <> ""
      If sFileDir <> "." and sFileDir <> ".." Then
          Idx = Idx + 1

          ' add a new record for this file
          rsFileInfo.AddNew
            rsFileInfo!ID = Idx
            rsFileInfo!FileName = sFileDir
          rsFileInfo.Update

          ' get the next file in the directory
          sFileDir = Dir
      End If
  Loop
  rsFileInfo.MoveFirst

End Sub

Sub cmdDisplayResults_Click()
  Do Until rsFileInfo.EOF
      MsgBox "File Number: " & rsFileInfo!ID & vbCrLf & "File Name:
" & rsFileInfo!FileName
      rsFileInfo.MoveNext
  Loop
End Sub
```

Understanding Performance Considerations

When you create applications that connect to a data source, especially in a multi-user environment, there are a number of performance issues that you should consider. These considerations include the number of open connections to a server, the way in which locking is managed, and the proper use of transactions.

Active Connections

Each connection you create to a data source, such as SQL Server, uses resources on both the client and the server. In addition, the number of connections available on a server is limited by the number of licenses purchased. Since each connection from a Visual Basic application appears as a separate connection, the number of available connections can be reduced quickly. SQL Server does not consider connections on a per-application basis. Therefore, consider using multiple recordsets from the same **Connection** object if you require more than one cursor.

Using Recordsets

Unless your application requires use of a recordset, consider using the **Execute** method of a **Connection** object or **Command** object to interact with the data source. SQL statements are more efficient and use less overhead than recordsets.

Sorting Records

Using an existing ADO recordset, your application can sort the returned records or search for a specific record without re-querying the data source. This helps limit network access and reduce server load. However, depending upon the size of the recordset, or the search requirements, it may be more efficient to re-query the data source with a more specific SQL statement.

Updating Data

When you use ADO, there are two techniques for updating data in an external data source. You can either execute SQL commands to update records, or you can use a **Recordset** object and issue various methods of the object to update records.

Unless you need to build a recordset, it is usually more efficient to execute the required modification through a SQL command. You can do this from either the **Connection** object or the **Command** object. However, a good understanding of SQL is required.

If your application has already created a recordset that can be updated, it may be easier to use the recordset methods **AddNew** or **Update** to modify the database. This technique is only available for single record updates, since only one record is available at a time when using a **Recordset** object. For multiple record updates, such as batch updates, consider using the **Execute** method of a **Command** object.

Transactions

Although transactions ensure data integrity, locks are created by the data source while a transaction is open. Commit or roll back the transaction as soon as possible to allow other applications access to the data.

Lab 5: Using ActiveX Data Objects

In this lab, you will add the **CAccount** class to the StateUBookstore project. This component will use ADO code to access the StateUBookstore database. The component will verify that the student has enough available credit to purchase a book.

To see the demonstration "Lab 5 Solution," see the accompanying CD-ROM.

Estimated time to complete this lab: **120 minutes**

To complete the exercises in this lab, you must have the required software. For detailed information about the labs and setup for the labs, see "Labs" in "About This Course".

> **Note** If you have not completed Lab 4 using the same computer on which you are currently working, you may need to register the
> *<install folder>*\Labs\Lab05\StateUControls.ocx before you start this lab.
>
> For information about registering components, see "Making the Component Available" on page 247 in Chapter 7, "Using COM Components."

Objectives

After completing this lab, you will be able to:

♦ Use the ADO **Connection** object to create a connection to a database.

♦ Create an ADO **Recordset** object that contains information from a database.

♦ Use the **Execute** method of a connection to update database information.

Prerequisites

Before working on this lab, you should be familiar with the following:

◆ Using the ADO Object model

◆ Working with class modules

Exercises

The following exercises provide practice working with the concepts and techniques covered in this chapter:

◆ Exercise 1: Creating the CAccount Class

In this exercise, you will create the **CAccount** class that handles the financial transaction for buying a book.

◆ Exercise 2: Implementing the Authorize Method

In this exercise, you will write code to initialize the **CAccount** class. You will also implement the **Authorize** method of the **CAccount** class.

◆ Exercise 3: Implementing the Debit Method

In this exercise, you will implement the **Debit** method of the **CAccount** class.

◆ Exercise 4: Using the CAccount Class

In this exercise, you will add code that uses the **CAccount** class you've created. This class will be used when a student attempts to buy a book from the State University Bookstore.

◆ Exercise 5: Testing the CAccount Class

In this exercise, you will test the lab solution using specific scenarios that will test different cases that the **CAccount** component should handle.

Exercise 1: Creating the CAccount Class

In this exercise, you will create the **CAccount** class that handles the financial transaction for buying a book. The following table shows the methods and properties you will implement for the **CAccount** class.

Name	Type	Purpose
Price	Property	The price of the book a student wants to purchase.
Authorize	Method	Looks up a student's account balance. If the balance plus the price of the book is less than $500, this method returns success.
Debit	Method	Adds the book price to a student's account balance.
Warning	Event	Sends notification that a student's account balance is greater than $450.
Memo	Property	A memo used when writing the account log.

▶ **Create the CAccount Class**

1. Open the StateUBookstore project.

2. Run the Class Builder Add-In.

3. Create a new class named **CAccount**.

4. Add the **Price** property as a **Public** property. Set the data type to **Double**.

5. Add the **Authorize** method. This method has an **Integer** argument called **iStudentID**. Set the return type to **Boolean**.

6. Add the **Debit** method. This method has an **Integer** argument called **iStudentID**. Set the return type to **Boolean**.

7. Add the **Warning** event. Add a **String** argument called **Message** to this event.

8. Add the **Memo** property as a **Public** property. Set the data type to **String**.

9. On the **File** menu, click **Update Project** to write changes into the StateUBookstore project.

10. Exit the Class Builder.

11. Open the Object Browser and examine the **CAccount** class. Make sure the properties and methods of the class look the way you expect them to.

12. Save the project.

Exercise 2: Implementing the Authorize Method

In this exercise, you will write code to initialize the **CAccount** class. You will also implement the **Authorize** method of the **CAccount** class.

▶ **Create a connection to the database**

1. In the General Declarations section of the **CAccount** class, declare a Private ADO **Connection** object.

2. In the **Initialize** event of the **CAccount** class, create a new instance of the ADO **Connection** object.

3. Add code to open the connection.

4. In the **Terminate** event of the **CAccount** class, add code to close the connection and release the **Connection** object variable.

To see an example of how your code should look, see Lab Hint 5.1 in Appendix B.

▶ **Implement the Authorize method**

The **Authorize** method will determine if a student has enough credit to purchase a book. It will look up a student's account balance in the StateUBookstore database. Students can owe the university a maximum of $500. If they have a balance including the book they are trying to buy of less than $500, the **Authorize** method will return **True**. If they are within $50 of their limit, they will be authorized, but the **CAccount** class will raise the Warning error to let students know they are close to their limit. If students are over their $500 limit, the **Authorize** method will return **False**.

1. Open the **CAccount** class module.

2. In the **Authorize** method, declare an ADO **Recordset** object called **rsAccountBalance**.

3. Declare two variables of type Double. One will hold the current account balance. Call it dBalance. The other will hold the account balance including the book price. Call it dPotentialBalance.

4. Declare a string variable called strWarning to hold a warning message used by the **Warning** event.

5. Create a new ADO **Recordset** object with the **Open** method using the following parameters:

Parameter	Value
Source	"Select AccountBalance from Students Where StudentID = " & str(iStudentID)
ActiveConnection	cnStateUBookstore
CursorType	adOpenStatic
LockType	adLockReadOnly

6. Set the dBalance variable equal to the value of the AccountBalance field in the recordset.

7. Set the dPotentialBalance variable equal to the account balance plus the book price.

8. Use a **Case** statement to evaluate the dPotentialBalance variable based on the following criteria:

Criteria	Result
Is <450	The **Authorize** method returns **True**.
Is <= 499	The **Authorize** method returns **True** and raises the **Warning** event because the student is within $50 of their $500 limit.
Is >= 500	The **Authorize** method returns **False** and raises the **Warning** event that the student does not have enough available credit.
All other values	The **Authorize** method returns **False**.

9. Close and release the recordset object variable.

To see an example of how your code should look, see Lab Hint 5.2 in Appendix B.

10. Test the class.

    To test the **CAccount** class, you may want to create a test procedure that creates an instance of the class, and calls the **Authorize** method for a student. Remember that you can use the Data View window to create a connection to the StateUBookstore database. With such a connection, you can open tables and evaluate the data to determine if your class is working correctly.

11. Save your work.

Exercise 3: Implementing the Debit Method

In this exercise, you will implement the **Debit** method of the **CAccount** class.

▶ **Change the Student AccountBalance**

The **Debit** method is called only after the book purchase transaction has been authorized. This method will add the book price amount to the student's account balance.

1. In the **Debit** method declare an ADO **Recordset** object called **rsStudent**.

2. Declare a variable of type Double called dCurrentBalance.

3. Declare a second variable of type Double called dNewBalance.

4. Create a new **Recordset** object with the **Open** method using the following parameters:

Parameter	Value
Source	"Select AccountBalance from Students Where Student ID = " & str(iStudentID)
ActiveConnection	cnStateUBookstore
CursorType	adOpenKeyset
LockType	adLockOptimistic

5. Set the dCurrentBalance variable equal to the value of the AccountBalance field in the recordset.

6. Set the dNewBalance variable equal to the account balance plus the book price.

7. Set the AccountBalance field's value equal to the new balance.

8. Call the **Update** method of the recordset to save the change.

9. Add an error handler to the **Debit** method that returns vbFalse and raises the **Warning** event with the error description of any error that occurs.

10. Return vbTrue from the **Debit** method to indicate success.

11. Close and release the **Recordset** object variable.

   To see an example of how your code should look, see Lab Hint 5.3 in Appendix B.

12. Save your work.

▶ **Record the book purchase**

1. After the student AccountBalance has been written, this transaction needs to be recorded in the AccountLog table.

2. Create a new private function in the class called **RecordPurchase**. It should take an **Integer** argument called **iStudentID**.

3. Declare a string variable called sSQLInsert. It will contain the SQL **Insert** statement.

4. Set the sSQLInsert text to a SQL Insert string to add a new record to the AccountLog table. Your code should resemble the following:

```
sSQLInsert = "INSERT INTO AccountLog(StudentID,LogDate,Amount,Memo)
" & _
                "VALUES(" & Str(iStudentID) & ", '" & Str(Now) & _
                "'," & Str(mvarPrice) & ",'" & mvarMemo & "')"
```

5. Call the **Execute** method of the active connection to insert the record into the AccountLog table.

6. Add a call to the **RecordPurchase** function at the end of the **Debit** method.

7. Test the class.

   If you created a test procedure in the previous exercise, you can add to that procedure to test the **Debit** method for the same student.

8. Save your work.

Exercise 4: Using the CAccount Class

In this exercise, you will add code that uses the **CAccount** class you've created. This class will be used when a student attempts to buy a book from the State University Bookstore.

▶ **Add code to handle buying a book**

1. In the code for the **frmStateUMain** form, add a new procedure called **PurchaseBook.**

2. In the click event for the **cmdBuyBook** button, call the **PurchaseBook** procedure.

3. In the double click event of the **DataRepeater** control, call the **PurchaseBook** procedure.

▶ **Authorize the book purchase**

1. In the general declaration section of the main form module, declare a **CAccount** object called **actCurrent** using the **WithEvents** keyword.

2. In the **PurchaseBook** procedure, create a new instance of the **CAccount** class.

3. Declare a Boolean variable called bAuth to handle the return value from the **Authorize** method.

4. Set the **Price** property of the **actCurrent** object using the price of the book currently selected in the **DataRepeater** control. Your code should resemble the following:

```
actCurrent.Price = drClassBookList.RepeatedControl.Price
```

5. Call the **Authorize** method of the **actCurrent** object and set the return value equal to bAuth.

6. If the **Authorize** method returned **False,** display a message box that the student is not authorized to buy the book.

7. If the **Authorize** method returned **True,** implement the following:

   a. Declare a boolean variable called bDebit to handle the return value from the **Debit** method.

   b. Set the **Memo** property of the **actCurrent** object to some useful information about the purchase. For example:

```
actCurrent.Memo = "Book Purchase: " & _
            RTrim(drClassBookList.RepeatedControl.BookName)
```

   c. Call the **Debit** method and set the return value equal to bDebit.

   d. Display a message box stating the results of the **Debit** method. If it returns **True,** the account was increased by the book amount, if it returns **False,** the purchase did not occur.

▶ **Handle the Warning event**

1. Add the event handler for the **Warning** event of the **actCurrent** object.

2. In the event handler, add code to display the message passed into the event.

3. Save your work.

Exercise 5: Testing the CAccount Class

In this exercise, you will test the lab solution using specific scenarios that will test different cases that the **CAccount** component should handle. Throughout this exercise you should use the Data View window or some other query tool to check the value of a student's AccountBalance as you test the **Authorize** and **Debit** methods of the **CAccount** class.

> **Note** This exercise depends on the data in the StateUBookstore being the same data as delivered in the StateUBookstore database scripts that were provided on your CD.

▶ **Test for a student not authorized to buy a book**

1. Run the StateUBookstore application.

2. Enter the Student ID 23.

3. Attempt to buy any of the books for this student's classes.

   You should receive a message that this purchase would put the student over the credit limit.

▶ **Test for a student who can buy this book with a warning**

1. Run the StateUBookstore application.

2. Enter the Student ID 39.

3. Attempt to buy any of the books for this student's classes.

   You should receive a message that this purchase would put the student within $50 of the $500 limit.

   You should receive a second message notifying you that the charge has been incurred.

▶ **Test for a student who can buy this book with no warning**

1. Run the StateUBookstore application.

2. Enter the Student ID 15.

3. Attempt to buy any of the books for this student's classes.

You should receive a second message notifying the charge that has been incurred.

Self-Check Questions

To see the answers to the Self-Check Questions, see Appendix A.

1. Which of the following code examples turns off a filter?

    A. rsStudents.Filter = " "

    B. rsStudents.Filter = Nothing

    C. rsStudents.Filter = adFilterNone

    D. rsStudents.Filter = adDisableFilter

2. Which of the following is not a component of the ADO object model?

    A. TableDef

    B. Recordset

    C. Connection

    D. Command

3. Which cursor location must be used when implementing a disconnected recordset?

    A. Server-side

    B. Client-side

    C. Dynamic

    D. Static

4. Which Recordset method is used to save changes to a data source?

    A. AddNew

    B. Save

    C. Update

    D. Edit

5. Which method is used to add a new field to a dynamic recordset?

A. Update

B. Insert

C. AddNew

D. Append

6. Which two lines of code bind a text box to a Recordset object?

A. Set txtStudentCity.DataSource = rsStudent

```
txtStudentCity.DataField = "City"
```

B. Set txtStudentCity.DataSource = rsStudent

```
txtStudentCity.Text = "City"
```

C. Set txtStudentCity.Text = rsStudent

```
txtStudentCity.DataField = "City"
```

D. Set txtStudentCity.DataField = rsStudent

```
txtStudentCity.DataSource = "City"
```

Chapter 6:
Advanced Data Access Issues

...er, you will learn about database concepts for creating
...ient/server applications. Using the techniques introduced in
..., and what you learned in Chapter 5, "Using ActiveX Data
...you will implement features such as client-side or server-side
...d support for Microsoft SQL Server stored procedures. In
...managing referential integrity errors and ensuring data
...will be discussed.

...ctives

...completing this chapter, you will be able to:

...scuss SQL Server security implementations.

...escribe different cursor locations and when to use a specific
...ursor type.

...se a stored procedure to execute a statement on a database.

...Handle referential integrity errors.

...Describe ways to enforce data integrity.

Overview of SQL Server Security

The behavior of your application when connecting to a SQL Server database depends upon the type of security on the server.

In this section, you will learn how Microsoft SQL Server manages security.

Understanding SQL Server Security

To develop a client application that establishes a connection to a data source, you must plan the way in which the connection is made. This includes determining the security mode of the designated data source, and whether it requires a user ID and password.

SQL Server Security Modes

Security is necessary to protect the information contained in the database. You usually implement one of two primary security options:

- Standard security mode
- Integrated security mode

Standard Mode

Standard security mode is the default security mode for SQL Server. Standard mode uses the SQL Server security model for every connection to the database. It supports non-trusted environments, such as the Internet. For example, if you implement a solution that allows users to connect to a SQL Server over the Internet, users will not necessarily first connect to a Windows NT server for authentication. SQL Server will perform its own authentication in this situation. The system administrator or database owner can create user IDs, aliases, user names, and groups for each database on the server. When this mode is in use, the user must enter a user ID and password combination that has been established for the database.

When using standard mode, you can pass security information to a data source in one of the following three ways:

- Hard-code all connection information.
- Prompt the user for some information and hard-code the rest.
- Prompt the user for all information.

Integrated Mode

Integrated security mode allows SQL Server to use Microsoft Windows NT authentication mechanisms to validate users for all connections to the database. You can use integrated security in network environments in which all clients support trusted connections. A trusted connection is one that recognizes users who have been granted system administrator status, have valid Windows NT accounts, or otherwise have access to the database.

Integrated security allows applications to take advantage of Windows NT security capabilities, which include encrypted passwords, password aging, domain-wide user accounts, and Windows-based user administration.

With integrated security, users maintain a single user ID and password for both Windows NT and SQL Server.

For more information about SQL Server security terms, read the article "Security Terminology" in Platform SDK Help.

Using SQL Server Security and ADO

Regardless of which ADO technique you use for connecting to a SQL Server, you must send a user ID value and a password value. The user ID and password are passed through ADO directly to the server for validation.

For more information about connection techniques, see "Connecting to a Data Source" on page 172 in Chapter 5, "Using ActiveX Data Objects."

Note In the event that SQL Server is using Integrated Security, the values of user ID and password are ignored.

If an invalid user ID or password is provided, the connection will fail and a runtime error will result. If no password is required for the user ID, the password argument can be left out of the connection information.

Connecting to a Secure SQL Server

Unless your application hard-codes the user ID and password values, you must prompt the user for these values before connecting to the database. The following example code prompts the user for a user name and password.

```
Sub cmdConnect_Click()

    Dim sUsername As string
    Dim sPassword As string
    Dim cnStateUBookstore As Connection

    Set cnStateUBookstore = New Connection
    sUsername = InputBox("Please enter your user name:")
    sPassword = InputBox("Please enter your password:")
    With cnStateUBookstore
        .Provider = "SQLOLEDB"
        .ConnectionString = "User ID=" & sUsername & _
                            ";Password=" & sPassword & _
                            ";Data Source=MSERIES1;" & _
                            "Initial Catalog=StateUBookstore"

        .Open
    End With

End Sub
```

Using Cursors

When a **Recordset** object is created, specific records based on a SQL query are returned. This grouping of records is called a cursor because it indicates the current position in the result set, just as the cursor on a computer display indicates the current position on the screen. You can specify four types of cursors and two different locations. In this section you will learn about a cursor's features, and how to implement the appropriate cursor for your application's needs.

Choosing a Cursor Type

Cursors are created in a computer's memory. Using ADO and certain databases, such as Microsoft SQL Server, you can specify on which computer the cursor is created.

You can implement four types of cursors: forward-only, static, dynamic, and keyset. Depending on their functionality, certain cursors use more system resources than others.

Selecting where the cursor should be built (its location) and the functionality of the cursor (its type) occurs when the recordset is first opened. The cursor type affects the performance and overhead of the cursor.

The location and type of the cursor cannot be changed unless the recordset is first closed and then reopened.

Forward-Only Cursors

The default recordset cursor type is forward-only. A forward-only cursor provides support exclusively for the **MoveNext** navigation method. Any other navigation method generates a run-time error. Due to the limited capabilities of a forward-only cursor, it is very efficient and uses the least amount of overhead.

Since forward-only is the default, you do not need to specify a cursor type when opening a recordset. However, it is a recommended practice to specify the cursor type. To explicitly create a forward-only cursor, set the **CursorType** property of the recordset to **adOpenForwardOnly**. The following sample code opens a forward-only recordset. To copy this code for use in your own projects, see "Creating a Forward-Only Cursor" on the accompanying CD-ROM.

```
Sub cmdOpenRecordset_Click()
  Dim rsPublishers As Recordset
  Set rsPublishers = New Recordset
  With rsPublishers
      .Open "SELECT pub_id FROM Publishers", cnStateUBookstore, _
            adOpenForwardOnly
  End With
End Sub
```

Static Cursors

A static cursor does not detect changes made to the recordset, the order in which the records are returned by the cursor, or the changes made to the values in each record in the recordset after the cursor is opened. For example, suppose a static cursor fetches a record and then another application updates that record. If the static cursor uses the record again, the values seen by the static cursor are unchanged, in spite of the changes that the other application made. In order for a static cursor to reflect changes made to its records, it must be closed and reopened.

You can use a static cursor when you need more flexible navigation, but do not need to see changes to the data.

To create a static cursor, set the **CursorType** property of a recordset to **adOpenStatic**. The following sample code opens a static recordset. To copy this code for use in your own projects, see "Creating a Static Cursor" on the accompanying CD-ROM.

```
Sub cmdOpenRecordset_Click()
  Dim rsPublishers As Recordset
  Set rsPublishers = New Recordset
  With rsPublishers
      .Open "SELECT pub_id FROM Publishers", cnStateUBookstore, _
              adOpenStatic
  End With
End Sub
```

Dynamic Cursors

Dynamic cursors are the most functional of the cursor types, but use the most overhead. A dynamic cursor can detect changes made to records in the recordset and their order. For example, suppose a dynamic cursor fetches two records, and then another application updates one of the records, deletes the other, and adds a new record that satisfies the query criteria. If the dynamic cursor attempts to fetch these records again, it will return the updated value of the first record, it will not return the deleted record, and it will return the new record.

You can use a dynamic cursor when you need a cursor that will always provide live data.

To create a dynamic cursor, set the **CursorType** property of the recordset to **adOpenDynamic**. The following sample code opens a dynamic recordset. To copy this code for use in your own projects, see "Creating a Dynamic Cursor" on the accompanying CD-ROM.

```
Sub cmdOpenRecordset_Click()
  Dim rsPublishers As Recordset
  Set rsPublishers = New Recordset
  With rsPublishers
      .Open "SELECT pub_id FROM Publishers", cnStateUBookstore, _
              adOpenDynamic
  End With
End Sub
```

Keyset Cursors

A keyset cursor lies between a static and dynamic cursor in its ability to detect changes. Like a static cursor, it does not always detect changes to its records and order of the recordset. For example, if the cursor is fully populated, new records are not included without refreshing the recordset. Like a dynamic cursor, however, it does detect changes to the values of records in the recordset.

You can use a keyset cursor when you need to be able to see changes to the data in the recordset but do not need to see additions or deletions of records.

To create a keyset cursor, set the **CursorType** property of the recordset to **adOpenKeyset**. The following sample code opens a keyset recordset. To copy this code for use in your own projects, see "Creating a Keyset Cursor" on the accompanying CD-ROM.

```
Sub cmdOpenRecordset_Click()
  Dim rsPublishers As Recordset
  Set rsPublishers = New Recordset
  With rsPublishers
      .Open "SELECT pub_id FROM Publishers", cnStateUBookstore, _
              adOpenKeyset
  End With
End Sub
```

Choosing a Cursor Location

You can build cursors on the server or the client. Which location is preferable will depend on the size of the cursor and the capabilities of the server data source.

Server-Side Cursors

Server-side cursors are the default in ADO. If the data source you are connecting to does not support server-side cursors, a client-side cursor must be created. To explicitly specify the creation of a server-side cursor, set the **CursorLocation** property of the **Recordset** object to **adUseServer**. If a server-side cursor is created, the values of the records contained in the recordset are stored on the server.

Using a server-side cursor can increase an application's performance since the overhead on the client is limited and the amount of network traffic is reduced.

Creating a Server-Side Cursor

Server-side cursors are specified in the **CursorLocation** property. The following sample code opens a server-side cursor. To copy this code for use in your own projects, see "Creating a Server-Side Cursor" on the accompanying CD-ROM.

```
Sub cmdOpenRecordset_Click()
  Dim rsStudents As Recordset
  Set rsStudents = New Recordset
  With rsStudents
      .CursorLocation = adUseServer
      .Open "SELECT StudentID FROM Students", cnStateUBookstore
  End With
End Sub
```

Client-Side Cursors

Client-side cursors are built by setting the **CursorLocation** property of the **Recordset** object to **adUseClient**. If a client-side cursor is created, the values of the records contained in the recordset are stored on the client's computer. This allows for the creation and management of disconnected recordsets and can be used to move the overhead of cursor management off the server.

> **Note** When you set the **CursorLocation** property to **adUseClient,** the client cursor engine supports only "static" cursor types, no matter what's reported by the **CursorType** property.

For information about disconnected recordsets, see "Using Disconnected Data" on page 196 in Chapter 5, "Using ActiveX Data Objects."

If the size of the recordset it too large, using a client-side cursor can slow an application's performance. Since most client machines have strict limitations on resources, use of client-side cursors should be restricted to small recordsets.

Creating a Client-Side Cursor

Server-side cursors are specified in the **CursorLocation** property. The following sample code opens a client-side cursor. To copy this code for use in your own project, see "Creating a Client-Side Cursor" on the accompanying CD-ROM.

```
Sub cmdOpenRecordset_Click()
  Dim rsStudents As Recordset
  Set rsStudents = New Recordset
  With rsStudents
      .CursorLocation = adUseClient
      .Open "SELECT StudentID FROM Students", cnStateUBookstore
  End With
End Sub
```

Practice: Using Cursors

In this practice, you will use different cursor types and locations and observe their effects on an application.

▶ **Create a default cursor**

1. Start Visual Basic and open the project Cursors.vbp located in the <*install folder*>\Practices\Chapter06\Using Cursors folder.

2. Open the code window for the **cmdConnect** click event.

> **Note** Change the **Data Source** name of MSERIES1 to that of your SQL Server.

3. Add the following code to create a default cursor:

```
rsPublishers.Open "Select pub_id, pub_name, city, state from Pub-
lishers", cnStateUBookstore, adOpenForwardOnly
```

4. Save your work.

5. Run the application and use a navigation button other than **Next** to move to a new record. Observe the error code generated.

6. Stop the application.

▶ **Create a scrollable cursor**

1. Open the code window for the **cmdConnect** click event.

2. Change the cursor type created to **adOpenKeyset**.

3. Save your work.

4. Run the application and attempt to navigate the recordset using a navigation button other than **Next**.

5. Stop the application.

▶ **Create a client-side cursor**

1. Open the code window for the **cmdConnect** click event.

2. Change the cursor location from the default, server-side to **adUseClient**.

3. Set the cursor type to **adOpenStatic**.

4. Save and test your work.

Enforcing Data Integrity

Ensuring data integrity is a critical element of developing professional applications. Techniques such as record locking, transaction management, implementing data source features, and handling referential integrity errors help maintain data consistency.

In this section, you will learn about various techniques for ensuring data integrity.

Using Record Locking

When you build a recordset, select a locking option to manage the user's access to records in a data source. In a multi-user environment, locking ensures that no two users can change the same record at the same time. Note that the combination of the cursor location, cursor type, and locking option affects the updateability of a recordset.

Use the **LockType** property to set the locking option for the recordset. The following table describes the options of the **LockType** property.

Locking Option	Description
adLockReadOnly	The data is read-only and cannot be altered. This is the default option.
adLockPessimistic	The provider ensures successful editing of the records, usually by locking records at the data source immediately upon editing.
adLockOptimistic	The provider uses optimistic locking, locking records only when you call the **Update** method.
adLockBatchOptimistic	The records are locked in batch update mode, as opposed to immediate update mode. This option is required for client-side cursors, including disconnected recordsets.

Note Specifying a forward-only cursor that uses read-only locking is the most efficient implementation of a cursor and should be used whenever possible. This type of cursor is sometimes called a "firehose cursor."

Specifying a Locking Option

You specify a locking option when you open a recordset. Set the **LockType** property of the recordset to one of the locking constants to control how the data source locks the records. The following sample code opens a new recordset and uses pessimistic locking. To copy this code for use in your own projects, see "Specifying a Locking Option" on the accompanying CD-ROM.

```
Sub cmdOpenRecordset_Click()
  Dim cnStateUBookstore As Connection
  Dim rsStudents As Recordset
  Set cnStateUBookstore = New Connection
  With cnStateUBookstore
      .Provider = "SQLOLEDB"
      .ConnectionString = "User ID=sa;" & _
                          "Data Source=MSERIES1;" & _
                          "Initial Catalog=StateUBookstore"
      .Open
  End With
  Set rsStudents = New Recordset
  rsStudents.Open "SELECT StudentID FROM Students", _
                  cnStateUBookstore, adOpenKeyset, _
                  adLockPessimistic
End Sub
```

Using Database Transactions

Transactions help ensure data integrity by grouping one or more SQL statements together. A transaction is an "all or nothing" proposition; either all of the statements are committed, or none of them are. If either command fails, you can roll back both commands, returning the data source to its original state. If both commands are successful, you can commit the changes and make them permanent.

There are two categories of transactions: implicit and explicit.

Implicit Transactions

Implicit transactions do not allow you to group multiple commands together. Instead a transaction is built around each individual command. Using implicit transactions, you cannot programmatically roll back or commit the changes. However, you can trap for a run-time error if the command were to fail. Your program can then resubmit the individual change.

If you do not explicitly turn on a transaction, implicit transactions are used automatically. SQL Server will use auto-commit mode and build a transaction around each individual command.

Tip For more information on how SQL Server implements and manages transactions, read the article "Application Development Using Transact-SQL" in SDK Platform Help.

Explicit Transactions

Explicit transactions allow your application to manage multiple SQL statements as if they were a single command. When you use an explicit transaction, your application groups commands into a single action.

For example, you can use an explicit transaction if your application transfers money between bank accounts. The act of transferring money consists of two operations: removing money from one account (a debit) and then adding it to another account (a credit). If there are any network problems or other errors that prevent the credit from occurring, the money will be removed from the first account without being added to the second.

Your application can manage explicit transactions by using one of three transaction methods: **BeginTrans**, **RollbackTrans**, or **CommitTrans**. When you create an explicit transaction with the **BeginTrans** method, all statements that follow are automatically a part of that transaction. When you use the **RollbackTrans** or **CommitTrans** methods, the transaction is closed and a new one can be created.

Creating an Explicit Transaction

Transactions are managed at the level of the **Connection** object. Any **Recordset** objects or **Command** objects created when a transaction is enabled automatically share the transaction.

The following sample code creates a new transaction and closes it appropriately. To copy this code for use in your own projects, see "Creating an Explicit Transaction" on the accompanying CD-ROM.

```
Sub cmdMakeChanges_Click()

    Dim cnStateUBookstore As Connection
    Set cnStateUBookstore = New Connection

    With cnStateUBookstore
        .Provider = "SQLOLEDB"
        .ConnectionString = "User ID=sa;" & _
                            "Data Source=MSERIES1;" & _
                            "Initial Catalog=StateUBookstore"
        .Open
    End With

    ' A Transaction space is created
    cnStateUBookstore.BeginTrans

    ' Turn on the error handler
    On Error Goto Error_Handler

    ' SQL Commands are executed in the transaction
    cnStateUBookstore.Execute "INSERT INTO Authors..."
    cnStateUBookstore.Execute "DELETE FROM Publishers..."

    ' If all commands are successful, commit them
    cnStateUBookstore.CommitTrans

Exit Sub

Error_Handler:

    ' If an error occured, roll back the changes
    cnStateUBookstore.RollbackTrans
    MsgBox "An error occured changing the records.", vbExclamation

End Sub
```

SQL Server Data Integrity Features

SQL Server provides a number of features that help ensure data integrity in the database. From Visual Basic, ADO can automatically take advantage of these features. Depending on the feature, a trappable run-time error will occur if data integrity is violated, prompting the user for corrective action without terminating the program. Developers typically must work with the SQL Server database administrators at their sites to identify how specific data integrity issues should be handled in their applications.

Note It is usually more efficient for a client application to validate input data before sending it to the database.

For more information about data integrity concepts, read the article "Understanding Database Objects" in Platform SDK Help.

Referential Integrity Constraints

Constraints are the preferred way to restrict data being sent to a SQL Server. A constraint applies to a table's field or fields. Constraints provide the following advantages:

◆ Multiple constraints can be associated with a field, and a constraint can be associated with multiple fields.

◆ Constraints are created by using the SQL Server CREATE TABLE statement and reside with the table definition.

◆ Constraints can be used to enforce referential integrity.

For more information about referential integrity, see "Handling Referential Integrity Errors" on page 230 in this chapter.

The five types of constraints are:

◆ PRIMARY

◆ UNIQUE

◆ FOREIGN KEY

◆ DEFAULT

◆ CHECK

Validation Rules

Rules are database objects that specify the acceptable values for a specific field based on simple criteria. Rules only support the individual fields being tested. They do not support references to other tables. A rule can specify one of the following:

◆ A set of values

◆ A range of values

◆ A format

You must first create a rule and then bind it to a field in order to use it. When bound to a field, the rule specifies the acceptable values that can be applied to that field. You can bind only one rule per field.

Field Defaults

Defaults provide a convenient way to ensure that a field has a reasonable value for every record, even when you insert a new record without a specified value for the field. In a SQL Server database, each field in a record must contain a value, even if that value is a null value. You determine whether a field can accept null values by the specified data type, default, or constraint.

Defaults specify the value that SQL Server inserts when the user does not enter a value. For example, in a table with a field named "price," you can instruct SQL Server to enter a null value if the user does not know the price of an item. You must first create a default and then bind it to a field in order to use it.

An alternate, and preferred, method to creating a default is to create a default constraint. Constraints are the preferred method of restricting field data because the constraint definition is stored with the table and is deleted (dropped) automatically when the table is deleted. However, it is more efficient to use defaults when the default will be used repeatedly for multiple fields.

Handling Referential Integrity Errors

Referential integrity preserves defined relationships among tables when you enter and delete records in those tables. For example, assume your database contains two tables, Customers and Orders. Each customer in the Customers table can have multiple records in the Orders table. In the event that a Customer record is deleted, all matching records in the Orders table will be left with an invalid Customer ID. This is an example of a referential integrity violation because the integrity of the database has been violated.

Trapping for Referential Integrity Violations

If a referential integrity violation occurs, your application will receive a run-time error. Depending on the data source, the command that violates the integrity will fail. Therefore, if this type of error occurs, the data source will retain its original state and your application must respond accordingly.

Note Referential integrity error codes are specific to the data source your application is using. The errors are also specific to the kind of referential integrity error encountered, such as foreign key violation, duplicate key, and so forth.

Tip In order to verify the error code a given referential integrity error will generate in your application, force a situation that will generate the error you want to trap for and then check the error value returned by the data source.

The sample code on the following page attempts to delete a record in a transaction that would result in a referential integrity violation. To copy this code for use in your own projects, see "Trapping Referential Integrity Errors" on the accompanying CD-ROM.

```
Sub cmdDeleteRecords_Click()

  Dim cnStateUBookstore As Connection
  Dim errStateU As Errors

  Set cnStateUBookstore = New Connection

  With cnStateUBookstore
      .Provider = "SQLOLEDB"
      .ConnectionString = "User ID=sa;" & _
                          "Data Source=MSERIES1;" & _
                          "Initial Catalog=StateUBookstore"
      .Open
  End With

  On Error Goto Error_Handler:

  cnStateUBookstore.BeginTrans
      ' this command will generate a foreign key violation error
      cnStateUBookstore.Execute "DELETE FROM Books WHERE
          BookID = 14"
  cnStateUBookstore.CommitTrans

Exit Sub

Error_Handler:

    ' trap for the foreign key violation from SQL Server using
    ' the OLE DB Provider for SQL Server.
  If Err.Number = -2147217900 Then

      ' show the database errors
      For Each errStateU In cnStateUBookstore.Errors
          MsgBox "Database Error: " & _
                  errStateU.Number & " " & _
                  errStateU.Description
      Next

      ' the transaction will be rolled back
      cnStateUBookstore.RollbackTrans
  End If

End Sub
```

Executing Statements on a Database

You can execute a statement on a Microsoft SQL Server directly, or by using a stored procedure. In this section, you will learn how to execute statements against a data source.

Executing Statements Directly

Your application can run SQL commands by executing them directly. These commands either return records, in the form of a recordset, or they affect the value of records.

To see the demonstration "Executing Statements Directly," see the accompanying CD-ROM.

For information on returning records in a recordset, see "Retrieving Data from a Data Source" on page 176 in Chapter 5, "Using ActiveX Data Objects."

To execute commands that affect the value of records, such as updating current data and adding or deleting new records, use the appropriate SQL command and the **Execute** method of either the **Connection** object or the **Command** object.

Executing Directly Using the Connection Object

If the sample code being executed will be called only once from your application, you can use the **Execute** method of the active connection. This is the most efficient technique for one-time execution of SQL commands. If your application will call the same command more than once, consider using a **Command** object. The following sample code creates a **Connection** object that updates records in the Products table. To copy this code for use in your own projects, see "Executing a Statement with a Connection Object" on the accompanying CD-ROM.

```
Sub cmdUpdateRecords_Click()

  Dim cnStateUBookstore As Connection
  Dim sSQL As String

  Set cnStateUBookstore = New Connection

  With cnStateUBookstore
      .Provider = "SQLOLEDB"
      .ConnectionString = "User ID=sa;" & _
                          "Data Source=MSERIES1;" & _
                          "Initial Catalog=StateUBookstore"

      .Open
  End With

  sSQL = "INSERT INTO Authors(First_Name, Last_Name) " & _
      "VALUES ('Suanne', 'Nagata')"

  cnStateUBookstore.Execute sSQL

End Sub
```

Executing Directly Using the Command Object

For SQL commands that will be called more than once from the same application, use the **Command** object to build the query. Set the **Prepared** property to **True**. This technique improves the performance of your application since the command is prepared and then saved in memory. Initially, this is slower than using the **Connection** object but improves performance for subsequent calls. The following sample code creates a **Command** object and executes a SQL statement. To copy this code for use in your own projects, see "Executing a Statement Using the Command Object" on the accompanying CD-ROM.

```
Sub cmdUpdateRecords_Click()
  Dim cnStateUBookstore As Connection
  Dim comBooks As Command
  Set cnStateUBookstore = New Connection
  With cnStateUBookstore
      .Provider = "SQLOLEDB"
      .ConnectionString = "User ID=sa;" & _
                          "Data Source=MSERIES1;" & _
                          "Initial Catalog=StateUBookstore"
      .Open
  End With

  Set comBooks = New Command
  With comBooks
      .Prepared = True
      .ActiveConnection = cnStateUBookstore
      .CommandType = adCmdText
      .CommandText = "UPDATE Books SET Price = Price * 1.1"
  End With

  comBooks.Execute
End Sub
```

Note If the **Prepared** property of a **Command** object has been set to **True**, you can re-execute the statement using the **Execute** method.

Overview of Stored Procedures

Stored procedures are routines that are stored on the server and can be executed from a single call from a client. They are complex routines that you create using a scripting language called Transact SQL that are compiled and stored in a SQL Server database.

Stored procedures are useful when building a client/server application that accesses a SQL Server database. Stored procedures can be written to validate, modify, insert, and/or delete data. They can encapsulate business rules and integrity rules such that the rules do not need to be addressed on the client or in a middle tier component.

Stored procedures differ from an ordinary SQL statement because they are pre-parsed and pre-normalized. When a stored procedure is created, SQL Server analyzes it and prepares an internal, normalized structure that is stored in a system table. The first time the stored procedure is executed, a query plan is created and compiled. The compiled plan stays in memory on the server until it is forced out by other memory needs. This means that subsequent calls to the stored procedure result in much better performance than re-creating the same SQL command each time it is needed.

Advantages of Stored Procedures

Stored procedures can streamline the execution of a query because of their ability to:

◆ Accept parameters.

◆ Return values of parameters to a calling procedure or client.

◆ Return a status value that indicates success or failure, as well as the reason for the failure.

◆ Call other stored procedures.

◆ Encapsulate business functionality so that all applications can use and perform the procedures consistently.

◆ Make execution faster and more efficient. Once they are compiled, no syntax checking is required when they are executed.

◆ Store the compiled version on the server and use it for subsequent calls, thus reducing network traffic.

◆ Be called from different client applications.

Calling a Stored Procedure

You call stored procedures by using the ADO **Command** object. In order to call a stored procedure use the following main steps:

1. Create an ADO **Command** object and set its **ActiveConnection** property to use a connection to the database containing the stored procedure you want to call.

2. Specify that the command is a stored procedure by setting the **CommandType** property to **adCmdStoredProc**.

3. Specify which stored procedure you want to call by setting the **CommandText** property to the name of the stored procedure.

4. If you need to send data to or receive data from the stored procedure you can use the **Parameters** collection of the **Command** object.

    a. Use the **Append** and **CreateParameter** methods to create parameters to hold the data.

    b. Use the Direction argument of the **CreateParameter** method to specify the type of parameter you want to create.

5. To run the stored procedure, call the **Command** object's **Execute** method.

6. If the stored procedure returns data, you can receive the output either in a recordset or in parameters. More complex stored procedures can return a combination of recordsets and output parameters in a single call.

The rest of this topic provides detailed information about how to implement the steps to use a stored procedure.

To see the demonstration "Using a Stored Procedure to Return Author Information," see the accompanying CD-ROM.

Creating a Command to Call a Stored Procedure

Create an ADO **Command** object and set the **ActiveConnection** property to use a connection to the database containing the stored procedure you want to call.

To specify that the command will call a stored procedure, set its **CommandType** property to **adCmdStoredProc**. Use the **CommandText** property to specify the name of the stored procedure to call.

If you need to send to or receive data from the stored procedure, create parameters and set input values as required before executing the statement.

Parameters

Your application can pass specific data to a stored procedure by using parameters. The following table describes the three types of parameters available to you.

Type	Used...	Direction argument	Comment
Input	By your application to send specific data values to a stored procedure.	adParamInput	This is the default parameter type.
Output	By a stored procedure to send specific values back to the calling application.	adParamOutput	Differs from a recordset in that only one value is returned, not a complete record or group of records. This is a very efficient way to interact with a database.
Input/ Output	By a stored procedure to both retrieve information sent by your application and to send specific values back to the application.	adParamInputOutput	

Creating a Parameter

To create a parameter on the **Command** object, use the **Append** and **CreateParameter** methods. The **CreateParameter** method requires two arguments — the name of the parameter and its data type. You will also want to specify the optional Direction argument to indicate how the parameter is used by the stored procedure. The following example code adds an input parameter called StudentID with a data type of integer to the **Parameters** collection for the **Command** object called **comGetUserName**:

```
comGetUserName.Parameters.Append _
    comGetUserName.CreateParameter("StudentID", _
    adInteger, adParamInput)
```

> **Note** When creating a parameter, you can either give it a useful name or reference it by its index. If you choose to give it a name, the name does not have to match the parameter's name in SQL Server.

For a complete listing of ADO parameter data types read the article "Type Property (ADO)" in Platform SDK Help.

Specifying a Value for a Parameter

Once an input parameter has been added to the **Parameters** collection of the **Command** object, set the **Value** property to specify the data that should be sent to the server. The following example code sets the StudentID parameter equal to 10:

```
comGetUserName.Parameters("StudentID").Value = 10
```

Retrieving a Value from a Parameter

If you need to retrieve a value from a stored procedure that returns an output parameter, use the **Parameters** collection to find the value of the output parameter. The following example code retrieves the value of an output parameter to a variable:

```
sUsername = comGetUserName.Parameters("UserName").Value
```

The following sample code creates a new **Command** object and calls an existing stored procedure that uses parameters. To copy this code for use in your own projects, see "Accessing a Stored Procedure" on the accompanying CD-ROM.

```
Dim rsAuthorInfo As Recordset

Sub cmdGetStudentsByMajor_Click()

    Dim cnStateUBookstore As Connection
    Dim comStudentMajor As Command

    ' Instantiate the object variables
    Set cnStateUBookstore = New Connection
    Set comStudentMajor = New Command
    Set rsStudentInfo = New Recordset
```

code continued on next page

code continued from previous page

```
    ' Establish a connection to the database
    With cnStateUBookstore
        .Provider = "SQLOLEDB"
        .ConnectionString = "User ID=sa;" & _
                            "Data Source=MSERIES1;" & _
                            "Initial Catalog=StateUBookstore"
        .Open
    End With

    ' Create the Command object
    With comStudentMajor
        .CommandType = adCmdStoredProc

        ' set the name of the stored procedure
        .CommandText = "StudentMajor"

        ' create and append the input parameter
        .Parameters.Append
comStudentMajor.CreateParameter("MajorID", adInteger)

        ' set the initial value of the parameter
        .Parameters("MajorID").Value = txtMajorID.Text

        ' set the connection
        .ActiveConnection = cnStateUBookstore
    End With

    ' call the stored proc and save the results in a recordset
    Set rsStudentInfo = comStudentMajor.Execute

End Sub
```

Lab 6: Advanced Data Access Issues

In this lab, you will call a SQL Server stored procedure and use its return value. You will also handle referential integrity errors that may be raised by the database.

To see the demonstration "Lab 6 Solution," see the accompanying CD-ROM.

Estimated time to complete this lab: **45 minutes**

To complete the exercises in this lab, you must have the required software. For detailed information about the labs and setup for the labs, see "Labs" in "About This Course."

Note If you have not completed Labs 4 through 5 using the same computer on which you are currently working, you may need to register *<install folder>*\Labs\Lab06\StateUControls.ocx before you start this lab.

For information about registering components, see "Making the Component Available" on page 247 in Chapter 7, "Using COM Components."

Objectives

After completing this lab, you will be able to:

◆ Use a SQL Server stored procedure from ADO code.

◆ Write ADO code to manage database transactions.

Prerequisites

Before working on this lab, you should be familiar with the following:

◆ Using the ADO **Object** model

◆ Using a SQL Server stored procedure

Exercises

The following exercises provide practice working with the concepts and techniques covered in this chapter:

◆ Exercise 1: Using a Stored Procedure

In this exercise, you will use a stored procedure in the StateUBookstore SQL Server database. You will pass the stored procedure an argument and it will return a value as an output parameter.

◆ Exercise 2: Using Transactions

In this exercise, you will add code to wrap the functionality of the **CAccount** class in a database transaction.

Exercise 1: Using a Stored Procedure

In this exercise, you will use a stored procedure in the StateUBookstore SQL Server database. You will pass the stored procedure an argument and it will return a value as an output parameter. You'll use the value from the stored procedure in Lab 7.

▶ **Create a procedure to call the stored procedure**

1. In the code module for the main form, create a new **Function** procedure called **GetBookID** that returns an integer.

2. In the **GetBookID** procedure, declare and instantiate an ADO **Command** object called **comGetBookID**.

3. Set the **ActiveConnection** property of the command to the connection to the StateUBookstore database established in the Data Environment.

4. Set the **CommandType** property of the command to **adCmdStoredProc**.

5. Set the **CommandText** property of the command to the name of the stored procedure "sp_GetBookID."

6. Use the **Parameters** collection of the command to add two parameters to the collection with the following parameters:

Name	Data Type	Direction	Size	Value
@BookTitle	adVarChar	Input	50	RTrim(drClassBookList. RepeatedControl. BookName)
@BookID	adInteger	Output n/a	n/a	

7. Invoke the **Execute** method of the command to call the stored procedure.

8. Return the output parameter's value as the return value for the **GetBookID** procedure.

To see an example of how your code should look, see Lab Hint 6.1 in Appendix B.

▶ **Use the GetBookID procedure**

1. Call the **GetBookID** procedure from the **PurchaseBook** procedure in the conditional case that a student has been authorized, but before the account has been debited.

2. Display the return value from this procedure in a message box.

You will add functionality to decrement bookstore inventory with this BookID in Lab 7.

Exercise 2: Using Transactions

The **CAccount** class **Debit** method changes the student AccountBalance and adds a record to the AccountLog table. In this exercise, you will add code to wrap the functionality of the **CAccount** class in a database transaction.

▶ **Add Database transaction code**

1. Open the **CAccount** code module and locate the **Debit** method.

2. Before the recordset is created, add code to call the **BeginTrans** method of the ADO **Connection** object to start the database transaction.

3. After the record has been written to the AccountLog table to record this book purchase, add code to call the **CommitTrans** method of the ADO **Connection** object to commit the database transaction.

4. In the error handler for the **Debit** method, add code to call the **RollbackTrans** method of the ADO **Connection** object to roll back any changes to the database.

5. Test the transaction handling by stepping through each line of code.

You can test whether the database changes have been rolled back by adding code after the student's AccountBalance has been updated that generates an error to force the error handler to run. To see the transaction work, you will need to evaluate the value of the student's account balance in the Data View window or some other query tool.

Self-Check Questions

To see the answers to the Self-Check Questions, see Appendix A.

1. **Which of the following cursors should you use to provide constant live access to the data?**

   A. Keyset cursor

   B. Dynamic cursor

   C. Static cursor

   D. Forward-only cursor

2. What happens when a referential integrity violation occurs?

   A. Your application will continue to execute.

   B. You will be prompted to ignore the error and continue working in the application.

   C. The data source will retain its original state and your application must respond accordingly.

   D. The data source accepts the change and your application receives an error message.

3. Transactions can only be managed from which of the following objects?

   A. Connection object

   B. **Command** object

   C. Recordset object

   D. ADO does not support transactions

4. Which of the following is NOT a feature of SQL Server integrated security?

   A. Windows NT groups

   B. Windows NT user names

   C. Non-trusted environments

   D. Single user name/password combinations for both Windows NT and SQL Server

5. Which of the following lock type options must be used with disconnected recordsets?

   A. adLockPessimistic

   B. adLockOptimistic

   C. adLockReadOnly

   D. adLockBatchOptimistic

6. Which is NOT a benefit of stored procedures?

   A. They can accept parameters.

   B. They should only be called once for best performance.

   C. They can call other stored procedures.

   D. They encapsulate business functionality.

Chapter 7:
Using COM Components

 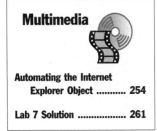
Component Object Model (COM) components are units of code that provide specific functionality. COM components can be either internal components, which are compiled into a project and are available only to that project, or external components, which are compiled into an executable (.exe) or dynamic-link library (.dll). Any client application can use an external component. Client applications use a component in the same way, whether it was compiled in a .dll or an .exe.

In Chapter 3, "Using Class Modules," you learned how to create COM components that are compiled inside a project, and are available only to that project. In Chapter 4, "Building ActiveX Controls," you learned how to create and use ActiveX controls. ActiveX controls are COM components that typically have a user interface and are hosted by a form.

In this chapter, you'll learn how to use external COM components to extend the functionality of your application. Although COM components are typically libraries of classes, entire applications such as Microsoft Excel or Microsoft Internet Explorer are also COM components. Client applications use Automation to take advantage of the services that such components expose.

In Chapter 8, "Building COM Components," you will learn how to create COM components that can be reused by other applications.

Objectives

After completing this chapter, you will be able to:

- List the main steps required to use an external COM component in a Microsoft Visual Basic application.

- Create a Visual Basic client application that uses a COM component.

- Create a Visual Basic application that handles events from a COM component.

- Create a Visual Basic application that automates Internet Explorer.

Introduction to Using COM Components

COM supplies a mechanism that allows binary software components, derived from any combination of pre-existing components you have developed and components from different software vendors, to connect to and communicate with each other in a well-defined manner.

As you define the functionality required by an application you're designing, look for places where you can use pre-existing COM components instead of having to write the code to implement a given functionality yourself. When you use COM components in a Visual Basic project, you do not have to understand all of the inner details that make these components work together; just how to use the component that adds the functionality you need to your application.

If you are interested in learning more about the inner workings of COM, see David Chappell's *Understanding ActiveX and OLE*. Other good books about COM include *Inside COM* by Dale Rogerson, and *Developing ActiveX Components with Visual Basic 5.0 - A Guide to the Perplexed* by Dan Appleman.

For current information about COM, go to the Microsoft COM Web site at http://www.microsoft.com/com/.

Creating a Client Application

In this section, you will learn how to create a Visual Basic client application that uses an external COM component. Using an external component in a Visual Basic application requires four main steps:

1. Making the component available to your application.

2. Declaring an object variable to hold an instance of the class you are reusing.

3. Creating the object.

4. Using the object.

Making the Component Available

In Chapter 3, "Using Class Modules," you learned how to create and use components that are internal to a project. By adding the class module and its properties, methods, and events for the component to your project, you provided both the code and the information needed to use the component internally. You then used the Object Browser to view information about the component.

When you want to use an external component in a client application, you must first ensure that the actual component is available and that information about its use is known to your application.

Registering a Component

When you run the installation program for a component, it adds any required files and typically registers the component. Registering the component places the information needed to use the component in the registry on your computer.

If you are going to use a component that does not have an installation program, you will need to run the Regsvr32 utility to register the component yourself. The following table lists the name and location of this utility on computers using different Windows operating systems.

Operating System	Location	Name
Microsoft Windows 95	*Windows 95 directory*\System	**Regsvr32.exe**
Microsoft Windows NT	*Windows NT directory*\System32	**Regsvr32.exe**

The following example command shows how to register a hypothetical Payroll component on a computer:

```
Regsvr32.exe  C:\StateUBookstore\payroll.dll
```

For more information about the Regsvr32 utility, see "Registering a Component" on page 278 in Chapter 8, "Building COM Components."

Setting References

Once a component has been registered, you can make the information about the component in the registry available to your Visual Basic project. To do so, set a reference to the component's type library. The library contains a description of all objects, methods, events, and properties for a COM component. A type library can be either an .olb or .tlb file or part of the .exe or .dll that the type library describes.

▶ **To set a reference to a type library**

1. On the **Project** menu, click **References**.

   Visual Basic displays the **References** dialog box.

2. Click the reference to the type library you want to use, and then click **OK**.

Once you have set a reference to a type library, you can find the specific object you want and information about its methods and properties in the Object Browser. For more information about the Object Browser, see "Using the Object Browser" on page 82 in Chapter 3, "Using Class Modules."

Note There are special situations in which you cannot set a reference to an object's library because the type of object you will use in your application is not determined until run time. For information about using objects whose type is determined at run time, see "Declaring Object Variables" in this chapter.

Declaring Object Variables

Before you can create an instance of a component to use in a client application, you must declare an object variable to refer to the object. You declare an object variable as either specific or generic, depending on how you will use the variable.

Specific Object Variables

In most cases, you will know at design time the type of object you want to create and use in your application. It is much more efficient in these cases to use specific object variables to point to the objects you create.

The following example code declares a variable **ie** in the General Declarations section that will hold a pointer to Internet Explorer objects only.

```
Dim ie As InternetExplorer
```

> **Note** A specific object variable refers to a particular object type and can only hold pointers to that type. If you try to store a different object type in that variable, an error will result.

Because you have set a reference to the object's library, Visual Basic detects an object variable at design time when you write code for the client application. Visual Basic can display information about the available methods and properties, as well as the syntax of each method or property call. Another advantage is that you can use the Object Browser to view information about the object's methods, properties, and events.

Generic Object Variables

There are cases when you do not know at design time the specific type of object your application will use. In these situations, you can use generic object variables to hold pointers to any type of object. For example, you might want to write a function that acts on any one of several different classes of objects. In this case, you must declare the variable **As Object**.

The following example code uses the **Object** data type to declare a generic object variable:

```
Dim objGeneric As Object
```

Since the specific object to be used will not be known until run time, you cannot set a reference to a library for the object in Visual Basic. This results in the disadvantages described in the next subsection "Variable Types and Binding." Therefore, you should only use generic variables when absolutely necessary.

Variable Types and Binding

Before a client application can use an object's methods, properties, or events, the client application must be bound, or connected, to the object. The type of variable you choose will determine the type of binding used between the client application and the object. The following table summarizes how the choice of variable type and type of binding affects you as a developer and your application.

Object Variable	Binding Type	Binding at ...	Implications
Specific	Early	Design time	Visual Basic checks the syntax of calls that use specific object variables. The compiler can produce more efficient code to access the object at run time.
Generic	Late	Run time	No information is known about the object at design time. Additional work is required by Visual Basic to access the object run time, causing a negative impact on the client application's performance.

For more information about early and late binding, read the article "Speeding Object References" in Visual Basic Help.

Creating Objects for Components

Once you have made the external component available to your application and have declared an object variable to hold an instance of the component, you can create the object.

In Visual Basic there are three ways to create an object to access an external component:

◆ Use the **New** keyword with a **Set** statement.

◆ Use the **GetObject** function.

◆ Use the **CreateObject** function.

The rest of this topic describes the appropriate use of each of the ways to create an object to hold an instance of an external COM component.

Using the New Keyword with the Set Statement

If you have set a reference to the type library for the external component and can use a specific object variable (early binding), then use the **New** keyword with the **Set** statement to create an instance of the class you want to use in your application.

The following example code shows using the **New** keyword with the **Set** statement to create an instance of the Internet Explorer application:

```
Sub StartIE()

  Static ie As InternetExplorer
  Set ie = New InternetExplorer
  ie.Visible = True

End Sub
```

> **Note** A client application that uses the preceding example code must have set a reference to the Microsoft Internet Controls object library (Shdocvw.dll).

Never use the **New** keyword in a declaration statement to create objects for external components because it creates extremely inefficient code. The reason is that using the **New** keyword in a declaration statement defers creation of the object until the first use. That means every time you use the object in the client application, Visual Basic must check to see if the object has been created.

Using the GetObject Function

When you want to create an instance of an object that has been saved to a file, use the **GetObject** function.

The following example code creates an instance of a Microsoft Word document object called Contract.doc and displays it in Print Preview mode:

```
Sub PreviewContract()

  Static wdContract As Word.Document
  Set wdContract = GetObject("C:\Contract.doc", "Word.Document")

  wdContract.Parent.Visible = True
  wdContract.PrintPreview

End Sub
```

> **Note** A client application that uses the preceding example code must have set a reference to the Microsoft Word 8.0 Object Library (Msword8.olb).

For more information about the **GetObject** function, read the article "GetObject Function" in Visual Basic Help.

Using the CreateObject Function

If you must use a generic variable in your application because you do not know the specific object type until run time (late binding), use the **CreateObject** function to instantiate the class.

The syntax for the **CreateObject** function is as follows:

CreateObject(class,[servername])

The following table describes the arguments of the **CreateObject** function in more detail.

Argument	Description	Class Argument Syntax	Description of Argument Parts
class	Required; **Variant** (**String**). The application name and class of the object to create.	appname.objecttype	
			appname
			Required; **Variant** (**String**). The name of the application providing the object.
			objecttype
			Required; **Variant** (**String**). The type or class of object to create.
servername	Optional; **Variant** (**String**). The name of the network server where the object will be created.		

For more information about the **CreateObject** function, read the article "CreateObject Function" in Visual Basic Help.

Using Components

After you have created an instance of the component, you can then use the component to provide useful information and services to the client application.

Using the Properties and Methods of a Component

The code you use to access the properties and methods of an external COM component is no different than code you use to access properties and methods of an internal component. The following example code shows calling the **Refresh** method of an Internet Explorer object from the **Click** event of a client application's **Refresh** button:

```
Private Sub cmdRefresh_Click()

    ie.Refresh

End Sub
```

For more examples of using the properties and methods of an external component, see "Using Microsoft Internet Explorer Properties" on page 256 and "Using Microsoft Internet Explorer Methods" on page 257 in this chapter.

Receiving Messages from Components

Client applications often want to take specific action when certain component events occur. To receive notification of COM component events, use the **WithEvents** keyword when you declare the variable for the component. The following example code shows how to declare a variable for an Internet Explorer object so you can trap and handle its events:

```
Dim WithEvents ie As InternetExplorer
```

To handle a given event, add the appropriate event handler to your application. The following example code shows an event handler for the Internet Explorer object that causes the client application to display the message "Download begun" every time the **DownloadBegin** event is fired by the instance of Internet Explorer referenced by the variable name **ie**:

```
Private Sub ie_DownloadBegin()

    lblStatus.Caption = "Download begun..."

End Sub
```

For more information about using events, see "Handling Events" on page 94 in Chapter 3, "Using Class Modules."

Another way a component can send asynchronous messages to a client is by using Callback procedures. This technique allows a COM component to send a given message to a specific client application. For more information about how COM components can communicate with client applications, read the article "Asynchronous Call-Backs and Events" in Visual Basic Help.

Using Microsoft Internet Explorer

In "Creating a Client Application" on page 246 in this chapter, you learned the major steps required to create a client application that uses an external COM component.

In this section, you will learn how to apply this knowledge to automate the Internet Explorer component from a client application.

The main steps to using Internet Explorer from a client application are:

1. Create an instance of the **InternetExplorer** application object.

2. Use properties, methods, and events of the **InternetExplorer** object.

3. Release the **InternetExplorer** object when the client application exits.

To see the demonstration "Automating the Internet Explorer Object," see the accompanying CD-ROM.

To view the complete code of the demonstration application used in this chapter, open the project *<install folder>*\DemoCode\ControlIE\ieController.vbp.

Creating an Instance of Microsoft Internet Explorer

You can use the Object Browser, as well as information about the Internet Explorer object's properties, methods, and events in the Platform SDK documentation, to learn how to use the Internet Explorer component. The following illustration shows using the Object Browser to view information about the Internet Explorer component.

You will use properties, methods, and events from a single class, the **InternetExplorer** class, from the Microsoft Internet Controls object library to control a stand-alone instance of Internet Explorer from a client application. In Chapter 10, "Building Internet Applications," you will learn how to create a Visual Basic application that uses the **WebBrowser** control, another class contained in this same object library.

To create an instance of the **InternetExplorer** object, you follow three main steps:

1. Set a reference to Microsoft Internet Controls (Shdocvw.dll).

2. Declare an object variable to use the **InternetExplorer** object.

   The following example code shows how to declare an object variable called **ie** in the General Declarations section of the client application for the **InternetExplorer** object:

```
Dim WithEvents ie As InternetExplorer
```

3. Create an instance of the Internet Explorer application that you will control from the client.

The following example code shows how to create an instance of the Internet Explorer application:

```
Private Sub cmdStartIE_Click()

    Set ie = New InternetExplorer
    ...
End Sub
```

Using Microsoft Internet Explorer Properties

The following example code shows how to create a stand-alone instance of the Internet Explorer application referenced by a variable called **ie** and then set several of its properties:

```
Private Sub cmdStartIE_Click()

    Set ie = New InternetExplorer

    ' set all the UI to invisible
    ie.ToolBar = False
    ie.StatusBar = False

    ' set starting size and location
    ie.Width = 635
    ie.Height = 500
    ie.Left = 162

    ' make ie visible
    ie.Visible = True

End Sub
```

The following table describes properties of the **InternetExplorer** object that are used in the prjIEController demonstration project for this chapter.

Property	Description
Height	Returns or sets the vertical dimension, in pixels, of the Internet Explorer application's frame window.
Left	Returns or sets the distance between the internal left edge of the Internet Explorer application's frame window and the left edge of the screen.
StatusBar	Returns or sets a value that determines whether the status bar is visible.
ToolBar	Returns or sets a value that determines whether the toolbar is visible.
Visible	Returns or sets a value indicating whether the object is visible or hidden.
Width	Returns or sets the horizontal dimension, in pixels, of the Internet Explorer application's frame window.

For more information about the **InternetExplorer** object's properties, read the article "InternetExplorer Object" in Platform SDK Help.

Using Microsoft Internet Explorer Methods

The following example code calls the **InternetExplorer** object's **Navigate** event from an instance of the Internet Explorer application referenced by a variable called **ie**:

```
Private Sub cmdOpenPage_Click()

    ie.Navigate txtURL.Text

End Sub
```

The following table describes methods of the **InternetExplorer** object that are used in the prjIEController demonstration project for this chapter.

Method	Description
Navigate	Navigates to the resource identified by a Uniform Resource Locator (URL) or to the file identified by a full path.
Quit	Closes the Internet Explorer application.
Refresh	Reloads the page currently displayed in the Internet Explorer application's main frame window.
Stop	Cancels any pending navigation or download operation and stops any dynamic page elements, such as background sounds and animations.

For more information about the **InternetExplorer** object's methods, read the article "InternetExplorer Object" in Platform SDK Help.

Handling Microsoft Internet Explorer Events

Once you have declared a variable for the **InternetExplorer** object using the **WithEvents** keyword, you can use the Visual Basic Code window to add code to handle events for the **InternetExplorer** object.

▶ **To add an event procedure for the InternetExplorer object**

1. Open the Visual Basic Code window in your project.

2. From the **Object** box list, choose the variable name you used for the **InternetExplorer** object, and then in the **Procedures/Events** box list, click the name of the event for which you wish to add an event procedure.

The following illustration shows selecting **BeforeNavigate2** from the list of **ie** events.

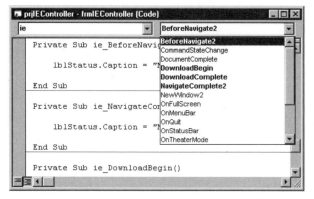

3. Add the code you want to run when the event is fired.

The following example code shows an event handler for the **DownloadComplete** event of the **InternetExplorer** object referenced in the client application using the variable **ie**:

```
Private Sub ie_DownloadComplete()

    lblStatus.Caption = "Download complete..."

End Sub
```

The following table describes events of the **InternetExplorer** object that are used in the prjIEController demonstration project for this chapter.

Event	Description
BeforeNavigate2	Occurs when the Internet Explorer application is about to navigate to a different URL. The container has an opportunity to cancel the pending navigation.
DownloadBegin	Occurs when a navigation operation is beginning. This event is fired shortly after the **BeforeNavigate2** event, unless the navigation is canceled. Note that **DownloadBegin** event will have a corresponding **DownloadComplete** event.

table continued on next page

Event	Description
DownloadComplete	Occurs when a navigation operation finishes, is halted, or fails. Unlike **NavigateComplete2**, which is fired only when a URL is successfully navigated to, this event is always fired after a navigation starts. Note that any **DownloadBegin** event will have a corresponding **DownloadComplete** event.
NavigateComplete2	Occurs after the browser has successfully navigated to a new location. The document might still be downloading (and in the case of HTML, images may still be downloading), but at least part of the document has been received from the server, and the viewer for the document has been created.

For more information about the **InternetExplorer** object's events, read the article "InternetExplorer Object" in Platform SDK Help.

Releasing the Internet Explorer Object

Before exiting the client application, remember to clean up memory used by the instance of the **InternetExplorer** object you created. The following example code sets the object variable **ie** used to reference the instance of the **InternetExplorer** object to **Nothing** before unloading the main form of the client application:

```
Private Sub Form_Unload(Cancel As Integer)

    On Error Resume Next

    ' if Internet Explorer is closed, ignore the error...
    ie.Quit

    ' clean up ie object variable
    Set ie = Nothing

End Sub
```

Lab 7: Using COM Components

In this lab, you will use a COM component that has been provided. It will handle changing the bookstore inventory when a student purchases a book.

To see the demonstration "Lab 7 Solution," see the accompanying CD-ROM.

Estimated time to complete this lab: **45 minutes**

To complete the exercises in this lab, you must have the required software. For detailed information about the labs and setup for the labs, see "Labs" in "About This Course."

> **Note** If you have not completed Labs 4 through 6 using the same computer on which you are currently working, you may need to register *<install folder>*\Labs\Lab07\StateUControls.ocx before you start this lab.
>
> For information about registering components, see "Making the Component Available" on page 247 in this chapter.

Objectives

After completing this lab, you will be able to:

◆ Register and set a reference to a COM component.

◆ Use the Object Browser to get information about a COM component.

◆ Call a COM object's methods, and set its properties.

Prerequisites

Before working on this lab, you should be familiar with the following:

◆ Setting a reference to a COM Component

◆ Using the Object Browser

Exercises

The following exercises provide practice working with the concepts and techniques covered in this chapter:

♦ Exercise 1: Maintaining Book Inventory

In this exercise, you will use a component that maintains bookstore inventory. During the book purchase transaction, this component's **DecrementInventory** method will be called to lower the inventory for the book being purchased.

♦ Exercise 2: Testing Inventory Handling

In this exercise, you will test the inventory handling capabilities of the application.

Exercise 1: Maintaining Book Inventory

In this exercise, you will use a component that maintains bookstore inventory. During the book purchase transaction, this component's **DecrementInventory** method will be called to lower the inventory for the book being purchased.

▶ **Prepare to use the COM component**

1. In the *<install folder>*\Labs\Lab07\HandleInventory Solution folder, locate the file named HandleInventory.dll.

   This file is the COM component that contains the **CBook** class you will use to maintain the bookstore inventory.

2. Open a command window and use Regsvr32 to register the COM component.

3. Open the StateUBookstore project.

4. Set a reference to the **HandleInventory** component.

5. Open the Object Browser and look at the **CBooks** class in the **HandleInventory** component.

▶ **Add inventory handling**

1. Open the code module for the frmStateUMain form. In the General Declarations section of the code module, declare a module-level variable of type **CBooks** called **bkCurrent**.

2. In the code module for the frmStateUMain form, locate the **PurchaseBook** procedure.

   If the student has been authorized to buy the book, the first thing that must occur in this solution is the decrement of the bookstore inventory. The

DecrementInventory method of the **CBooks** class will return an error if the book is currently out of stock—in which case, the purchase should not occur.

In this scenario, the inventory change and the debit of the account do not take place within a transaction. For information on using components that participate in a transaction, consult the *Mastering Enterprise Development Using Visual Basic 6* title.

3. Add code to create the **bkCurrent** object in the **PurchaseBook** procedure.

4. Add code to set the **DataSource** and **InitialCatalog** properties of the **bkCurrent** object to the Data Source and Initial Catalog of the StateUBookstore database.

5. Locate the call to **GetBookID** from Lab 6 that displays the **BookID** in a message box. Change this line of code to set the **BookID** property of the **bkCurrent** object to the value returned from the **GetBookID** function.

6. Declare a boolean variable called bInventoryResult to contain the return value from the **DecrementInventory** method of the **bkCurrent** object.

7. Set the bInventoryResult variable equal to the return value from a call to the **DecrementInventory** method of the **bkCurrent** object.

8. Evaluate the result of the **DecrementInventory** method and display a message box to the user indicating the result. The following table describes the return values.

Return value	Result
True	Book inventory was decremented; continue with book purchase.
False	Book inventory was not decremented; do not continue with book purchase.

9. The **CBooks** class can also raise the error "vbObjectError + 998." If the object raises this error, it means that no books were in stock. Handle the error, set bInventoryResult to **False**, and do not continue with book purchase.

10. Save your work.

Exercise 2: Testing Inventory Handling

In this exercise, you will test the inventory handling capabilities of the application.

▶ **Test buying a book that is in stock**

1. Run the StateUBookstore application.

2. Enter the student ID 8.

3. Attempt to buy the book titled "Emperors in China."

    The book should be purchased successfully.

▶ **Test buying a book that is out of stock**

1. Run the StateUBookstore application.

2. Enter the student ID 39.

3. Attempt to buy the book titled "An Introduction to Algebra."

    You should be notified that this book is out of stock.

Self-Check Questions

To see the answers to the Self-Check Questions, see Appendix A.

1. Which type of binding results in the fastest execution?

   A. Late

   B. Early

   C. Run-time

   D. Mixed

2. Which one of the following must be done before an external COM component can be used by an application?

   A. You must set a reference to the component's type library in your application.

   B. You must save and compile the application.

   C. The component must be registered.

   D. You must view the COM Component in the Object Browser.

3. What must you do to make sure the Visual Basic compiler can validate the syntax of a call made to an object at design time?

A. The component must be registered.

B. Set a reference to the component's type library in your application.

C. You must save and compile the application.

D. You must view the object in the Object Browser.

4. Which of the following ways would you use to create an instance of an object that has been saved to a file?

A. Use the **CreateObject** function.

B. Use the **GetObject** function.

C. Use the **New** keyword with the **Set** statement.

D. Use the **MakeObject** function.

5. Which Visual Basic tool can you use to find out information about the properties, methods, and events of a COM component you plan to use in your application?

A. The Data View window

B. The Visual Data Manager

C. The Object Browser

D. The Visual Component Manager

6. Which of the following declaration statements will allow you to add code to respond to events fired by a COM component?

A. Dim SampleDoc As New Word.Document

B. Static SampleDoc As Word.Document

C. Dim SampleDoc As Object

D. Dim WithEvents SampleDoc As Word.Document

7. What is the name of the type library that contains the InternetExplorer class?

A. Ie4com.dll

B. Shdocvw.dll

C. Brwser401.exe

D. InetBrowse.dll

Student Notes:

Chapter 8:
Building COM Components

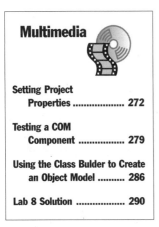

In Chapter 4, "Building ActiveX Controls," you learned how to create ActiveX controls. An ActiveX control is a Component Object Model (COM) component that typically has a user interface and is hosted by a form. You can also create COM components that are stand-alone applications that provide functionality to other applications through Automation.

In Chapter 3, "Using Class Modules," you learned how to create class modules that are compiled within a Microsoft Visual Basic application. In this chapter, you will learn how to build COM components that can be shared by many applications. You will learn how to compile a COM component both as a separate executable program and a dynamic-link library (DLL).

Objectives

After completing this chapter, you will be able to:

◆ Compile a project with class modules into a COM component.

◆ Create an object model in a COM component.

◆ Debug and test a COM component.

Introduction to COM Components

A COM component is a unit of executable code, such as an .exe, .dll, or .ocx file, that follows the COM specification for providing objects. A COM component exposes objects that can be used by other applications.

You can create three types of COM components with Visual Basic: ActiveX controls, Active documents, and COM executable programs and DLLs.

ActiveX Controls

ActiveX controls (formerly known as OLE controls) are standard user-interface elements that allow you to rapidly assemble reusable forms and dialog boxes.

For information about developing ActiveX controls, see Chapter 4, "Building ActiveX Controls" on page 113.

Active Documents

Active documents are COM components that must be hosted and activated within a document container. Active document technology is an extension to OLE documents. It enables generic shell applications, such as Microsoft Internet Explorer, to host different types of documents.

For information about developing Active documents, see "Creating Active Documents" on page 330 in Chapter 10, "Building Internet Applications."

COM Executable Programs and DLLs

COM executable programs and DLLs are libraries of classes. Client applications use COM objects by creating instances of classes provided by the COM .exe or .dll file. Clients call the properties, methods, and events provided by each COM object.

In Visual Basic, the project templates you use to create a COM executable program or COM DLL are referred to as ActiveX EXE and ActiveX DLL, respectively.

For more information about using COM objects in your Visual Basic application, see Chapter 7, "Using COM Components" on page 245.

Visual Basic handles much of the complexity of creating COM .exe and .dll files, such as creating a type library and registering the component, automatically. For more information about creating a COM DLL, read the article "Creating an ActiveX DLL" in Visual Basic Help. For more information about creating a COM executable program, read the article "Creating an ActiveX EXE Component" in Visual Basic Help.

Distributing Components

When you create COM components, you can run different parts of an application on multiple computers at the same time. A standard application resides on one computer, while an application that uses functionality in many code components can run on many computers at the same time.

However, there are many issues, such as memory management and thread pooling, that make it difficult to create a reliable, effective remote component.

Using MTS

Microsoft Transaction Server (MTS), part of Windows NT and Internet Information Server (IIS), provides much of the distributed infrastructure for you so that creating and using remote COM components is much more manageable. For more information about using MTS, read the article "Visual Basic and Microsoft Transaction Server" in Visual Basic Help.

Consider the following guidelines when creating a component to be used with MTS:

◆ Set the **MTSTransactionMode** property of the class module to support transactions.

◆ Make it a COM DLL.

◆ Make it stateless.

◆ Pass arguments by value (**ByVal**) whenever possible. The **ByVal** keyword minimizes trips across networks. For more information about passing arguments by value, see "Writing Procedures" on page 12 in Chapter 1, "Understanding Visual Basic Development."

◆ Use methods that accept all of the property values as arguments. Avoid exposing object properties. Each time a client accesses an object property, it makes at least one round-trip call across the network.

◆ Avoid passing or returning objects. Passing object references across process and network boundaries wastes time.

◆ Enable Microsoft Transaction Server to run simultaneous client requests through objects by making them apartment threaded. In Visual Basic, you make objects apartment threaded by selecting the **Apartment Threaded** threading model in the **Project Properties** dialog box. For more information about the apartment threading model, read the article "Apartment-Model Threading in Visual Basic" in Visual Basic Help.

A comprehensive discussion of Microsoft Transaction Server is beyond the scope of this course. Another course in the Mastering Series curriculum, *Mastering Enterprise Development Using Visual Basic 6,* covers using MTS as the application infrastructure for your COM DLLs in more detail.

For more information about Microsoft Mastering Series courses, go to the Microsoft Mastering Series Web site at msdn.microsoft.com/mastering/.

Creating COM Components

A COM component is a library of code that is compiled into either an executable program or a dynamic-link library (DLL). In Visual Basic, COM components are composed of one or more class modules in a Visual Basic project.

In this section, you will learn about the different choices you make when you create a COM component, and how these decisions affect the performance and security of the client applications that use your component.

In-Process vs. Out-of-Process Components

Components can be designed and built to provide services from different locations, depending on the intended use of the component.

For example, a user interface component would probably be best located as close to an individual client as possible, while a component that supplies statistical calculations of remote data would probably be best located on a separate computer.

In-Process vs. Out-of-Process Components

Components can be run in any one of three places: in the same address space as the client (in-process), on the same computer (out-of-process), or on a remote computer. The following table defines the differences between these types of locations for components.

Type of Component	Location
In-process	An in-process component is implemented as a dynamic-link library (DLL). It runs in the same process space as its client application. This enables the most efficient commnication between client and component, because you need only call the function to obtain the required functionality. Each client application that uses the component starts a new instance of the component.
Out-of-process	An out-of-process component is implemented as an executable file, and runs in its own process space. Communication between the client and component is slower because parameters and return values must be marshaled across process boundaries from the client to the component, and back again. However, a single instance of an out-of-process component can service many clients, share global data, and insulate other client applications from problems that one client might encounter.
Remote	Remote components are also out-of-process components, but they are located on a separate computer. While communication time between a client and a remote component is much slower than with a local component, remote components allow processing to be done on a separate, and possibly more powerful computer. The component can also be located closer to the work it is doing. For example, a component can be located closer to a remote database with which it interacts.

When you work with out-of-process and remote components, you should ensure that the client minimizes the number of calls to objects created from the component. For example, a well-designed component should have a way to pass data in bulk with as few calls as possible.

Component Project Templates

In Visual Basic, you can build code components to run in-process (COM DLL) or out-of-process (COM executable program).

When you create a new project in Visual Basic, you can choose among a number of project templates on which to base the new project. In the **New Project** dialog box, choose **ActiveX EXE** to create an out-of-process component, or **ActiveX DLL** to create an in-process component. Selecting either type sets a number of default values that are important to creating components.

Tip You can change the project type later by changing the project properties.

Setting Project Properties

When you create a new ActiveX DLL or ActiveX EXE project, you can set a number of properties for your project. These properties affect how your code component will run.

To see the demonstration "Setting Project Properties," see the accompanying CD-ROM.

You set properties for the project in the **Project Properties** dialog box, which you access from the **Project** menu. All of the options described in this topic are found on the **General** tab of the **Project Properties** dialog box, as shown in the following illustration.

Project Type

The **Project Type** field provides four options: Standard EXE, ActiveX EXE, ActiveX DLL, and ActiveX Control. When you create a new ActiveX DLL or ActiveX EXE project, Visual Basic automatically sets the **Project Type** property.

The project type determines how some of the other project options can be used. For example, options on the **Component** tab are not available when the project type is set to Standard EXE.

Startup Object

For most components, you set the **Startup Object** field to (**None**). If you want code to run when the component is loaded, rather than when an instance of a class is created, you can set the **Startup Object** property to **Sub Main**. You must then add a standard module to your project, and add a **Sub** procedure named **Main** to that module.

Project Name

The **Project Name** field indicates the name that a client application uses to refer to the component.

The following code sample shows a client application creating an instance of a class named **CEmployee** in a COM component named StateUComponent. To copy this code for use in your own projects, see "Creating an Instance of a Class" on the accompanying CD-ROM.

```
Public Sub CreateEmployee()

    'Use the project name to create an instance of the class
    Dim empCurrent As StateUComponent.CEmployee
    Set empCurrent = New StateUComponent.CEmployee

End Sub
```

Project Description

The **Project Description** field enables you to enter a brief description of the COM component and the objects that it provides. The contents of this field appear in the **References** dialog box for any client application that is selected in the **Available References** list. This string also appears in the Description pane at the bottom of the Object Browser.

Unattended Execution

Selecting the **Unattended Execution** check box indicates that the component is expected to run without user interaction. Unattended components do not have a user interface. Any run-time functions, such as messages that normally result in user interaction, must be written to an event log. This setting is most useful for components running on remote computers, particularly servers, that often run unattended by users.

Threading Model

The **Threading Model** list box allows you to specify whether your component is single threaded or apartment threaded. When creating components for MTS, you should make them apartment threaded because MTS works best with this model.

Setting the Instancing Property

When you design an object in a component, you must set its **Instancing** property to specify whether or not the object will be available for use by client applications, and whether or not multiple instances of the object can be created. You need to set the **Instancing** property for each class module in the component.

Although a client does not have any control over the instancing of the component, the **Instancing** property can significantly influence the performance of the client. For example, if your client must share an instance of a component, its performance may be slower.

Instancing Property

The **Instancing** property determines if applications outside a project can create new instances of a class, and if so, how those instances are created.

The available instancing options are different in COM executable and COM DLL components, as shown in the following illustration.

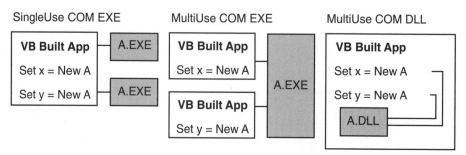

The following table defines each of the **Instancing** property settings.

Setting	Description
Private	Other applications are not allowed access to type library information about the class, and cannot create instances of it. **Private** objects are used only within a component.
PublicNotCreatable	Other applications can use objects of this class only if a component creates the objects first. Other applications cannot use the **CreateObject** function or the **New** operator to create objects of this class. You set the **Instancing** property to this value when you want to create dependent objects.
SingleUse	Allows other applications to create objects from the class. Every object of this class that is created by a client will start a new instance of the component.
GlobalSingleUse	Similar to the SingleUse setting, except that properties and methods of the class can be invoked as though they were global functions.
MultiUse	Allows other applications to create objects from the class. One instance of a component can provide any number of objects created in this way, regardless of how many applications request them.
GlobalMultiUse	Similar to the MultiUse setting, except that properties and methods of the class can be invoked as though they were global functions. Explicitly creating an instance of the class first is not necessary because one will automatically be created.

Declaring Friend Properties and Methods

You can create components that contain more than one class module. If you want instances of these classes to communicate with each other, but you do not want to make them available to other client applications that use these components, you can use the **Friend** keyword. This declares the properties and methods of the **Friend** class as available only to the other classes within the component.

The **Public** properties and methods in a class can be called by other objects, and they can also be called by client applications. The **Private** properties and methods cannot be called from outside a component, and they are also not visible to other objects within the component.

Properties and methods declared with the **Friend** keyword are visible to other classes in the application, but are not visible outside your application because **Friend** procedures are not added to the type library or to the public interface.

Tip Only properties created with property procedures can be made **Friend** properties.

In the following example code, the **FormatSalaryInfo** method in **CEmployee** is a friend method to other classes in the same application:

```
' Code in CEmployee can be called from other class modules but not
' from outside the project.
Friend Sub FormatSalaryInfo()
  ' code to process salary info
End Sub
```

For more information about using Friend properties and methods, read the article "Private Communications Between Your Objects" in Visual Basic Help.

Compiling a Component

Once you have built the class modules for a COM component, you are ready to compile it. Your component is compiled as either an .exe or .dll file, depending on the settings in the **Project Properties** dialog box.

Type-Library ID

The type library for your component is used by the Object Browser when clients using your COM component early-bind their object variables. When you compile a COM component, Visual Basic creates a type library with a unique type-library ID. This ID is entered into the registry when you register your code component and is used to link the type library to the actual .exe or .dll file for your COM component.

The **Project Compatibility** field in the **Project Properties** dialog box is selected by default. In this setting, Visual Basic reuses the same type-library ID each time you compile a code component.

If you make a change that is incompatible with the version of your server specified in the **Project Compatibility** field (for example, if you delete a property), Visual Basic displays a warning and generates a new type-library ID to indicate that your component has changed.

Version Compatibility

COM standards require that once you create a version of a COM component that is used by others, you don't change the characteristics of that component. To facilitate making improvements to COM components, Visual Basic provides version compatibility that enables you to enhance components while maintaining compatibility with programs compiled with earlier versions of a component.

In Visual Basic, you select version compatibility options by clicking **Project Properties** on the **Project** menu, and then clicking the **Component** tab of the **Project Options** dialog box.

Under **Version Compatibility**, you can select one of three options, as shown in the following table.

Option	Result
No Compatibility	Each time you compile a component, new type library information is generated. There is no relationship between versions of a component. Applications that currently use one version cannot use subsequent versions. Use this compatibility option when you start a new project, or when you do not want to enforce compatibility with an earlier version of the component.
Project Compatibility	Each time you compile a component, new type library information is generated, but the type-library ID remains the same so that your test projects can maintain their references to the component project. Use this compatibility option when you start a new project, or if you are working on components without changing their methods or properties.
Binary Compatibility	When you compile a component using Binary Compatibility, Visual Basic preserves the type library information from the previous version. Components that currently use an earlier version will continue to work. Use this compatibility option when you want to ensure that an upgrade to a component will work with clients currently using an earlier version of the component. Visual Basic warns you when changes to your component would make the new version incompatible with previously compiled versions.

For more information about how to use these compatibility options, read the articles "When Should I Use Version Compatibility" and "Levels of Binary Version Compatibility" in Visual Basic Help.

Registering a Component

Before you can use a COM component, it must be registered. The process to register a component differs for out-of-process and in-process components. When you register a COM component it adds information to the Windows registry to identify itself as an available COM component to clients on that system.

There are several ways to register an out-of-process component (.exe file):

♦ Compile the component.

Visual Basic registers the component as it compiles the component.

♦ Run the component.

It automatically registers itself each time it runs.

♦ Run the component with the /Regserver command-line argument.

The component ends immediately after registering itself.

♦ Create a Setup program.

When you run the Setup program, the component is registered.

There are several ways to register an in-process component (.dll file):

♦ Compile the component

Visual Basic registers the component as it compiles the component.

♦ Run Regsvr32.exe.

Regsvr32 is a utility that will register a .dll. Pass the .dll file name as an argument to the Regsvr32 utility as shown in this example code:

```
Regsvr32.exe C:\StateUBookstore\payroll.dll
```

Regsvr32.exe is located on the Visual Basic CD-ROM in the \Tools folder.

♦ Create a Setup program.

When you run the Setup program, the component is registered.

Unregistering the Component

When a component is no longer needed, it can be removed from the registry.

To remove an .exe entry from the registry, run the component with the /UnRegserver command line argument, as shown in the following example code:

```
StateUEmployee.exe /UnRegserver
```

To remove a .dll entry from the registry, run Regsvr32.exe, including the /u option and the name of the .dll file, as shown in the following example code:

```
Regsvr32.exe /u C:\StateUBookstore\payroll.dll
```

You can also uninstall a component using its Setup program.

Testing a Component

Microsoft Visual Basic offers different scenarios for testing and debugging in-process and out-of-process components. For in-process components, you test and debug a component within a single instance of Visual Basic. For out-of-process components, you run two copies of the development environment.

For more information about testing and debugging a COM component, read the article "Testing and Debugging ActiveX Components" in Visual Basic Help.

Testing

To test a COM component, you create a test project that will use the component. Depending on whether your component is a DLL or an executable program, you create the test project within the current instance of Visual Basic, or in a separate instance.

Testing a COM DLL

To test a COM DLL, you can add a Standard EXE project to the project group, and test the in-process component within a single instance of Visual Basic. You can then step directly from the test project's code into the in-process component's code.

To see the demonstration "Testing a COM Component," see the accompanying CD-ROM.

Testing a COM Executable Program

To test a COM executable program, you must run the component within one instance of Visual Basic, and run the test application in a second instance of Visual Basic. In this case, you cannot step directly from one component into the other, but you can still use all of the other Visual Basic debugging tools.

Debugging

Once you have set up a test project and established a reference to the component, you can debug the component just as you would any Visual Basic application. You can step between the client application and component, and use the standard debugging tools to set break points, step through code, use watch expressions, and so on.

Handling Missing References

In the course of debugging components, you may see an error message indicating that the component's type-library ID has changed, and the test project cannot locate the component. To continue, you clear the missing reference.

▶ **To clear a missing reference**

1. On the **Project** menu, click **References**.

   In the **References** dialog box, the word **MISSING** will appear next to the name of the component.

2. Clear the check mark next to the name of the missing component, and then click **OK**.

Component Design Considerations

After you decide you need to create a COM component, you'll want to carefully consider the design of that component before building it. By carefully designing your application, you can build a component that is not only immediately useful, but can also be reused in other solutions. Consider the following recommendations when designing a COM component:

◆ Avoid using global data.

   In a Visual Basic application, data declared as **Public** in a standard module is global data, and is available to the entire application. Class module data, on the other hand, exists separately for each instance of the class created by a client application.

Avoid using global data in standard modules in your component.

For more information, read the article "Standard Modules vs. Class Modules" in Visual Basic Help.

◆ Use Public, Private, and Friend properties and methods.

As you saw in Chapter 3, "Using Class Modules," you can create Public, Private, and Friend properties and methods of an object. This becomes very useful in creating an object model:

- Public properties and methods can be used by all objects within the component and all clients of the component.

- Private properties and methods can only be used in the object where they are declared.

- Friend properties and methods can be used by all objects within the component, but not by any clients of the component.

◆ Name properties, methods, and events intuitively.

Choosing names for properties, methods, and events that clearly reflect their purpose will make your code easier to use and maintain.

◆ Incorporate robust error handling.

When you formulate a strategy for error handling, keep in mind that your component will likely be reused in other applications and environments.

◆ Include thorough documentation.

Since other developers may be using and maintaining your component, be sure to document its features thoroughly, both in your code and in a separate help file or manual.

For more information about designing a COM component, read the article "General Principles of Component Design" in Visual Basic Help.

COM Executable Component Design Considerations

If you are creating a COM executable component, there are some things to consider to make it work more efficiently with client applications:

◆ When a client application sets individual properties of objects in the component, the application makes separate calls to the component for each property. If the client application and the component are located on separate computers, this requires multiple network calls.

◆ It's a good idea to create a method in a class to set multiple properties of the object. A client application makes one call to the method, passing in arguments for each property they want to set, which causes only one network call.

Using Visual Component Manager

Visual Component Manager allows you to easily publish, find, and catalog components, including ActiveX controls, COM Components, HTML and ASP pages, and Visual Basic source code. With Visual Component Manager you publish components to a repository database, where they can easily be located, inspected, retrieved, and reused. The Enterprise version of Visual Component Manager makes it easy for teams of developers to share components, enabling effective component and code reuse both within a development team, and across an entire organization.

▶ **To add Visual Component Manager to the Visual Basic toolbar**

1. On the **Add-ins** menu, click **Add-in Manager**.

2. In the list of available add-ins, select **Visual Component Manager**.

3. Under **Load Behavior**, select the **Load on Startup** check box, and then click **OK**.

    The Visual Component Manager toolbar button appears on the Standard Visual Basic toolbar, as shown in the following illustration.

Publishing a Component

Publishing a component means storing it in a Visual Component Manager repository database along with attributes and search keywords that make it easy for others to find and reuse it.

When you publish a component, you add it to a Microsoft Repository database. This can be a local database on your own workstation, or it can be a shared database on a network server. A shared database gives everyone who has access to that server the ability to find and reuse your component.

Note Microsoft Repository creates a default repository database for you when it is installed. This database is managed by Microsoft Jet. Its location is determined by the default value of the *Current Location* registry key.

▶ **To publish a component**

◆ On the **Tools** menu, point to **Publish,** and then click **Source Files** or **Build Outputs**. When you click **Source Files,** you publish the project's source code files; when you click **Build Outputs,** you compile and publish the files that are generated at compile time.

The Visual Component Manager Publish Wizard appears, and walks you through a series of steps that allow you to publish a project for reuse.

Creating an Object Model

When you create a COM component, you may want to provide many different objects for the client application to use. You create an object model to define the relationship between the objects in your component, and to define how the client application will create these objects.

In this section, you will learn what an object model is, and how to create one in a Visual Basic component.

Understanding Object Models

When you design a COM component, you can structure the objects that it offers into an object model.

An object model defines the relationship among objects available from a component. An object model organizes the objects into a hierarchy that represents which objects contain other objects. This structure makes the component easier to use.

For example, Microsoft Excel exposes many objects such as charts, worksheets, and cells. Excel also organizes these objects into an object model that mimics the hierarchical relationship between these objects in the application. For example, a workbook contains many worksheets, and a worksheet contains many cells. The following illustration shows a simplified view of Excel's object model.

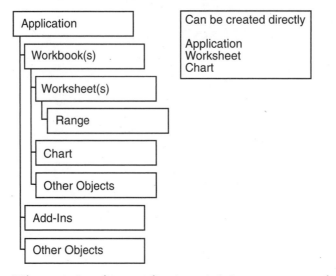

When creating client applications, it is important to understand the relationships between objects in the object model and how you create them. Some objects may be publicly createable (with **New** and **CreateObject**), and some objects are created by invoking a method of another object. For example, the **Application** object in Excel is publicly createable, while its contained **Range** object is not.

For more information about creating objects that are publicly createable, see "Setting the Instancing Property" on page 274 in this chapter.

Building an Object Model for Your COM Component

An object model defines the relationship between objects in a component. Some objects are dependent on other objects. These dependent objects exist only within the context of another object. For example, in Excel, a **Button** object cannot exist without a parent **Worksheet** object. So a client application cannot use the **CreateObject** function or the **Set** *object* = **New** class statement to create a **Button** object. Instead, the **Worksheet** object provides an **Add** method that creates a new **Button** object contained by the worksheet.

You can create a COM component that provides an object model. By defining the relationships between the objects that you use in your program, an object model organizes the objects in a way that makes programming easier.

To create an object model for a COM component, you use the following steps:

1. Create a top-level object by setting the **Instancing** property of the class to **SingleUse** or **MultiUse**.

2. Create dependent objects by setting the class **Instancing** property to **PublicNotCreatable**.

You can also provide a method for the top-level object that creates a dependent object and returns a reference to the newly created object. For example, in **CEmployee** class you could write an **AddDirectReport** function that creates a new instance of a dependent class and returns an object variable that points to the newly created dependent object. In the following sample code, the **AddDirectReport** method creates an instance of the **CDirectReport** class. To copy this code for use in your own projects, see "Building an Object Model" on the accompanying CD-ROM.

```
Public Function AddDirectReport(sFirstName As String, sLastName As
String) As CDirectReport

  ' declare the dependent class object
  Dim drpCurrent As CDirectReport

  ' create the direct report object
  Set drpCurrent = New CDirectReport

  ' set the direct report's properties
  drpCurrent.FirstName = sFirstName
  drpCurrent.LastName = sLastName

  ' return the new direct report object
  AddDirectReport = drpCurrent

End Function
```

For more information about creating object models, read the article "Organizing Objects: The Object Model" in Visual Basic Help.

Storing Objects in a Collection

When you create an object model, you may want to give the client application access to an object type by creating a collection of objects of that type. Creating a collection of objects enables related objects to be stored together. In Visual Basic, the **Collection** object is a predefined object. It can be created in the same way as other objects, as shown in the following example code:

```
Dim Skills As New Collection
```

The **Collection** data type has predefined **Add** and **Remove** methods and a **Count** property.

You can use the Class Builder in Visual Basic to create an object model for a COM component that uses collections. To see the demonstration "Using the Class Builder to Create an Object Model," see the accompanying CD-ROM.

The following example code creates a new **CSkill** object and adds the object to the **Skills** collection:

```
Public Sub AddSkill(sSkillName As String, sDescription As String)

    ' declare a CSkill object
    Dim curSkill As CSkill

    ' create a new CSkill object
    Set curSkill = New CSkill

    ' set properties of the skill
    curSkill.SkillName = sSkillName
    curSkill.Description = sDescription

    ' add this skill object to the collection
    Skills.Add Item:=curSkill, Key:=curSkill.SkillName

End Sub
```

Storing related objects in a collection enables you to work with those objects as a group. For example, you could use the **Skills** collection created in the previous code example to display the description for each skill as follows:

```
Private Sub ShowDescriptions()

 Dim curSkill as CSkill

 ' show description for each skill
 For Each curSkill In empCurrent.Skills

    MsgBox curSkill.Description

 Next curSkill

End Sub
```

Adding Error Handling

This section describes the two ways of providing error information to a client application: raising an error that the application must handle, and returning an error code to the application. It also explains how to raise errors to a client application to provide the client with error information.

For more general information on error handling, see "Debugging and Error Handling" on page 22 in Chapter 1, "Visual Basic Essentials."

Error Handling Styles

Handling errors requires close communication between client applications and components. If possible, a component and its clients should handle errors, rather than displaying a message to the user.

When a client application calls a method of an object provided by a component, the method can provide error information in the following ways:

◆ Raise an error that the client application must handle. In this case, the client uses conventional error-handling statements to handle errors that are raised.

◆ Return an error code that the client application must test for and handle.

Using a Raised Error

In a code component, a method calls the **Raise** method of the **Err** object to raise an error to the client application. The client implements an error handler to trap the error.

For more information on raising run-time errors, see "Raising Run-Time Errors" in this chapter.

Using a Return Value

In a code component, a method can return a value to the client application. The client examines the return value to determine if an error occurred, and if so, which one.

With this type of error handling, developers of client applications must always test the return value after calling a method of an object in a component.

For information about error handling in components and clients, read the article "Generating and Handling Errors" in Visual Basic Help.

Raising Run-Time Errors

When you create a component, you can provide error messages to the client application. To pass an error back to a client application, you use the **Raise** method in a component. For the error to be raised in the client, you must call **Raise** from your method's error-handling routine or with error handling disabled.

The **Raise** method has the following syntax:

Err.Raise (Number, Source, Description, HelpFile, HelpContext)

To generate an error number, add the constant **vbObjectError** to the error number. The resulting number is returned to the client application. This ensures that your error numbers do not conflict with the built-in Visual Basic error numbers.

The following code sample shows error handling from a component. To copy this code for use in your own projects, see "Component Error Handling Code Sample" on the accompanying CD-ROM.

```
Private mvarSalary As Double

Public Property Let Salary(ByVal dNewSalary As Double)

    If dNewSalary < 0 Then
        Err.Raise 12345 + vbObjectError, "CEmployee", "Salary must
be positive"
    Else
        mvarSalary = dNewSalary
    End If

End Property

Public Property Get Salary() As Double

    Salary = mvarSalary

End Property
```

Client Code

```
Private Sub SetSalary_Click()

    ' declare an employee object
    Dim empCurrent As CompanyComponent.CEmployee

    On Error GoTo HandleError

    ' create the employee and set the salary property
    Set empCurrent = New CompanyComponent.CEmployee

    ' an error could occur here
    empCurrent.Salary = CDbl(txtSalary.Text)

Exit Sub
HandleError:

    If Err.Number = 12345 + vbObjectError Then
        MsgBox "Salary must be positive.", ,Err.Source
    End If

End Sub
```

Breaking on Errors

You can change the way Visual Basic enters Break mode when an error occurs in your code component. To do this, you set **Error Trapping** options on the **General** tab of the **Options** dialog box.

Visual Basic provides three options for setting breakpoints, as shown in the following table.

Option	Description
Break on All Errors	Any error causes the project to enter break mode, whether or not an error handler is active, and whether or not the code is in a class module.
Break in Class Module	Any unhandled error that has been produced in a class module will cause the project to enter Break mode at the line of code in the class module that produced the error. When you debug a COM component project by running a client application from another project, set this option in the COM component project to break on errors in its class modules, instead of returning the error to the client application.
Break on Unhandled Errors	If an error handler is active, the error is trapped without entering Break mode. If there is not any active error handler, the error causes the project to enter Break mode. An unhandled error in a class module will cause the project to enter Break mode on the line of code that invoked the offending procedure of the class.

Lab 8: Building COM Components

In this lab, you will turn the Account component you created in Lab 5 into an ActiveX EXE component.

To see the demonstration "Lab 8 Solution," see the accompanying CD-ROM.

Estimated time to complete this lab: **30 minutes**

To complete the exercises in this lab, you must have the required software. For detailed information about the labs and setup for the labs, see "Labs" in "About This Course."

> **Note** If you have not completed Labs 4 through 7 using the same computer on which you are currently working, you may need to register *<install folder>*\Labs\Lab08\StateUControls.ocx and *<install folder>*\Labs\Lab08\HandleInventory.dll before you start this lab.
>
> For information about registering components, see "Making the Component Available" on page 247 in Chapter 7, "Using COM Components."

Objectives

After completing this lab, you will be able to:

◆ Build a COM component that can be used from other applications.

◆ Register a COM component.

Prerequisites

Before working on this lab, you should be familiar with the following:

◆ Using a COM component in a Visual Basic application, as discussed in Chapter 7, "Using COM Components."

◆ Creating properties, methods, and events for class modules, as shown in "Adding Properties, Methods, and Events" on page 84 in Chapter 3, "Using Class Modules."

Exercises

The following exercises provide practice working with the concepts and techniques covered in this chapter:

◆ Exercise 1: Creating the StateUFinance COM Component

In this exercise, you will take the **Account** class from Lab 5 and compile it as an ActiveX DLL.

◆ Exercise 2: Using the StateUFinance COM Component

In this exercise, you will test the StateUBookstore application to ensure that it runs with the new COM component.

Exercise 1: Creating the StateUFinance COM Component

In this exercise, you will take the **CAccount** class from Lab 5 and compile it as an ActiveX DLL.

▶ **Remove the CAccount class module**

1. Open the StateUBookstore project and remove the **CAccount** class module.

2. Close the StateUBookstore project and save your changes.

▶ **Create a COM component from a class module**

1. Start a new ActiveX DLL project and name it StateUFinance.

2. Remove the default class module, **Class1,** from the project.

3. Add the **CAccount** class module to the project.

   a. On the **Project** menu, click **Add Class Module.**

   b. In the **Add Class Module** dialog box, on the **Existing** tab, select the **Account** class module and click **Open.**

4. Set the **Instancing** property of the **Account** class to **MultiUse.**

5. Add a reference to Microsoft ActiveX Data Object 2.0.

6. Make the StateUFinance.dll.

7. Set the **Compatibility** property for the project to **Binary Compatibility,** and select the StateUFinance.dll component you just created.

   For more information on setting component properties, see "Compiling a Component" on page 276 in this chapter.

8. Save and close the project.

Exercise 2: Using the StateUFinance COM Component

In this exercise, you will test the StateUBookstore application to ensure that it runs with the new COM component.

▶ **Test the client application**

1. Open the StateUBookstore project.

2. Add a reference to the **StateUFinance** COM component you just created.

Note You don't need to change the code to create an object of the type **StateUFinance.CAccount** since there is no other component with a **CAccount** class.

3. Run the State University Bookstore application to make sure it runs as it did before.

4. Save your changes to the StateUBookstore project.

Self-Check Questions

To see the answers to the Self-Check Questions, see Appendix A.

1. Which project template would you select to build an in-process COM component?

    A. ActiveX Control

    B. ActiveX DLL

    C. ActiveX EXE

    D. Standard EXE

2. Which action results in the registration of a COM component?

    A. The COM component is run for the first time.

    B. The COM component is installed on a computer using Setup.

    C. The COM component is run with the /REGSERVER command-line argument.

    D. All of the above.

3. Which of the following Instancing property settings should you choose if you want one instance of your component to provide objects to multiple-client applications?

A. SingleUse

B. MultiUse

C. Private

D. PartialUse

4. When raising errors from a COM component, what constant should you add to the error code you raise?

A. vbCustomError

B. None

C. vbObjectError

D. vbErrorFromObject

5. Which of the following makes a Friend method unique?

A. It will not be available to other classes within the same component or to other client applications.

B. It will be available only to the other classes within the component and not to client applications.

C. It will be available to the other classes within the component and to client applications.

D. It will not be available to other classes within the component, but it will be available to other client applications.

Chapter 9:
Optimizing and Deploying Applications

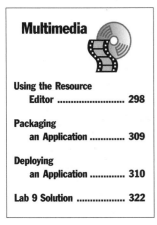

Multimedia

Before distributing your application to users, you may want to improve the speed of your application, make it easier to internationalize, or include online documentation to describe the functionality your application provides. If you are developing an ActiveX control, you may want to license your control to regulate its use by other developers. If you are distributing a control over the Internet, you need to understand the security issues involved and how to address them.

In this chapter, you will learn how to optimize the usability and performance of an application, and how to use the tools provided with Visual Basic to develop applications more efficiently. You will also learn about security issues involved in using ActiveX controls on HTML pages, and how to ensure the security of the controls you distribute.

When you deploy your application, you distribute not only your application's executable file, but also any supporting files that your application requires, such as DLLs and custom controls. These files must be copied to the appropriate locations and registered on the user's computer. The easiest way to do this is to create a Setup program for your users. In this chapter, you will learn how to create a Setup program using the Microsoft Visual Basic Package and Deployment Wizard.

Objectives

After completing this chapter, you will be able to:

◆ Describe a variety of techniques for optimizing the performance of an application.

◆ Use the **GetSetting** and **SaveSetting** statements to save application-specific information to the registry.

◆ Use resource files.

◆ Create a Setup program using the Package and Deployment Wizard.

◆ Package an ActiveX control for use on a Web site.

Optimizing an Application

When you optimize an application, you typically spend time improving its run-time speed and memory usage. You may also want to fine-tune your application's usability. For example, you can add code so that your users can save their current preferences and working environment settings. In subsequent sessions, users will not have to reconfigure their application at startup.

In this section, you will learn about a number of coding techniques that you can use to enhance the performance of your application. You will also learn how to save application settings, how to use resource files to make internationalization of your application more efficient, and how to create a help file for your application.

Saving Application Settings

You can make your applications easier to use by saving information about user activity or preferences each time a user runs your application. You can then use this information in subsequent sessions. For example, you can save the name of the last database the user opened, and then use that name as the default database the next time your user opens a database.

In Windows 3.1 and earlier, program settings were commonly stored in .ini files. In Windows NT and Windows 95, program settings are stored in the registry.

To save and retrieve application settings, you can use the Visual Basic statements **SaveSetting** and **GetSetting**.

Using SaveSetting

To write an entry to the registry, use the **SaveSetting** function with the following syntax:

SaveSetting (appname, section, key, setting)

The following example code saves customer ID information to the appropriate key in the Windows 95 registry:

```
Dim iCustID As Integer
Private Sub Form_Unload()
  iCustID = CInt(txtCustID.Text)
  SaveSetting _
      "OrderApp", "CustSection", "CustID", iCustID
End Sub
```

Using GetSetting

To read a setting from the registry, use the **GetSetting** function with the following syntax:

GetSetting (appname, section, key, [default])

The following example code obtains customer ID information from the appropriate key in the Windows 95 registry. If there is no value for **CustID** in the registry, the value 0 is returned.

```
Dim iCustID As Integer
Private Sub Form_Load()
  iCustID = GetSetting _
      ("OrderApp", "CustSection", "CustID", "0")
End Sub
```

Both **GetSetting** and **SaveSetting** use the following default location on Windows 95:

```
HKEY_CURRENT_USER\Software\VB and VBA Program
Settings\<appname>\<section>
```

Both **GetSetting** and **SaveSetting** use the following default location on Windows NT:

```
HKEY_USERS\<user section>\Software\VB and VBA Program
Settings\<appname>\<section>
```

To add your own hierarchy of data in the registry, add directory structure to the **Section** argument of **GetSetting** and **SaveSetting**. You can also remove a setting in the registry by using **DeleteSetting**, or retrieve a whole section of the registry by using **GetAllSettings**. For more information about managing application settings in the registry, read the article "Managing Application Settings" in Visual Basic Help.

Using Resource Files

If you are planning to distribute your application to an international market, you can reduce the amount of time it takes to translate and internationalize your application. Rather than using literal data in your code, you can store data, such as strings and bitmaps, in a resource file. Your application then uses functions to load these resources at run time. You can easily change the data in a resource file, eliminating the need to change the actual application code.

For more information about using resource files, read the article "Working with Resource Files" in Visual Basic Help.

To see the demonstration "Using the Resource Editor," see the accompanying CD-ROM.

Creating Resource Files

You can create and modify resource files using the Resource Editor add-in that comes with Visual Basic.

▶ **To add the Resource Editor to the Tools menu**

1. On the **Add-Ins** menu, click **Add-In Manager**.

2. In the list of available add-ins, select **VB 6 Resource Editor**.

3. Under **Load Behavior**, select the **Loaded/Unloaded** check box, and then click **OK**.

Note If you also select the **Load on Startup** check box, the Resource Editor will automatically be available on the **Tools** menu every time you start a new project or open an existing project.

4. On the **Tools** menu, click **Resource Editor** to start the Resource Editor.

There are five types of resources supported by Visual Basic resource files; string tables, cursors, icons, bitmaps, and custom resources. The following illustration shows a resource file that contains all five types of resources.

In the resource editor, you add the resources your application will use. Each specific resource or string in a string table is assigned a unique resource identifier. To use the data in the resources or strings, refer to their identifiers in your application code.

▶ To add a resource to a resource file

♦ In the Resource Editor, click the toolbar button that corresponds to the type of resource you want to add.

The following table shows the toolbar button that corresponds to each type of resource.

To perform this action	Use this toolbar button
Edit String Table	
Add Cursor	
Add Icon	
Add Bitmap	
Add Custom Resource	

Use the string table editor to add string resources for the different languages that your application supports. Each string table represents one language, and each string identifier represents a phrase that appears in your application.

Id	English (United States)	French (Standard)
101	First Name	Prénoms
102	Last Name	Nom

▶ **To add a string table in the string table editor**

1. In the string table editor, click the **Add String Table** toolbar button as shown in the following illustration.

A new column appears in the string table editor.

2. Double-click the column header and choose a language from the dropdown list.

▶ **To add strings to a string table**

◆ In an existing row of the string table, press **Enter**.

A new row is inserted immediately below the row that was active.

– or –

Click the **Insert New Row** toolbar button as shown in the following illustration.

Using Resource Functions

Visual Basic provides several functions that enable you to load information from a resource file at run time, as shown in the following table.

Function	Purpose
LoadResString	Loads a string.
LoadResPicture	Loads a picture. The second argument to **LoadResPicture** determines the type of data to load (0=bitmap, 1=icon, 2=cursor).
LoadResData	Loads general data, such as a .wav file.

The following example code illustrates how to use the **LoadResString** function to fill the caption of a label:

```
Private Sub Form_Load()

  lblFirstName.Caption = LoadResString(101)
  lblLastName.Caption = LoadResString(102)

End Sub
```

Note The Visual Basic resource functions look at the current Windows Regional Setting to determine which string table to use. Be sure to test your application with each regional setting that your application supports.

Tuning Application Performance

Optimizing your application means making sure it is as efficient as possible. You optimize your application throughout the development process, starting with the design phase. A poorly designed application may run slowly, no matter what you do to try to improve performance.

Optimization is a tradeoff. If you improve one area of performance, you can cause poorer performance in another area. For example, if you keep forms loaded but hidden, they will be displayed quickly, but they will consume memory while they are loaded.

If your user's computer does not have enough memory, your application may run more slowly. Determine the factors that are most important to your user, and develop your application accordingly.

Optimizing Speed

To improve the speed of your application, consider the following techniques.

Optimizing Actual Speed

The following suggestions describe how to optimize the speed of your application:

◆ Some data types are faster at calculation speed than others. Use the simplest data type possible.

◆ Accessing a variable is faster than accessing a property. If you are accessing a property in a loop, set the property to a variable first, and then use the variable in the loop.

Optimizing Apparent Speed

The following techniques will make your application appear faster to the user:

◆ Use progress indicators to inform the user of the status of a task.

◆ Use a mouse cursor, such as the hourglass cursor, to indicate that processing is occurring.

◆ Write components that utilize asynchronous processing.

For more information about asynchronous processing, read the article "Asynchronous Call-Backs and Events" in Visual Basic Help.

Optimizing Display Speed

To make display operations faster, use the following techniques:

◆ Use the form's **AutoRedraw** property appropriately.

If your application generates complex graphics that change frequently, you will get better performance if you set **AutoRedraw** to **False**, and handle repainting graphics manually.

◆ Use an **Image** control instead of a **PictureBox** control.

An **Image** control requires less overhead than a **PictureBox**. If you only need to display a picture and respond to a **Click** event, use an **Image** control.

◆ If a form is used frequently, keep the form hidden rather than unloaded. A hidden form displays more quickly than an unloaded form.

Reducing Memory Size

To reclaim memory from an application, consider the following suggestions:

◆ Reclaim data from strings

When you no longer need the data in a long string, set the string to " " to reclaim the memory used by the string. When you no longer need the data in a dynamic array, use **Erase** or **ReDim Preserve** to discard unneeded data, and reclaim the memory used by the array. **Erase** eliminates an array; **ReDim Preserve** shrinks the size of the array without losing the data in the array.

- Reclaim data from pictures

  When you no longer need the picture displayed in a **PictureBox** object, use the **LoadPicture** function with an empty string parameter to clear the object.

For more information about designing applications to maximize performance, read the article "Designing for Performance and Compatibility" in Visual Basic Help, or go to the Microsoft Visual Basic Tips and Tricks Web site at http://msdn.microsoft.com/vbasic/techmat/tntgtg/.

Compiling to Native Code

You can compile your code either to standard Visual Basic pseudocode (p-code) format or to native code format.

P-code is an intermediate step between the high-level instructions of a Visual Basic application and the low-level native code that your computer's processor executes. At run time, Visual Basic translates each p-code statement to native code. By compiling directly to native code format, you eliminate the intermediate p-code step. However, you will still need to distribute the Visual Basic run-time DLL with your application.

Native code compilation provides several options for optimizing and debugging that are not available with p-code. The performance of your application will benefit from native code compilation if your code includes complex mathematical calculations and looping.

▶ **To compile a project to native code**

1. In the Project window, select the project you want to compile.

2. On the **Project** menu, click **Project Properties**.

3. In the **Project Properties** dialog box, click the **Compile** tab.

4. Select the compile options you want to use, and then click **OK**.

   For additional native code options, click the **Advanced Optimizations** button.

The following illustration shows the native code options available in the **Project Properties** dialog box.

Native Code Optimizations

There are several native code optimizations from which you can choose.

◆ Fast Code

Maximizes the speed of the compiled executable by instructing the compiler to favor speed over size.

◆ Small Code

Minimizes the size of the compiled executable by instructing the compiler to favor size over speed.

◆ Favor Pentium Pro

Optimizes executable for Pentium Pro (P6) processor. The executable will still run on earlier processors, but not as efficiently.

◆ Create Symbolic Debug Info

Generates debugging information in the compiled executable. The executable can then be debugged with the Visual C++ or compatible debugger.

Optimizing an Executable

You can further optimize a native code executable by clicking the **Advanced Optimizations** button on the **Compile** tab of the **Project Properties** dialog box, and selecting further optimization options.

The following illustration shows the advanced native code optimization options in the **Advanced Optimizations** dialog box.

The following advanced optimization options are available:

◆ Assume No Aliasing

An alias is a name that refers to a memory location that is already referred to by a different name. This occurs when using **ByRef** arguments that refer to the same variable in two ways.

If you do not use aliasing you can turn on this optimization and the compiler will create faster code.

◆ Remove Array Bounds Checks

Turns off checking for valid array indexes and the correct number of array dimensions.

This will create code that does faster array manipulations. However, if your program accesses an array with an index that is out of bounds, unexpected behavior or program crashes may occur.

◆ Remove Integer Overflow Checks

Turns off checking to insure that numeric values assigned to integer variables (Byte, Integer, Long, and Currency) are within the correct range for the data type.

This will speed up integer calculations. However, if data type capacities are overflowed, no error will be returned, and incorrect results may occur.

- ◆ Remove Floating Point Error Checks

    Turns off checking to insure that numeric values assigned to floating-point variables (Single and Double) are within the correct range for the data type, and that division by zero or other invalid operations do not occur.

    This will speed up floating-point calculations. However, if data type capacities are overflowed, no error will be returned, and incorrect results may occur.

- ◆ Allow Unrounded Floating Point Operations

    Allows the computer to compare the results of floating-point expressions without first rounding those results to the correct precision.

    Comparisons are more efficient without rounding, so this option will speed up some floating-point operations. However, this might introduce errors because floating-point numbers are stored at a higher precision than expected.

    Do not use this option if you perform comparisons of the results of floating-point expressions.

- ◆ Remove Safe Pentium FDIV Checks

    Turns off generation of special code to check for the floating-point division bug in some Pentium processors.

For more information about advanced native code options, click the **Help** button in the **Advanced Optimizations** dialog box.

Creating a Help File for an Application

Including online documentation with your application enhances its usability and reduces support costs. The Visual Basic CD includes Microsoft HTML Help Workshop to help you create help files for your application.

You can use HTML Help Workshop to create standard help topics to provide conceptual and procedural information for your application. You can also provide context-sensitive help for the controls and dialog boxes in your application. For information about how to use HTML Help Workshop, read the article "Using HTML Help Workshop" in HTML Help Workshop Help.

You start the HTML Help Workshop by clicking **HTML Help Workshop** on the **Start** menu. If you did not choose to install HTML Help Workshop when you installed Visual Basic, you can install it from your Visual Basic or Visual Studio CDs.

▶ **To install HTML Help Workshop**

◆ In the \HtmlHelp folder on Disc 1 of your Visual Basic or Visual Studio CDs, double-click **htmlhelp.exe**.

– or –

Install the most current version of HTML Help Workshop from the Microsoft HTML Help Web site. For information, go to the Microsoft HTML Help Web site at www.microsoft.com/workshop/author/htmlhelp.

Deploying an Application

When you distribute your application, you should provide users with a Setup program to perform some or all of the following tasks:

◆ Copy the necessary files to the user's computer.

◆ Place the files in the appropriate folders.

◆ Register files.

◆ Create a **Start** menu item or group.

◆ Create an icon on the user's desktop.

In this section you will learn how to use the Package and Deployment Wizard provided by Visual Basic to create a Setup program for an application. For information about creating a Setup program for an ActiveX control, see "Packaging a Control for the Internet" on page 319 in this chapter.

Using the Package and Deployment Wizard

When you have finished writing, debugging, and testing your application, you're ready to distribute it to your users. The Visual Basic Package and Deployment Wizard steps you through the process of determining which files need to be distributed, compressing them into a Cabinet file (.cab file), and creating a Setup program.

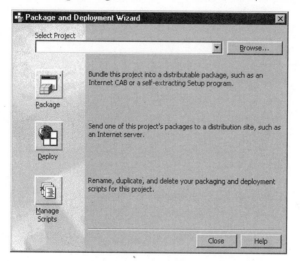

The Package and Deployment Wizard stores the information it gathers about your application every time you run the wizard, and saves it in a script file that you can name. The next time you run the wizard, you can choose to use the settings in an existing script file so that you don't have to step through each screen of the wizard again.

To start the Package and Deployment Wizard, click the **Start** menu, point to **Programs**, and then point to **Microsoft Visual Basic 6.0**. Point to **Microsoft Visual Basic 6.0 Tools**, and then click **Package & Deployment Wizard**.

You can also add the wizard to the **Add-Ins** menu. If you start the Package and Deployment Wizard from the **Add-Ins** menu, it uses the current active project.

▶ **To add the Package and Deployment Wizard to the Add-Ins menu**

1. On the **Add-Ins** menu, click **Add-In Manager**.

2. In the list of available add-ins, select **Package and Deployment Wizard**.

3. Under **Load Behavior**, select the **Loaded/Unloaded** check box, and then click **OK**.

Note If you select the **Load on Startup** check box, the Package and Deployment Wizard will automatically be available on the **Add-Ins** menu every time you start a new project or open an existing project.

If you need to customize your Setup program to include functionality that is not supported by the Package and Deployment Wizard, you can use the Setup Toolkit that comes with Visual Basic. For information about customizing a Setup program for your application, read the article "The Setup Toolkit" in Visual Basic Help.

Packaging an Application

The first step in preparing your application for distribution is to package it for convenient handling. The Package and Deployment Wizard gathers information about all the files used by your application, and compresses them into a Cabinet file (.cab file).

To see the demonstration "Packaging an Application," see the accompanying CD-ROM.

The Package and Deployment Wizard offers the following options for packaging your application:

◆ Standard Setup Package

You can choose to package your application into a single .cab file for distribution on a network folder or CD-ROM, or you can package your application into multiple .cab files of a specific size to fit on a number of floppy disks.

◆ Internet Package

Your application is compressed into a single .cab file that is posted to a Web site. You can choose to have some components downloaded from an alternate Web site if you always want your users to download the most current version of the component.

◆ Dependency File

You can also use the Package and Deployment Wizard to create a dependency file that lists the run-time components required by your application.

For information about a particular step in the Package and Deployment Wizard, click the **Help** button in the wizard dialog box.

To determine which files to include in your Setup program, the Package and Deployment Wizard checks the references and custom controls that you have loaded in your project. It then reads the VB6Dep.ini file in the *<install folder>*\Visual Studio\VB98\Wizards\PDWizard folder to determine which files are required for each reference or custom control.

For example, if you have set a reference to the **Microsoft Common Dialog** control, the Package and Deployment Wizard includes the appropriate .ocx file in your Setup program.

Note The Package and Deployment Wizard recognizes controls and references, whether you use them in your application or not. If controls or type libraries that you have not used in your application appear in the **Install Locations** step of the wizard, and you know you did not use any of these, you should delete the unused files. Either remove the tools and references from your source files manually and then run the wizard again, or clear the check boxes in the list box in the wizard.

The Package and Deployment Wizard also enables you to manually add or remove files from the list of files that need to be distributed.

Distributing an Application

Once your application has been packaged, you are ready to distribute it to your users. The Package and Deployment Wizard provides support for distributing your application on a network folder, CD-ROM, floppy disks, or an Internet server.

To see the demonstration "Deploying an Application," see the accompanying CD-ROM.

Your application must be packaged into one or more Cabinet files (.cab files) before you can deploy your application. For information about packaging your application, see "Packaging an Application" on page 309 in this chapter.

The Package and Deployment Wizard offers the following options for deploying your application:

◆ Folder

The .cab file and supporting setup files are copied to a local or network folder for distribution.

◆ Web Publishing

The .cab file is copied to a Web site, and your application is distributed across the Internet by using automatic code download from Microsoft Internet Explorer version 3.0 or later.

For more information about distributing an application from a Web site, read the article "Deployment Features" in Visual Basic Help.

For information about a particular step in the Package and Deployment Wizard, click the **Help** button in the wizard dialog box.

Understanding Setup Files

The Package and Deployment Wizard creates all of the files necessary to install your application on a user's computer.

The following list describes some of the necessary files:

◆ Cabinet file (.cab file)

The Package and Deployment Wizard compresses your application files into one or more .cab files for distribution. The Setup program then extracts application files from this .cab file and copies them to the appropriate locations on a user's computer.

◆ Setup.exe

The Package and Deployment Wizard copies Setup.exe from a Visual Basic folder to your application's distribution site. The user runs Setup.exe to install your application.

Setup.exe copies the bootstrap files, and then executes the main Setup program (usually named Setup1.exe) listed in Setup.lst.

◆ Setup.lst

The Package and Deployment Wizard creates the Setup.lst file. This file contains the list of files required by your application, and contains general information such as default folders and the required disk space.

The following example code illustrates what a sample Setup.lst file might contain:

```
[Bootstrap]
File1=1,,setup1.ex_,setup1.exe,$(WinPath),...
..
[Files]
File1=1,,GRID32.OC_,GRID32.OCX,$(WinSysPath),,$(Shared)..
..
[Setup]
Title=LoanSheet
DefaultDir=$(ProgramFiles)\Loan
```

◆ Setup1.exe

The Package and Deployment Wizard includes Setup1.exe, the main Setup program, in the .cab file that contains your application files. Setup1.exe copies and registers application files, and creates startup icons. Setup1.exe also increments the reference count for shared files in the registry.

◆ St6Unst.log

The Setup program creates an application log file (St6Unst.log) that is copied to the application folder, and includes the following information:

- Folders that were created.

- Files that were installed. The log indicates if a file was not copied because a newer version of the file was already found on the disk.

- Registry entries that were created.

- **Start** menu entries that were created.

- DLLs, .exe files, or .ocx files that were self-registered.

◆ St6Unst.exe

The Setup program also copies an application removal utility (St6Unst.exe) to the Windows folder. The application removal utility removes the application files and icons or groups, and it decrements the reference count for shared components. If a reference count is zero, the utility prompts the user to remove the shared component.

Note The application removal utility depends on an accurate log file and an accurate registry entry to perform its function.

If your application uses a shared component that you know is already on the user's system, you should still include the component with your Setup program. This ensures that the reference count for the component is incremented when the user installs your application.

To remove an application with either Microsoft Windows NT or Windows 95, click the **Add/Remove Programs** icon in the Control Panel.

Deploying an ActiveX Control

In Chapter 4, "Building ActiveX Controls" you learned how to create an ActiveX control. In this section, you will learn about the different ways you can deploy an ActiveX control.

If your ActiveX control will be used on an HTML page, there are a number of issues that you should take into account, such as the security of your control and proper use of your control by other developers. You will learn how to use an ActiveX control on an HTML page, and how to manage Internet distribution and security issues such as licensing controls, marking controls as safe, and signing controls.

Options for Distributing Controls

The way you distribute a control depends on how the control will be used. An ActiveX control can be used in many different types of applications, such as Microsoft Office or Visual Basic applications, or as part of a Web site. You can either distribute it as a compiled component, or include the source code of the control as part of your application.

Distributing Controls as Compiled Components

To distribute a compiled control (.ocx file) with an application, you must create ActiveX controls as public classes. Users of your control can then include the compiled control in the Setup program of their application.

The advantages of distributing a compiled control are:

◆ You keep the implementation of the control confidential.

◆ Users of your control cannot change the implementation of the control.

◆ You can make bug fixes and feature upgrades to the control and then ship the newly compiled control to all users of the control.

Distributing Controls as Source Code

You can also include a .ctl file in any Visual Basic project. When the application is compiled, the source code of the control is compiled as part of the application's executable file.

The advantages of distributing controls as source code are:

◆ There is no .ocx file to distribute.

◆ Debugging is easier because you only need to debug features of the specific application.

◆ You don't have to worry about whether your application will work with future versions of the control, because the version your application uses is compiled as part of the application.

The disadvantages of distributing controls as source code are:

◆ Fixing bugs in the control's source code requires recompiling the entire application.

◆ Multiple applications require additional disk space because each application includes all of the source code for a control.

◆ Each time you use the source code in an application, there will be an opportunity to fix bugs or enhance the code. It may become difficult to keep track of which version of a control was used in which version of which application.

Adding a Control to an HTML Page

If you want to distribute an ActiveX control over the Internet, you can use the Package and Deployment Wizard to create an Internet download for the control. For more information about using the Package and Deployment Wizard to deploy a control, see "Packaging a Control for the Internet" on page 319 in this chapter.

When you create an Internet download for a control, an HTML template is created. You can then modify the template to include download information for your users, and post the template as a Web site on the Internet. This template enables you to specify your control by using the <OBJECT> tag.

The <OBJECT> tag is an element of HTML that provides a standardized way to add objects to an HTML page. The HTML template created by the Package and Deployment Wizard contains the appropriate <OBJECT> tag for your ActiveX control.

For more information about HTML syntax and other Internet related topics, go to the Authoring page of the Site Builder Network site at http://www.microsoft.com/workshop/author/.

Parameters of the <OBJECT> Tag

The <OBJECT> tag contains a number of parameters that define an object, its location, and how it appears on an HTML page.

This following example code shows how to use the parameters of the <OBJECT> tag:

```
<OBJECT
  CLASSID="clsid:6A7A58F2-3DFC-11D0-A520-0080C776418A"
  WIDTH=200
  HEIGHT=200
  ID=MyControl
  CODEBASE="MySetup.cab#version=1,0,0,0">
</OBJECT>
```

The following table lists some of the standard parameters used with the <OBJECT> tag.

Parameter	Definition
CLASSID	A unique class identifier used to identify the control. The ClassID is stored in the system registry.
ID	A string that specifies the object name so you can refer to the object in code.
CODEBASE	A Uniform Resource Locator (URL) that points to a file containing the implementation of an object. For Visual Basic controls, you specify a URL that points to your .cab file, relative to the location of your HTML page. If the HTML page and .cab file are in the same folder on your Web server, the CODEBASE parameter refers to the name of the .cab file.

Licensing an ActiveX Control

To protect your ActiveX controls, Visual Basic provides licensing capabilities. Licensing your controls prevents other developers from using an instance of your control to create their own control. You can include licensing protection for any controls you want to distribute on the Internet, as well as providing licensing for ActiveX controls distributed as stand-alone components.

Licensing Controls for Standard Distribution

You can use Visual Basic to create licensed ActiveX controls. A licensed control contains a key that prevents it from being used at design time. This prevents other developers from including your control as part of their application without obtaining its license.

Adding Licensing to a Control

To add licensing to a control, select the **Require License Key** option in the **Project Properties** dialog box, as shown in the following illustration.

When you compile the .ocx file, Visual Basic creates a .vbl file that contains the licensing key for your control.

The Package and Deployment Wizard creates a Setup program that automatically registers any .vbl files in the system registry. When a user runs the Setup program, the default option for a .vbl file is **Do not install this file**. This is because you usually want the end-user to have the license file registered but not installed on his or her computer. This option ensures that you can include your controls in applications you distribute, but users of the application will only be able to access the run-time version of the control.

For more information about licensing controls, read the article "Licensing Issues for Controls" in Visual Basic Help.

Using Licensed Constituent Controls

If you use a licensed constituent control as a part of a control that you build, you must require developers using your control to have the constituent control installed, or ask that the constituent control vendor include the licensing key with their control's Setup program.

For information about constituent controls that you can use, read the article "Controls You Can Use as Constituent Controls" in Visual Basic Help.

Licensing Controls for the Internet

Licensing a control for distribution on the Internet is different from licensing a control as part of a stand-alone application. Internet licensing involves the following two steps:

1. Create a license package (.lpk) file.

   When you license a control for use on a Web page, you create a licensing package file. This file stores the run-time licensing information for all components on the page.

2. Create a reference to the licensing package file on your HTML page.

   When a user attempts to use a licensed control on a Web page, the Internet Explorer License Manager checks the information in the .lpk file to ensure that the proper license is being used. If someone tries to use your control on a Web page that does not include the .lpk file, the control will not appear on the page.

For more information about licensing controls for the Internet, read the article "Licensing for ActiveX Components" in Visual Basic Help.

Creating an .lpk File

You create a licensing package file by using the utility program Lpk_Tool.exe. This program is available as part of the Microsoft Internet Client SDK. For information about downloading Internet Client SDK, go to the Microsoft Internet Client SDK Web site at msdn.microsoft.com/msdn/sdk/inetsdk/asetup.

The licensing information for all controls on a page must be in a single .lpk file.

Creating a Reference to an .lpk File

You provide the name of the .lpk file in the HTML code of your Web page by using the **License Manager** object. The <OBJECT> tag is included in the sample HTML page created by the Package and Deployment Wizard. The following example code shows how to use an <OBJECT> tag for licensing:

```
<OBJECT CLASSID="clsid:5220cb21-c88d-11cf-b347-00aa00a28331">
  <PARAM NAME="LPKPath" VALUE="MyLicenseFile.LPK">
</OBJECT>
```

Testing an .lpk File

When you compile a licensed ActiveX control on your computer, the license information is written to your computer's registry. The control will load properly on your computer without using the .lpk file.

To make sure your control's licensing functionality works correctly, you should test it on a local computer before distributing it over the Internet. To test the licensing functionality, test it on a separate computer or remove the license information from your computer's system registry.

Signing an ActiveX Control

Because ActiveX controls can pose a security risk, a user can set browser options to only download controls that have been digitally signed by certain authors. If a control is not signed, or is signed by an author the user does not trust, the browser will not download and run the control.

To identify your control and assure users that the code has not been modified since it was signed, you can add a digital signature to your code. You add a digital signature by using the Authenticode technology, which is derived from public-key signature algorithms.

To sign your code, you work with a certificate authority (CA) to obtain a digital certificate, which provides users with information about the author of a control. The CA provides and renews your certificate, authenticates identity, and handles legal and liability issues when security is broken.

Signing Code

To sign code by adding a digital signature, you follow these steps:

1. Apply for a digital certificate over the Internet from a certificate authority.

   For instructions on how to obtain a certificate, go to the Microsoft Authenticode Web site at www.microsoft.com/workshop/security/authcode/certs.asp.

2. Install the ActiveX Software Development Kit (SDK). To download the ActiveX SDK, go to the Microsoft ActiveX SDK Web site at http://www.microsoft.com/workshop/misc/activexsdk/default.asp.

   The ActiveX SDK provides the tools and documentation necessary for code signing.

3. Sign your files.

   Use the Signcode.exe application included in the ActiveX SDK to apply your digital certificate to your code. Although you can sign most types of executable files, you will probably want to sign .cab files in particular because this applies the signature to the complete collection of compressed files.

Packaging a Control for the Internet

When you use an ActiveX control in a standard Visual Basic application, the control is installed on the user's computer when the user runs the Setup program for your application. When you use an ActiveX control on an HTML page, the control is downloaded from the Internet and registered on the user's computer when the user requests the Web page. Once the control is downloaded and registered, it remains on the user's computer and does not need to be downloaded again on subsequent requests for that page.

To make sure that your control can be downloaded from the Internet, you must package the control so it can be used in the HTML environment.

Using the Package and Deployment Wizard

The Package and Deployment Wizard handles most of the work involved with placing a control on a Web page, including the following tasks:

- Creating a .cab file.
- Marking your control as safe for scripting and initialization.
- Building an HTML template for using your control.

Creating a .cab File

When you use an ActiveX control on a Web page, the control must reside on an Internet server along with any dependent files or help information.

To simplify the distribution and installation of these files over the Internet, ActiveX controls can be compressed into a single .cab file. The Package and Deployment Wizard in Visual Basic can create this .cab file for you.

Marking a Control as Safe

A control is considered safe when it handles script and data passed to it during initialization in such a way that a malicious script or data cannot damage a user's computer.

When you are confident that your control's properties and methods cannot be used maliciously, you can use the Package and Deployment Wizard to mark your control as safe. In marking a control as safe for scripting, you are asserting that the control cannot do any damage, such as reformatting a hard drive, with an HTML script. Marking an ActiveX control as safe for initialization indicates that it cannot do any damage during initialization. In addition, you are guaranteeing that downloading your control will never corrupt a user's computer or obtain unauthorized information from the computer.

For information about how to create controls that are safe for scripting and initialization, read the article "Designing Controls for Use with HTML" in Visual Basic Help.

The following illustration shows the **Safety Settings** dialog box in the Package and Deployment Wizard.

In this dialog box, you can mark your component as safe for scripting and initialization.

For more information about marking components as safe, read the article "Safety Settings for ActiveX Components" in Visual Basic Help.

Building an HTML Template for Using Your Control

When you create an Internet download for a control, the Package and Deployment Wizard creates an HTML template for you. You can modify the template to include download information for your users, and then post the template as a Web site on the Internet. This template includes a reference to your control by using the <OBJECT> tag. For more information about the <OBJECT> tag, see "Adding a Control to an HTML Page" on page 314 in this chapter.

Lab 9: Deploying the StateUBookstore Solution

In this lab, you will deploy the StateUBookstore solution using the Package and Deployment Wizard.

To see the demonstration "Lab 9 Solution," see the accompanying CD-ROM.

Estimated time to complete this lab: **30 minutes**

To complete the exercises in this lab, you must have the required software. For detailed information about the labs and setup for the labs, see "Labs" in "About This Course."

> **Note** If you have not completed Labs 4 through 8 using the same computer on which you are currently working, you may need to register
> <*install folder*>\Labs\Lab09\StateUControls.ocx,
> <*install folder*>\Labs\Lab09\HandleInventory.dll, and
> <*install folder*>\Labs\Lab09\StateUFinance.dll before you start this lab.
>
> For information about registering components, see "Making the Component Available" on page 247 in Chapter 7, "Using COM Components."

Objectives

After completing this lab, you will be able to:

◆ Package and deploy a completed solution.

Prerequisites

Before working on this lab, you should be familiar with the following:

◆ Using the Package and Deployment Wizard

Exercises

The following exercises provide practice working with the concepts and techniques covered in this chapter:

◆ Exercise 1: Creating a Package and Setup Program

   In this exercise, you will package the StateUBookstore application and all of its COM components for deployment. You will also create a setup program so others can install the application.

◆ Exercise 2: Installing the StateUBookstore Application

In this exercise, you will install the StateUBookstore application using the setup program.

Exercise 1: Creating a Package and Setup Program

In this exercise, you will package the StateUBookstore application and all of its COM components for deployment. You will also create a setup program so others can install the application.

▶ Prepare the solution for packaging

1. Open the StateUBookstore project.

2. Make the StateUBookstore.exe file.

3. Close Visual Basic, and test the StateUBookstore.exe.

▶ Package the solution

1. From the **Start** menu, launch the Package and Deployment Wizard.

2. Select the StateUBookstore project and click **Package**.

3. Select **Standard Setup Package** as the type of package to create and click **Next**.

4. Choose a destination for the Package folder that will contain the StateUBookstore package and click **Next**.

5. In the Missing Dependency Information dialog box, check each of the files to indicate that they have no dependency information.

6. Check the list of files to verify that they all should be included in the package and click **Next**.

7. Choose to create a single .cab file and click **Next**.

8. Enter an installation title for the StateUBookstore setup program and click **Next**.

9. Determine the **Start** menu groups you want for the StateUBookstore application and click **Next**.

10. Accept the default installation locations for the StateUBookstore files and click **Next**.

11. Choose not to mark any of the files as shared components and click **Next**.

12. Name the installation script "StateUPackage" and click **Finish**.

▶ **Deploy the solution**

1. In the Package and Deployment Wizard, click **Deploy**.

2. Select the StateUPackage and click **Next**.

3. Chose **Folder** as the deployment method and click **Next**.

4. Chose a folder location to deploy the StateUBookstore solution and click **Next**.

5. Name the deployment script "StateUDeploy" and click **Finish**.

6. Close the Package and Deployment Wizard.

7. Look for the deployed files.

Exercise 2: Installing the StateUBookstore Application

In this exercise, you will install the StateUBookstore application using the setup program.

▶ **Install the StateUBookstore application**

1. Run the setup program you created in Exercise 1.

2. Test to see if the StateUBookstore application is on the **Start** menu.

3. Run the StateUBookstore solution and test its functionality.

Self-Check Questions

To see the answers to the Self-Check Questions, see Appendix A.

1. You have created a Setup program for your application using the Package and Deployment Wizard. Which file creates the startup icons?

A. Setup.exe

B. Setup1.exe

C. St6Unst.exe

D. Setup.lst

2. **Your application uses a complicated graphic to display order status statistics for the production department of your company, and the display is updated whenever an order is entered, constructed, packaged, or shipped. What can you do to improve the performance of your application's display operations?**

   A. Use a picture box instead of an image control.

   B. Set **AutoRedraw** to **True** so your status graphic is redrawn automatically.

   C. Make sure you unload rather than hide the status graphic when it is not being used so it will display more quickly when it is needed again.

   D. Set **AutoRedraw** to **False** and add code to refresh your status graphic.

3. **Your application retrieves data from text files in the form of many long strings. How can you reclaim the memory used by these strings when the data is no longer needed by your application?**

   A. Set the strings to " ".

   B. Use **Erase** to remove the strings from memory.

   C. Use **Remove** to erase the strings from memory.

   D. Use **PageStrings** to free memory and write the strings to a swap file.

4. **How can you retrieve an application setting from the registry?**

   A. Use the **GetAllSettings** function.

   B. Use the **SaveSetting** function.

   C. Use the **GetSetting** function.

   D. Use the **DeleteSetting** function.

5. **Which of the following options does the Package and Deployment Wizard offer when packaging your application?**

   A. Internet Package

   B. Dependency File

   C. Standard Setup Package

   D. All of the above

Student Notes:

Chapter 10: Building Internet Applications

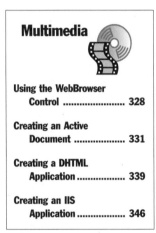
Using Microsoft Visual Basic, you can create applications that display HTML pages by using the **WebBrowser** control. You can create Active documents that can be hosted in Microsoft Internet Explorer or any other Active document container. You can also use Visual Basic to create Web applications that combine the security and convenience of COM components with the flexibility of HTML page design. In addition, you can choose whether their processing occurs primarily on the Web client or on the Internet server.

In this chapter, you will learn how to use Visual Basic to create different kinds of components and applications for the Internet.

Objectives

After completing this chapter, you will be able to:

- List the ways Visual Basic can enhance a Web site.
- Create applications that use the **WebBrowser** control.
- Explain what Active documents are.
- Create an Active document.
- Use the DHTML Page designer to create client-side COM components.
- Use the WebClass designer to create server-side COM components.

Using the WebBrowser Control

In Chapter 7, "Using COM Components," you learned how to control Internet Explorer from your Visual Basic application. Through the same DLL that provides access to Internet Explorer as a stand-alone application, you can also access the **WebBrowser** control. You can use the **WebBrowser** control to display and browse HTML documents within your Visual Basic application.

The **WebBrowser** control, like other ActiveX controls in Visual Basic, must be hosted within a form. It in turn can host documents the same way Internet Explorer hosts documents. Using this control, you have access to the Dynamic HTML (DHTML) document object model that you can use to manipulate open documents in the control. For information about the Dynamic HTML object model, read the article "Writing Code Using Dynamic HTML" in Visual Basic Help.

This section introduces the **WebBrowser** control and discusses its properties, methods, and events.

Introduction to the WebBrowser Control

The **WebBrowser** control adds browsing, document viewing, and data downloading capabilities to your Visual Basic applications. It enables users to browse sites on the World Wide Web, or folders on a local file system or network.

Navigation in the **WebBrowser** control is supported by means of hyperlinks and Uniform Resource Locators (URLs). The control maintains a history list that enables users to browse forward and backward through previously browsed sites, folders, and documents.

The control includes support for parsing and displaying HTML- and DHTML-encoded documents. It is also an Active document container and can host any Active document. Richly formatted documents, such as a Microsoft Excel spreadsheet or Microsoft Word document, can be opened and edited in-place within the **WebBrowser** control.

To see the demonstration "Using the WebBrowser Control," see the accompanying CD-ROM.

Uses of the WebBrowser Control

Some of the uses of the **WebBrowser** control include:

◆ Enabling users to navigate to and view HTML documents on an intranet or on the World Wide Web.

◆ Providing a single frame in which users can view and edit all types of Active documents.

◆ Creating a customized Web application based on the **WebBrowser** control.

Adding the WebBrowser Control to a Project

If the **WebBrowser** control is not already in the Toolbox for your project, you can add it by using the following steps.

▶ **To add the WebBrowser control to your project's Toolbox**

1. On the **Project** menu, click **Components**.

2. On the **Controls** tab, select **Microsoft Internet Controls**, and then click **OK**.

Basic Operations of the WebBrowser Control

To add common Web browser capabilities to an application, you can use the methods, properties, and events of the **WebBrowser** control described in the following table.

Interface element	Added functionality
Navigate method	Specifies a resource to view. The resource must be identified by a URL.
LocationURL and **LocationName** properties in the **NavigateComplete** event	Display the name and URL of a resource in the **WebBrowser** control.
GoBack, GoForward, GoSearch, and **GoHome** methods	Navigate to sites included in the **History** list.

table continued on next page

Interface element	Added functionality
Busy property	Determines whether the **WebBrowser** control is in the process of navigating to a new location or downloading a file.
Stop method	Cancels a navigation or download activity before it is finished.
Refresh method	Reloads a page that has already been displayed.
DownloadBegin, **ProgressChange**, and **DownloadComplete** events	Display status information during a Web page download.

Creating Active Documents

You can use Visual Basic to create applications that run within an Internet browser window. These applications are called Active documents.

In this section, you will learn about Active documents and Active document containers. You will learn how to implement Active documents in Visual Basic, and how to use Visual Basic to determine the container application and persist data in an Active document.

Introduction to Active Documents

Active documents are Visual Basic applications that can be hosted in Internet browser windows. Active documents can also be hosted in the Office Binder and other container applications that support OLE document objects.

Advantages of Active Documents

There are many reasons you might want to create your Internet or intranet application as an Active document.

Advantage	Description
Widely available container	Active documents enable a generic, widely available container application to host a variety of different document types. This allows users to work with information in any number of formats through common browser functionality.

table continued on next page

Advantage	Description
Visual Basic knowledge	If you are a skilled Visual Basic programmer, you already have the knowledge to create a solution. You do not have to learn HTML in order to create an application for the Internet.
Visual Basic programming environment	The full development environment is available to you, including the Visual Basic code window, debugger, and compiler.
Execution on a local computer	Active document technology enables computer-intensive processing to take place locally, and reduces the processing on a network.
Immediate visual feedback	Unlike coding in HTML, creating an Active document in Visual Basic provides immediate visual feedback about the layout of elements in your application.

Steps for Creating an Active Document

Creating an Active document is similar to creating any other kind of application in Visual Basic. The primary differences are that you use a **UserDocument** object instead of a form for the user interface, and you test your application in its container application.

To see the demonstration "Creating an Active Document," see the accompanying CD-ROM.

▶ **To create an Active document in Visual Basic**

1. Design the features and appearance of your document, and determine the properties, methods, and events it will provide.

2. Create a new Visual Basic project using either the **ActiveX Document DLL** or the **ActiveX Document EXE** project template.

   Create a .dll file if you want to create an in-process component. Create an .exe file if you want to create an out-of-process component. For more information, see "In-Process vs. Out-Of-Process Components" on page 270 in Chapter 8, "Building COM Components."

3. Add controls and code to the **UserDocument** object to implement the user interface of your document, and write code to implement its properties, methods, and events.

4. Compile your document to create a .vbd file, and test it with all potential target applications.

   For more information about binary data files and project files, read the article "Visual Basic Specifications, Limitations, and File Formats" in Visual Basic Help.

Using the UserDocument Object

In Visual Basic, you create an Active document by adding controls and code to a **UserDocument** object in an Active document designer. The **UserDocument** object is the foundation for all Active documents.

The **UserDocument** object is similar in functionality to the **UserControl** object. Like the **UserControl** object, the **UserDocument** object can raise events, and can support properties and methods. For information about the **UserControl** object, see "Creating an ActiveX Control" on page 114 in Chapter 4, "Building ActiveX Controls."

The **UserDocument** object also implements interfaces that enable it to be hosted within a document container.

The following illustration shows a new Active document project viewed in the Visual Basic Project Explorer.

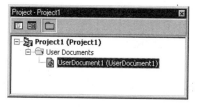

This project contains a user document, which is the default Visual Basic **UserDocument** object included in a new Active document project. You can add additional documents to a project.

▶ **To add a User Document to a project**

1. On the **Project** menu, click **Add User Document**.

2. In the **Add User Document** dialog box, click **User Document**, and then click **Open**.

Working with the **UserDocument** object is similar to working with a form. For example, you place controls on the **UserDocument** object to create the visual appearance of an Active document.

The following illustration shows a user document in design mode, along with the code module for the document.

Migrating a Form to an Active Document

You can always start a new Active document project, but you may have a form you want to migrate to an Active document. Visual Basic provides the ActiveX Document Migration Wizard to automate the process.

▶ **To use the ActiveX Document Migration Wizard**

1. Open the project that contains the form you want to convert.

2. On the **Add-Ins** menu, click **Add-In Manager**.

3. In the list of available add-ins, select **VB 6 Active Doc Migration Wizard**.

4. Under **Load Behavior**, select the **Loaded/Unloaded** check box to add the wizard to your project, and then click **OK**.

5. On the **Add-Ins** menu, click **ActiveX Document Migration Wizard**.

6. Follow the directions until the wizard has finished its task.

The wizard asks you to identify the form that you want to convert and to make a few choices, such as whether to remove the original form after conversion. It then performs the tasks described in the following table.

Form element	Action taken
Properties	Form properties are copied to a new **UserDocument** object.
Controls	All controls are copied from the form to the **UserDocument** object. Their names are retained.
Valid code	All code behind the form is copied to the **UserDocument** object.
Invalid code	Code that doesn't apply in the Active document situation (such as code to show, hide, load, and unload forms) is commented out.
Project file	The project type is switched to ActiveX Document DLL or ActiveX Document EXE, depending on the option you chose in the wizard.
Event handlers	Event handlers are copied to the **UserDocument** object, with "Form" replaced by "UserDocument" where appropriate. For example, "Form_Click()" becomes "UserDocument_Click()". In cases where there is no exact counterpart in the **UserDocument** object, the event handler is copied to the General section of the code window, leaving the original procedure name intact.

Working with an Active Document

There are some situations unique to Active documents that you may want to handle in your code. For example, a user may attempt to open your document in a container other than the one you intended. You can write code that determines the container and responds appropriately for that container.

Another common requirement for Active documents is the ability to store data associated with the page so that it is available the next time it is opened. In Visual Basic you can use the **PropertyBag** object to persist data in an Active document.

Determining the Container Application

To determine the container of an Active document, you use the **TypeName** statement with the **Parent** property of the **UserDocument** object, as shown in the following example code:

```
Dim strContainer As String
strContainer = TypeName(UserDocument.Parent)
```

The process of connecting an Active document to its container, or assigning it a site in the container, is called siting. When an Active document is sited on its container, the **Show** event occurs. You can use this event to determine the container being used. When a document is sited, the container properties become available.

The string value returned by the **Parent** property in Internet Explorer is **IWebBrowserApp**. The following sample code checks to see whether **IWebBrowserApp** is the string value returned by the **Parent** property of the **UserDocument** object. To copy this code for use in your own projects, see "Determining the Container Application" on the accompanying CD-ROM.

```
Private Sub UserDocument_Show()
  Dim strContainer As String
  strContainer = TypeName(UserDocument.Parent)

  If strContainer = "IWebBrowserApp" Then
      MsgBox "Confirmation: This document  " & _
      "works with Internet Explorer " & _
      "3.0 or later."
  Else
      MsgBox "Sorry, please open this "& _
      "document with Internet Explorer "& _
      "3.0 or later."
  End If

End Sub
```

Persisting Data in an Active Document

Users often navigate away from an Active document in Internet Explorer or another container, and then navigate back to it. They expect not to lose data or settings on that page, so you must ensure that property values are preserved for your Active document. You can do this by writing code that uses the **PropertyBag** object to persist data for that document.

Saving Property Values

You save property values in the **WriteProperties** event of the **UserDocument** object. This event is raised whenever the **PropertyChanged** method is invoked in your code.

The **WriteProperty** method takes three arguments: a string indicating the property to save, a value for the property, and a default value.

Tip Before saving the property value, the default value is compared with the property value. If they are the same, the property value doesn't have to be saved, because default values will be set automatically when the document is reopened. This keeps the data file from being cluttered with default entries unnecessarily.

The following example code shows how to save current property values by notifying the container that a property has changed, and then saving the value with the **WriteProperty** method of the **PropertyBag** object:

```
Private Sub txtEmpName_Change()
  'Notify container that Employee Name property has changed
  PropertyChanged "EmployeeName"
End Sub

Private Sub UserDocument_WriteProperties(PropBag As PropertyBag)
  PropBag.WriteProperty "EmployeeName", txtEmpName.Text, "No Name"
  PropBag.WriteProperty "EmployeeNumber", txtEmpNum.Text, "000"
End Sub
```

Reading Property Values

You retrieve property values in the **ReadProperties** event of the **UserDocument** object. This event is raised when the document is opened in its container.

The **ReadProperty** method takes two arguments: a string designating the property name and a default value. If a property value has been saved, the **ReadProperty** method returns the value. If a property value has not been saved, the method returns the default value.

The following example code shows how to use the **ReadProperty** method to return the saved value of the **EmployeeName** and **EmployeeNumber** properties:

```
Private Sub UserDocument_ReadProperties(PropBag As PropertyBag)
  txtName.Text = PropBag.ReadProperty("EmployeeName", "No Name")
  txtNum.Text = PropBag.ReadProperty("EmployeeNumber", "000")
End Sub
```

Creating DHTML Applications

With Visual Basic, you can create Web-based applications that perform their processing on the Web client, and combine the efficiency and security of COM components with the power of Dynamic HTML (DHTML).

DHTML is a technology built into Internet Explorer 4.0 that defines an object model for HTML pages. You can use DHTML to programmatically respond to events and modify elements on an HTML page at any time, not just while down-loading or refreshing the page. For more information about DHTML and its capabilities, read the article "Dynamic HTML in Visual Basic" in Visual Basic Help.

Client-side Web applications created in Visual Basic are called DHTML applications. In this section, you will learn how to use Visual Basic to develop DHTML applications.

Introduction to DHTML Applications

If you want to create a Web-based application that performs its processing on the Web client, you can develop a DHTML application in Visual Basic. A DHTML application consists of one or more HTML pages and a COM component that interacts with the page. The HTML page acts as the user interface for the application, and the COM component contains the functionality for the application.

The following illustration shows the parts of a DHTML application, and indicates where the processing for the application occurs.

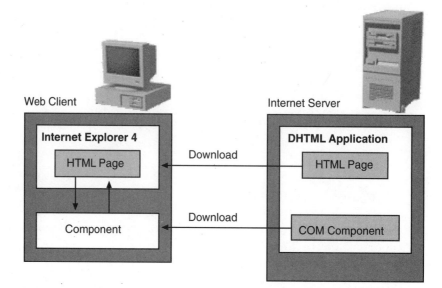

Using the DHTML Page designer, you can create a Web-based application as easily as you create a form-based application. Although the user interface for the application is an HTML page, you can create the page using visual tools instead of HTML tags. You also have access to the standard Visual Basic editing features and debugging tools to write and test the COM component used by your DHTML application.

The DHTML Page designer exposes the DHTML object model to you so that you can change the content and format of the HTML page as the user views the page. For more information about DHTML, read the article "Dynamic HTML in Visual Basic" in Visual Basic Help.

A DHTML application can run in Internet Explorer 4.0 or any other container that supports DHTML, such as a custom application built using the **WebBrowser** control. The processing associated with a DHTML application occurs on the Web client, although the application can make calls to a server.

Steps for Creating a DHTML Application

To see the demonstration "Creating a DHTML Application," see the accompanying CD-ROM.

▶ **To create a DHTML application in Visual Basic**

1. Create a new project in Visual Basic using the DHTML Application project template.

   Your project will contain a DHTML Page designer and a code module by default.

2. Create an HTML page or use an existing HTML page as the user interface for your application.

   There is a one-to-one relationship between DHTML Page designers and HTML pages in Visual Basic. If you want to use more than one HTML page in your application, add more DHTML Page designers to your project by clicking **Add DHTML Page** on the **Project** menu.

3. Assign a unique identifier to each element of the HTML page that you want to access programmatically.

4. Write code to add functionality to your application.

5. Test and debug your application as you would any other Visual Basic application.

   When you start your DHTML application from Visual Basic, it will run in Internet Explorer, but you will still debug your code in the Visual Basic IDE.

6. Compile your application, and use the Package and Deployment Wizard to package the .dll and supporting files for distribution.

   For more information about preparing an application for distribution, see "Deploying an Application" on page 307 in Chapter 9, "Optimizing and Deploying Applications."

Creating the User Interface

When you develop a DHTML application, you use the DHTML Page designer during design time to create and modify an HTML page that acts as your user interface. You must assign a unique identifier to each element of the HTML page that you want to modify or manipulate as an object in your code.

Using the DHTML Page Designer

The DHTML Page designer is a design-time tool in Visual Basic that enables you to quickly create and modify an HTML page that acts as the user interface in your DHTML application. The DHTML Page designer contains two panels. The panel on the right is where you edit the text on your HTML page and add controls to it, just as you would a form. The Treeview panel on the left displays an outline of the object model for the HTML page as it is created.

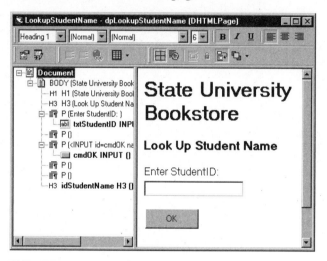

Working with HTML Pages

You can create a new HTML page as your user interface, or you can import an HTML page that was created in an external editor.

▶ **To import an existing HTML page into a DHTML Page designer**

1. Select the DHTML Page designer, and then click the **DHTML Page Designer Properties** toolbar button.

2. In the **Properties** dialog box, on the **General** tab, click **Save HTML in an external file,** and then click **Open.**

   The **Open** dialog box appears.

3. Select the HTML file you want to import, and then click **Open.**

4. In the **Properties** dialog box, click **OK.**

   The HTML file you imported is displayed in the right panel of the designer, and its object model is displayed in the left panel.

Before you can write code to the elements on your HTML page, you need to specify a value for the **Id** property in the Properties window for each element you want to treat as an object in your code.

> **Tip** Although Web browsers generally support multiple identifiers of the same value on an HTML page, Visual Basic requires identifiers to be unique on a page. Be sure if you are importing an HTML page that you verify the **Id** values are what you expect. Visual Basic will automatically increment **Id** values to ensure uniqueness.

The following illustration shows a command button selected in the DHTML Page designer. Its Properties window is open, displaying the **Id** value for that button. Notice the **Id** is also displayed in the left panel of the designer as part of the object model hierarchy.

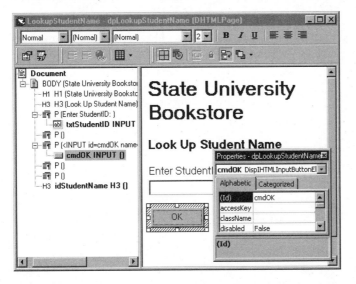

Writing Code in a DHTML Application

Once you have created the user interface for your DHTML application and specified **Id** values for the elements that you want to work with programmatically, you can write code to add functionality to your application.

Using DHTML Objects

The DHTML Page designer represents the elements of your HTML page in a hierarchy in the left panel of the designer. Each element in the hierarchy is a DHTML object. Although you will learn how to use a few specific objects in this chapter, discussing the Dynamic HTML object model in its entirety is beyond the scope of this course. For more information about the Dynamic HTML object model, read the article "Writing Code Using Dynamic HTML" in Visual Basic Help.

Any element of the HTML page that has an **Id** value is displayed in bold text in the left panel of the designer. You can double-click the bold text in the left panel, or double-click the object itself in the right panel of the designer to display the code window associated with that object. Then you can write code for the object just as you would write code for a control on a form.

Manipulating HTML Pages at Run Time

Using Dynamic HTML, you can manipulate the style and content of HTML pages at any time during run time of your DHTML application.

A common operation in DHTML applications is to dynamically change the text on an HTML page. To do this, use the **InnerText** property of the paragraph tag. The following example code sets the contents of the idStudentName paragraph to "Max Benson":

```
idStudentName.innerText = "Max Benson"
```

For more information about manipulating text in your HTML page, read the article "Handling Text in the Page Designer" in Visual Basic Help.

Using a DHTML Application

You can test and debug your DHTML application using the same powerful debugging tools that you are accustomed to using in Visual Basic. When you run your application from the Visual Basic environment, the HTML page that acts as the user interface is opened in Internet Explorer. However, you will still debug your code using the Visual Basic Integrated Development Environment (IDE).

Saving the HTML Files Associated with a DHTML Application

When you compile your application, Visual Basic generates a .dll file and saves the HTML files associated with your application. You can save HTML files as part of the Visual Basic project or as external files. You may want to save HTML files as external files if you have imported them from an existing Web site project.

▶ **To choose how to save an HTML file**

1. Select the DHTML Page designer, and then click the **DHTML Page Designer Properties** toolbar button.

2. In the **Properties** dialog box, on the **General** tab, choose **Save HTML as part of the VB project**, and then click **OK**.

   – or –

   In the **Properties** dialog box, on the **General** tab, choose **Save HTML in an external file**, and then click **OK**.

Deploying a DHTML Application

You can use the Visual Basic Package and Deployment Wizard to prepare your DHTML application for distribution. The wizard compresses the COM component and supporting HTML files that make up the DHTML application into a .cab file. It also provides you the opportunity to mark each page in your application as safe. For information about marking components as safe, read the article "Safety Settings for ActiveX Components" in Visual Basic Help.

The Package and Deployment Wizard can also copy the .cab file and other supporting files for your application to either a Web site or a folder for distribution to your users.

For more information about using the Package and Deployment Wizard, see "Using the Package and Deployment Wizard" on page 308 in Chapter 9, "Optimizing and Deploying Applications."

Practice: Creating a DHTML Application

In this practice exercise you will create a DHTML application.

▶ **Create a DHTML Application project**

1. Open Visual Basic and create a new project with the DHTML Application project template.

2. In the project window, open the Designers folder and double-click **DHTMLPage1**.

3. Click in the Treeview panel of the DHTML Page designer. Expand all of the objects that are currently in the DHTML page.

4. Add a title to your DHTML page by typing text in the right panel of the DHTML Page designer, and then press **Enter**.

5. Click in the Treeview panel of the DHTML Page designer and notice the change to the object model for this page.

6. Add a command button to the DHTML page.

7. Select the text of your title in the right panel of the designer. In the Properties window, change the **Id** property to **idTitle**.

8. Double-click the command button to open the code window for the button's **onclick** event.

9. In the **onclick** event, change the **innerText** property of the **idTitle** object to a new title.

10. Run the project, click **OK** to start your DHTMLPage component, and test the command button.

▶ **Change the background color**

1. Add another command button to the DHTML page.

2. In the command button's **onclick** event, set the **bgColor** property of the DHTML **Document** object to **"Green"**.

3. Run the project and test your work.

Creating IIS Applications

With Visual Basic, you can create Web-based applications that perform their processing on the server, and are accessible from Web browsers on any platform. You can combine the low overhead costs and other benefits of deploying an application over the Internet with the efficiency and security of COM components.

Server-side Web applications created in Visual Basic are called Internet Information Server (IIS) applications. In this section, you will learn how to use Visual Basic to develop IIS applications.

Introduction to IIS Applications

If you want to create a Web-based application that performs its processing on the Internet server, you can develop an Internet Information Server (IIS) application in Visual Basic. An IIS application consists of a COM component and a simple Active Server Page (.asp file). The COM component contains the functionality for the application. The .asp file exists only to instantiate the COM component on the Internet server.

The following illustration shows the parts of an IIS application, and indicates where the processing for the application occurs.

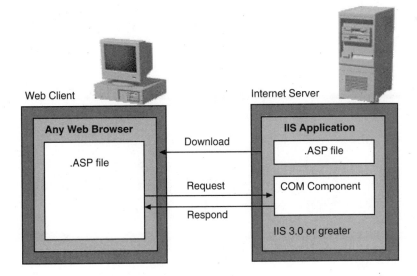

Using the WebClass designer, you can create a dynamic Web-based application without relying on script in an .asp file. Instead, you use the Active Server Page object model in your COM component to respond to events from the client browser. For information about the Active Server Page object model used by IIS applications, read the article "The Object Model for IIS Applications" in Visual Basic Help.

The user interface for an IIS application consists of one or more HTML pages. You can either create HTML pages in an external editor and import them into your project, or you can write code in your COM component to dynamically return content to the Web client. You use the standard Visual Basic editing features and debugging tools to write and test your COM component. The bootstrap .asp file used by your application is generated for you at compile time.

Steps for Creating an IIS Application

To see the demonstration "Creating an IIS Application," see the accompanying CD-ROM.

▶ **To create an IIS application in Visual Basic**

1. Create a new project in Visual Basic using the IIS Application project template.

   The project contains a WebClass designer and a code module by default. A reference is automatically set to the Microsoft Active Server Page Object Library.

> **Note** To use the IIS Application project template, you must have Internet Information Server or Personal Web Server installed on your computer. You can obtain either of these services by installing the NT Option Pack that is included on the Visual Basic CD.

2. Create custom webitems to represent each page in your application, or import existing HTML pages as webitems. For more information about webitems, see "Working with the WebClass Designer" on page 347 in this chapter.

3. Define the functionality of your application by adding code to the webitems and the **Start** event of your webclass.

4. Test and debug your application as you would any other Visual Basic application.

   When you start your IIS application from Visual Basic, it will run in Internet Explorer, but you will still debug your code in the Visual Basic IDE.

5. Compile your application, and use the Package and Deployment Wizard to package the .dll and supporting files for distribution.

For more information about preparing an application for distribution, see "Deploying an Application" on page 307 in Chapter 9, "Optimizing and Deploying Applications."

Working with the WebClass Designer

When you develop an IIS application in Visual Basic, you use a WebClass designer to define the COM component. A single webclass represents the entire Web application, which can contain multiple pages. Each page in the application is represented by a webitem. You can either create custom webitems using the WebClass designer, or you can import existing HTML pages to use as webitems.

Using the WebClass Designer

The WebClass designer is a design-time tool in Visual Basic that enables you to quickly create and modify the webitems that represent the pages in your application. The WebClass designer contains two panels. The Treeview panel on the left displays the webitems that make up the webclass. The Details panel on the right displays information about the currently selected item in the Treeview panel.

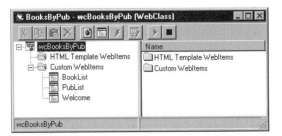

Adding Webitems to a Webclass

To add pages to your application, you add webitems to your webclass. Each webitem represents one page in your application. You can either create custom webitems or import existing HTML pages to use as webitems.

▶ **To create a custom webitem**

1. On the WebClass toolbar, click the **Add Custom WebItem** toolbar button.

A new webitem appears at the end of the list of custom webitems in the Treeview panel of the WebClass designer.

2. Type the name for the new webitem.

▶ **To import an existing HTML page as a webitem**

1. On the WebClass toolbar, click the **Add HTML Template WebItem** toolbar button.

   The **Add HTML Template** dialog box appears.

2. Select the HTML page you want to add as a webitem, and click **Open**.

   A new webitem appears at the end of the list of HTML template webitems in the Treeview panel of the WebClass designer. In the Details panel, the tags in the HTML page are listed as objects you can use in your code.

3. Type the name for the new webitem.

Writing Code in a Webclass

A webclass is a Visual Basic COM component that sends information to a Web browser from an Internet server. You use the built-in events of the webclass and the Active Server Page object model to respond to Web browser requests. Webitems in your webclass also have events, properties, and methods that you can use to define the functionality of your application. You can also add custom events to webitems.

Sending Information to the Web Browser

You use the Active Server Page object model in your COM component to communicate with the Web browser. In custom webitems, you use the **Write** method of the **Response** object to write string information to the Web browser. The following example code writes a heading to the Web browser:

```
Response.Write "<H1>Welcome to State University Bookstore</H1>"
```

For more information about the **Response** object, read the article "Response Object" in Platform SDK Help.

In HTML template webitems, you use the **WriteTemplate** method of the webitem to write the entire contents of the webitem to the Web browser. The following example code writes the contents of the webitem named **Welcome** to the Web browser:

```
Welcome.WriteTemplate
```

For more information about the **WriteTemplate** method, read the article "WriteTemplate Method" in Visual Basic Help.

For information about the different kinds of webitems you can use in a webclass, see "Working with the WebClass Designer" on page 347 in this chapter.

Using the Start Event of a Webclass

A webclass has several built-in events, including **Initialize, Start,** and **Terminate.** The **Start** event fires when the .asp file associated with the IIS application creates an instance of the webclass on the Web server.

Default code in the **Start** event uses the **Response** object to write out HTML in response to the Web client's request. The following sample code shows the default **Start** event code. To copy this code for use in your own projects, see "Webclass Start Event" on the accompanying CD-ROM.

```
Private Sub WebClass_Start()
  Dim sQuote As String
  sQuote = Chr$(34)
  'Write a reply to the user
  With Response
      .Write "<HTML>"
      .Write "<body>"
      .Write "<h1><font face=" & sQuote & "Arial" & sQuote & _
              ">WebClass1's Starting Page</font></h1>"
      .Write "<p>This response was created in the Start event of
WebClass1.</p>"
      .Write "</body>"
      .Write "</html>"
  End With
End Sub
```

You can add code to the **Start** event of your webclass to write directly to the Web browser or to navigate to the first webitem in your application.

Navigating Between Webitems in a Webclass

You use the **NextItem** property of the webclass to navigate between webitems in your application. When you navigate to a webitem using **NextItem**, a **Respond** event is fired for that webitem. You write code in the **Respond** event to display the next page to the user.

You may also want to provide a hyperlink in one webitem that jumps to another webitem in your webclass. To do this, you need a Uniform Resource Locator (URL) for that webitem, but you won't know the value of the hyperlink at design time. Use the **URLFor()** function to generate a hyperlink that points to another webitem at run time.

The following sample code uses the **NextItem** property of a webclass, the **Respond** event of a webitem, and the **URLFor()** function to enable navigation between webitems. To copy this code for use in your own projects, see "Navigating in a Webclass" on the accompanying CD-ROM.

```
Private Sub WebClass_Start()

    Set NextItem = Welcome

End Sub

Private Sub Welcome_Respond()

    With Response
        .Write "<HTML>"
        .Write "<BODY>"
        .Write "<H1>Welcome to State University Bookstore</H1>"
        .Write "<BR>"
        .Write "<A HREF=" & WebClass.URLFor(PubList) & ">Click here
to see the list of Publishers.</A>"
        .Write "<BR>"
        .Write "<A HREF=" & WebClass.URLFor(Welcome) & ">Home
Page</A>"
        .Write "</BODY>"
        .Write "</HTML>"
    End With

End Sub
```

Using Custom Events in a Webitem

You can also pass an event argument with the **URLFor()** function to specify a custom event that the webitem can handle. When a specific event argument is passed by the **URLFor()** function, it is handled by a built-in event in the webitem called **UserEvent**.

Custom events that you add to a webitem do not have to be declared. You just need to add code to the **UserEvent** event to handle the custom event arguments you expect to use. Anything that you can manipulate in the **UserEvent** code can be passed as an event name, even dynamically created information such as the key to a record in a database.

The following example code raises a custom event named **Status** for the webitem named **StatusInfo**:

```
Reponse.Write "<A HREF=" & WebClass.URLFor(StatusInfo, "Status") &
">Click here to get the Status</A>"
```

Using an IIS Application

You can test and debug your IIS application using the same powerful debugging tools that you are accustomed to using in Visual Basic. When you run your application from the Visual Basic environment, the HTML pages that act as the user interface are opened in Internet Explorer. However, you will still debug your code using the Visual Basic Integrated Development Environment (IDE).

Deploying an IIS Application

When you compile your application, Visual Basic generates a .dll file and a simple .asp file that instantiates your COM component on the Internet server. You can use the Package and Deployment Wizard to package your application for distribution. The wizard compresses the COM component and any supporting files into a .cab file, and provides you the opportunity to mark the component as safe. For information about marking components as safe, read the article "Safety Settings for ActiveX Components" in Visual Basic Help.

You can use the same wizard to deploy your .cab file and .asp file to a server on a network or to a folder. For more information about using the Package and Deployment Wizard, see "Deploying an Application" on page 307 in Chapter 9, "Optimizing and Deploying Applications."

Practice: Creating an IIS Application

In this practice exercise you will create an IIS application.

> **Note** To use the IIS Application project template, you must have Internet Information Server or Personal Web Server installed on your computer. You can obtain either of these services by installing the NT Option Pack that is included on the Visual Basic CD.

▶ **Create an IIS Application project**

1. Open Visual Basic and create a new project with the IIS Application project template.

2. In the project window, in the Designers folder, double-click **WebClass1**.

3. Add a custom webitem to the webclass. Name it **Welcome**.

4. Open the code module for the webclass.

5. Locate the **Start** event of the webclass.

6. Remove the default starting code, and add code that sets the **NextItem** property of the webclass to the Welcome webitem.

7. Locate the **Respond** event of the Welcome webitem.

8. Add code that uses the **Response** object to write a welcome message back to the web browser.

9. Run the application and test your work.

▶ **Navigate between webitems**

1. Add a custom webitem to the webclass. Name it **ShowDetails**.

2. In the **Respond** event of the Welcome webitem, add code to write a hyperlink to the ShowDetails webitem. Your code should resemble the following:

```
Response.Write "<A HREF=" & WebClass.URLFor(ShowDetails) &
">Details Page</A>"
```

3. In the **Respond** event of the ShowDetails webitem, add code to write a message back to the Web browser.

4. Run the application and test your work.

Self-Check Questions

To see the answers to the Self-Check Questions, see Appendix A.

1. Which of the following methods or events of the WebBrowser control do you use to display status information during a Web page download?

A. The **Navigate** method

B. The ProgressChange event

C. The NavigateComplete event

D. The **Refresh** method

2. Why should you create your Internet or intranet application as an Active document?

A. Widely available container

B. Immediate visual feedback

C. Execution on a local computer

D. All of the above

3. In a DHTML application, what must you do before you can write code to the elements on your HTML page?

A. Save your HTML page in an external file.

B. Specify a **className** in the Properties window for each element you want to treat as an object in your code.

C. Specify an **Id** in the Properties window for each element you want to treat as an object in your code.

D. Save your HTML page as part of the Visual Basic project.

4. Which project template should you use to create a Web application that performs its processing on the Internet server?

A. DHTML Application

B. ActiveX Document EXE

C. ActiveX Document DLL

D. IIS Application

5. Which of the following lines of code would you use to write the contents of the current HTML template webitem, named Welcome, to the Web browser?

A. Welcome.WriteTemplate

B. Set Me.NextItem = Welcome

C. Response.Write "<H1>Welcome</H1>"

D. Response.Write "<A HREF=" & Me.UrlFor(Welcome).& ">Welcome</A>"

Appendix A:
Self-Check Answers

Chapter 1

1. **You want to display the message "This is a text box" in a text box named txtMyBox by setting the value of the Text property with the following code:**

```
txtMyBox.Text = "This is a text box"
```

By mistake, you enter the code shown below:

```
txtMyBox = "This is a text box"
```

What is the result?

A. "This is a text box" is stored in a string variable named txtMyBox.

   Incorrect

   If you don't specify a property name when assigning a value to a control, you set the default property of the control.

B. The **Text** property of txtMyBox is set to "This is a text box".

   Correct

   The **Text** property of a text box is the default property.

C. The **Name** property of txtMyBox is set to "This is a text box".

   Incorrect

   If you don't specify a property name when assigning a value to a control, you set the default property of the control. The default property of a text box is not the **Name** property.

D. The **DataField** property of txtMyBox is set to "This is a text box".

   Incorrect

   If you don't specify a property name when assigning a value to a control, you set the default property of the control. The default property of a text box is not the **DataField** property.

For more information, see *Setting Properties*, page 10.

2. When creating a menu, how do you create a menu separation bar?

A. In the **Caption** text box, enter an ampersand (&).

   Incorrect

   An ampersand (&) in a menu item will make the letter after it the access key.

B. Select the **Menu Separator** check box.

   Incorrect

   There is no check box to indicate a menu separator.

C. In the **Caption** text box, enter a hyphen (-).

   Correct

   A hyphen (-) as the caption of a menu will create a menu separator.

D. In the **Caption** text box, enter the text "Separator".

   Incorrect

   Entering the text "Separator" as a caption will add a menu with that name.

For more information, see *Adding a Menu*, page 19.

3. Which line of code will enable an error trap and send code execution to an error handler to handle any run-time errors?

A. On Error HandleErrors

   Incorrect

   This statement will cause a syntax error.

B. On Error Goto 0

   Incorrect

   This statement will turn off error handling.

C. On Error Resume Next

   Incorrect

   This statement will establish inline error handling.

D. On Error Goto RunTimeErrorHandler

   Correct

   This statement will send execution after an error to an error trap called RunTimeErrorHandler.

For more information, see *Handling Run-Time Errors*, page 23.

4. What is the purpose of the .vbg file in a Visual Basic project?

A. The .vbg file contains information about the forms and modules in the current project.

Incorrect

Information about the files in a Visual Basic project are stored in the .vbp file.

B. The .vbg file contains information about the most recent projects you've worked on.

Incorrect

The recent project list is not stored in the .vbg file.

C. The .vbg file contains information about the projects in the current group.

Correct

The .vbg file stores information about the different projects in the project group.

D. The .vbg file contains a list of the most recent files you've opened.

Incorrect

The recent file list is not stored in the .vbg file.

For more information, see *Understanding the Files in a Visual Basic Project*, page 3.

5. Which Visual Basic debugging tool is used to monitor a particular variable or expression?

A. Watch window

Correct

The Watch window can monitor variables or expressions.

B. Breakpoint

Incorrect

Breakpoints will pause code execution.

C. Immediate window

Incorrect

The Immediate window can be used to evaluate variables or expressions, but will not monitor them if they change.

D. Call Stack dialog box

Incorrect

The Call Stack dialog box can be used to determine the procedures called during application execution.

For more information, see *Tools for Debugging*, page 22.

6. Why would you want to enter Break mode?

A. You want to step through a section of code line by line.

Incorrect

This is one reason to enter Break mode.

B. You want to interrogate all of the properties of an object at run time.

Incorrect

This is one reason to enter Break mode.

C. You want to change the value of a variable to test different scenarios.

Incorrect

This is one reason to enter Break mode.

D. All of the above.

Correct

All of the choices are ways to enter Break mode.

For more information, see *Tools for Debugging*, page 22.

7. How do you add a pre-built ActiveX control to the Toolbox?

A. On the **Project** menu click **Add User Control**. In the **Add User Control** dialog, select the control to include, and then click **OK**.

Incorrect

Clicking **Add User Control** on the **Project** menu will add a new User Control to the project.

B. Right click the Toolbox, and then click **Add Tab**.

Incorrect

Clicking **Add Tab** on the right mouse menu for the Toolbox will add a tab to the Toolbox.

C. On the **Project** menu click **Components**. In the Components dialog, select the control to include, and then click **OK**.

Correct

You add ActiveX controls to the Toolbox using the Components dialog.

D. On the **Project** menu click **References**. In the References dialog, select the control to include, and then click **OK**.

Incorrect

The References dialog is used to add references to COM components, not ActiveX controls.

For more information, see *Using Controls*, page 9.

Chapter 2

1. **When using the Data Environment designer, before you create a new command, you must first create:**

A. A parent command.

Incorrect

A parent command is only needed when creating a command hierarchy.

B. An ODBC data source.

Incorrect

A new command could be based on OLE DB instead of ODBC.

C. A connection to a data source.

Correct

You must have a connection to a data source before you can create a command for that connection.

D. A project group.

Incorrect

A Data Environment could be in a project that is not based on a project group.

For more information, see *Creating a Command*, page 49.

2. When using the Query Builder to create a query for a new command, what window do you click and drag tables from?

A. The Data Environment Designer window

Incorrect

The Data Environment window displays connections and commands.

B. The Command Properties window

Incorrect

The Command Properties window is one place you can open the Query Builder.

C. The Database Designer window

Incorrect

With the Database Designer window you can change the structure of your database.

D. The Data View window

Correct

The Data View window displays the objects that you can use to visually create queries.

For more information, see *Creating a Command*, page 49.

3. Which of the following data access methods is an OLE DB Consumer?

A. ADO

Correct

ADO is the interface that applications use to consume OLE DB data.

B. DAO

Incorrect

DAO is the interface to Jet and ODBC data.

C. RDO

Incorrect

RDO is the interface to remote ODBC data.

D. Jet

Incorrect

Jet is the database engine for Microsoft Access.

For more information, see *Understanding OLE DB*, page 40.

4. With the Data Environment, you can create commands that are related to each other. Which control can you use on a form to display the results of the command?

A. Microsoft FlexGrid control

Incorrect

The Microsoft FlexGrid control does not display related commands.

B. Microsoft Hierarchical FlexGrid control

Correct

The Microsoft Hierarchical FlexGrid control can be used to display the data returned by a command hierarchy.

C. Microsoft ADO Data control

Incorrect

The Microsoft ADO Data control is used as a data source.

D. Microsoft DataGrid control

Incorrect

The Microsoft DataGrid control does not display related commands.

For more information, see *Relating Commands*, page 52.

5. Which of the following properties does not need to be set when binding a control to a single field from a command in a Data Environment?

A. DataSource

Incorrect

The **DataSource** property must be set to the Data Environment name.

B. DataMember

Incorrect

The **DataMember** property must be set to the command name.

C. DataFormat

Correct

The **DataFormat** property is not a requirement for data binding.

D. DataField

Incorrect

The **DataField** property must be set to the name of the field in the command to which this control will be bound.

For more information, see *Creating Bound Forms*, page 54.

6. Which of the following is not an advantage of Format objects?

A. Format objects will save the data format in the database.
Correct

Using Format objects will not save data formatting in a database.

B. You can set formats either through code or at design time.
Incorrect

Formats can be set at design time and run time.

C. Format objects give you additional formatting types that are not supported by the Format function.
Incorrect

You can use Format objects to format Boolean, Binary, Object, Picture, and Checkbox types that are not supported by the **Format** function.

D. Format objects have **Format** and **Unformat** events that allow closer control over data formatting.
Incorrect

You can write code to a Format object's **Format** and **UnFormat** events for closer control over data formatting.

For more information, see *Using Format Objects*, page 58.

Chapter 3

1. How can you create a read-only property for a class?

A. Define a **Property Get** procedure and define a **Property Let** procedure with no arguments.
Incorrect

Arguments have no bearing on a property's availability.

B. Define a **Property Get** procedure and a **Property Let** procedure.

Incorrect

A property with both **Property Get** and **Property Let** procedures will be read-write.

C. Define a **Property Get** procedure without a **Property Set** or **Property Let** procedure.

Correct

Properties with only a **Property Get** procedure are read only.

D. Define a **Property Set** or **Property Let** procedure without a **Property Get** procedure.

Incorrect

Properties with only a **Property Set** or **Property Let** procedure are write only.

For more information, see *Creating Properties*, page 85.

2. How can you make a property that is an Object data type writeable?

A. Define a **Property Get** procedure and a **Property Let** procedure.

Incorrect

To make a non-object type property read-write, use a **Property Get** and **Property Let** procedure.

B. Define a **Property Set** procedure and a **Property Let** procedure.

Incorrect

You can not have both a **Property Set** and a **Property Let** procedure for the same property.

C. Define a **Property Get** procedure without a matching **Property Set** or **Property Let** procedure.

Incorrect

Properties with only a **Property Get** procedure are read-only regardless of the data type.

D. Define a **Property Get** procedure and a **Property Set** procedure.

Correct

Object properties are written using the **Property Set** procedure.

For more information, see *Creating Properties*, page 85.

3. Which of the following statements is true of class modules?

A. Only one class module can exist in a project.

Incorrect

Several class modules can exist in a single project.

B. Class modules provide functionality in the form of objects, and each class module defines one type of object.

Correct

A class module (.cls file) is similar to a standard code module (.bas file) in that it contains functionality that can be used by other modules within the application. The difference is that a class module provides functionality in the form of an object. Each class module defines one type of object.

C. Class modules contain methods that can be called only from other class modules.

Incorrect

All other modules within an application can use the properties, methods, and events of an object defined by a class.

D. You have access only to the methods of an object defined by a class module.

Incorrect

You have access to the properties, methods, and events of an object defined by a class module.

For more information, see *What Is a Class Module?*, page 76.

4. The example code below declares an event procedure that passes parameters to a client by value and by reference:

```
Public Event LimitChanged(ByVal iID As Integer, ByRef iLimit As
Integer)
```

What is the result if these parameters are changed when the event is handled?

A. If the **iLimit** argument is changed, the component will see the change.

Correct

The **iLimit** argument is passed by reference, so the value can be changed when the event is handled.

B. If the **iLimit** argument is changed, the component will not see the change.

Incorrect

If the **iLimit** argument were passed by value, the component would not see any changes to the value.

C. If the **iID** argument is changed, the component will see the change.

Incorrect

The **iID** argument is passed by value, so the component will not see any change to the value.

D. If the **iID** and **iLimit** arguments are both changed, the component will see both changes.

Incorrect

The **iID** argument is passed by value, so the component will not see any change to the value.

For more information, see *Adding Events to a Class*, page 90.

5. Why should you use COM components in your application?

A. COM components can be reused.

Incorrect

Reuse is one benefit of using COM components.

B. COM components hide programming complexity from other programmers.

Incorrect

Reduced complexity is one benefit of using COM components.

C. COM components make it easier for you to revise and update your applications.

Incorrect

Easier updating is one benefit of using COM components.

D. All of the above.

Correct

All of these are benefits of using COM components.

For more information, see *Advantages of Using COM Components*, page 75.

Chapter 4

1. Which action will create a design-time instance of an ActiveX control?

A. Running an application containing the control

Incorrect

This destroys the design-time instance of the control and creates a run-time instance. A design-time instance of a control is created when a control is placed on a form, and when you end an application containing a control at design time.

B. Closing a form containing the control

Incorrect

The design-time instance of an ActiveX control is destroyed when you close the form containing the control. Ending an application containing the control at design time and placing a control on a form creates a design-time instance of an ActiveX control.

C. Ending an application containing the control

Correct

A design-time instance of a control is created when you end an application containing the control and the form is opened in Visual Basic's design environment. A design-time instance will also be created when you place a control on a form.

D. Running a compiled application containing the control

Incorrect

Running a compiled application containing an ActiveX control creates a run-time instance of the control. A design-time instance is created when the control is placed on a form, and when you end an application containing the control at design time.

For more information, see *UserControl Events*, page 118.

2. How do you set up a property to be data-bound?

A. In the **Procedure Attributes** dialog box, check the **Property is data bound** check box for the data-bound property.

Correct

You set up data binding attributes for properties of controls in the **Procedure Attributes** dialog box.

B. Add the ADO Data control to your **UserControl** object.

Incorrect

When you data-bind a property of an ActiveX control, you enable that control to work with an ADO Data control or other data source in the application containing the control.

C. In the **Initialize** event of your control, connect to a known data source.

Incorrect

When you data-bind a property of an ActiveX control, you enable that control to work with an ADO Data control or other data source in the application containing the control.

D. Declare the data-bound property with the keyword **Data**.

Incorrect

Data is not a keyword.

For more information, see *Making a Control Bindable*, page 149.

3. What is the function of the code shown below?

```
Public Event UserNameKeyPress(KeyAscii As Integer)

Private Sub txtUserName_KeyPress(KeyAscii As Integer)
    RaiseEvent UserNameKeyPress(KeyAscii)
End Sub
```

A. It handles the **KeyPress** event for the **txtUserName** text box.

Incorrect

Although this code does handle the **KeyPress** event for the txtUserName text box, that is not the main function of the code.

B. It raises a **KeyPress** event whenever a user types in the **txtUserName** text box on the **UserControl**.

Incorrect

This code does not raise the event called **KeyPress**.

C. It raises a custom event, **UserNameKeyPress**, when a user types in the **txtUserName** text box.

Correct

This code raises a custom event, **UserNameKeyPress**, when the user types into the txtUserName text box.

D. It declares and raises an event for the **txtUserName** text box.

Incorrect

This code declares and raises an event for the **UserControl** object.

For more information, see *Raising Control Events*, page 132.

4. How do you notify Visual Basic that properties on a property page have changed?

A. Use the **Count** property of the **SelectedControls** collection to determine if the returned value is greater than one.

Incorrect

The **Count** property of the **SelectedControls** collection is used to determine whether multiple controls are selected.

B. Set the **Changed** property of the **PropertyPage** object to **True**.

Correct

Setting the **PropertyPage** object's **Changed** property to **True** notifies Visual Basic that properties have changed.

C. Add code to the **SelectionChanged** event.

Incorrect

The **SelectionChanged** event occurs when a property page is opened and when the list of selected controls changes.

D. Use the **WriteProperties** method of the **PropertyBag** object.

Incorrect

The **WriteProperties** method of the **PropertyBag** object saves the state of an object.

For more information, see *Implementing Property Page Behavior*, page 144.

5. When a user closes a property page, how do you write changed property values back to the currently selected controls?

A. Add code to the **ApplyChanges** event.

Correct

The **ApplyChanges** event is used to write any changed property values back to the currently selected controls.

B. Use the Connect Property Pages dialog box.

Incorrect

The **Connect Property Pages** dialog box is used to assign one or more property pages to a control.

C. Set the **PropertyPage** object's **Changed** property to **True**.

Incorrect

This will notify Visual Basic that properties have changed and enable the **Apply** button on the **Property Pages** dialog box.

D. Add code to the **SelectionChanged** event.

Incorrect

The **SelectionChanged** event is used to set the values of the controls on a property page that display property values for editing.

For more information, see *Implementing Property Page Behavior*, page 144.

6. How do you make a UserControl object a Data Source control?

A. Set the **DataSource** property of the control to the data source object.

Incorrect

The **DataSource** property of an ActiveX control is used to bind the control to data.

B. Write a function in the **UserControl** object called **GetDataMember**.

Incorrect

You will implement an event of the **UserControl** object called **GetDataMember** to return the data the control provides.

C. Drag the **UserControl** object into the Data Environment.

Incorrect

You can not drag a **UserControl** object into the Data Environment.

D. Set the **DataSourceBehavior** property of the control to **vbDataSource**.

Correct

Setting the **DataSourceBehavior** property of the control to **vbDataSource** will enable the control to provide data.

For more information, see *Creating a Data Source Control*, page 153.

Chapter 5

1. Which of the following code examples turns off a filter?

   A. rsStudents.Filter = " "

      Incorrect

      An empty string does not disable a filter.

   B. rsStudents.Filter = Nothing

      Incorrect

      Setting the filter property to Nothing does not disable a filter.

   C. rsStudents.Filter = adFilterNone

      Correct

      Using the adFilterNone constant disables an existing filter.

   D. rsStudents.Filter = adDisableFilter

      Incorrect

      adDisableFilter is not a supported constant.

For more information, see *Filtering Records*, page 189.

2. Which of the following is not a component of the ADO object model?

   A. TableDef

      Correct

      The **TableDef** object is part of DAO. It is not part of ADO.

   B. Recordset

      Incorrect

      The **Recordset** object is part of ADO.

   C. Connection

      Incorrect

      The **Connection** object is part of ADO.

   D. Command

      Incorrect

      The **Command** object is part of ADO.

For more information, see *Understanding the ADO Object Model*, page 165.

3. Which cursor location must be used when implementing a disconnected recordset?

A. Server-side

Incorrect

You cannot use a server-side cursor when creating a disconnected recordset.

B. Client-side

Correct

You must use a client-side cursor when creating a disconnected recordset.

C. Dynamic

Incorrect

Dynamic cursors do not specify the cursor location.

D. Static

Incorrect

Static cursors do not specify the cursor location.

For more information, see *Creating a Disconnected Recordset Object*, page 196.

4. Which Recordset method is used to save changes to a data source?

A. AddNew

Incorrect

AddNew is used to create a new record, but it does not save the new record to the data source.

B. Save

Incorrect

Save does not update changes to a data source.

C. Update

Correct

The **Update** method saves changes back to a data source.

D. Edit

Incorrect

The **Edit** method is not supported by the ADO **Recordset** object.

For more information, see *Using a Recordset*, page 194.

5. Which method is used to add a new field to a dynamic recordset?

A. Update

Incorrect

The **Update** method is not used to add new fields to a recordset.

B. Insert

Incorrect

The **Insert** method is not supported by the ADO **Recordset** object.

C. AddNew

Incorrect

The **AddNew** method is not used to add new fields to a recordset.

D. Append

Correct

Use the **Append** method to add a new field to a dynamic recordset.

For more information, see *Creating Dynamic Recordsets*, page 201.

6. Which two lines of code bind a text box to a Recordset object?

A. `Set txtStudentCity.DataSource = rsStudent`
   `txtStudentCity.DataField = "City"`

Correct

Both the **DataSource** and **DataField** properties must be set.

B. `Set txtStudentCity.DataSource = rsStudent`
   `txtStudentCity.Text = "City"`

Incorrect

You do not set the text property when binding controls to a recordset.

C. `Set txtStudentCity.Text = rsStudent`
   `txtStudentCity.DataField = "City"`

Incorrect

You do not set the text property when binding controls to a recordset.

D. `Set txtStudentCity.DataField = rsStudent`
   `txtStudentCity.DataSource = "City"`

Incorrect

The **DataSource** property must be set to the object and the **DataField** property must be set to the field name.

For more information, see *Presenting Data to the User*, page 184.

Chapter 6

1. **Which of the following cursors should you use to provide constant live access to the data?**
   A. Keyset cursor

      Incorrect

      A keyset cursor stops providing access to new records after it is fully populated.

   B. Dynamic cursor

      Correct

      Only the dynamic cursor provides live access to the data. However, it uses the most overhead.

   C. Static cursor

      Incorrect

      Static cursors do not provide live access to the data. You must close and reopen the cursor to refresh the data.

   D. Forward-only cursor

      Incorrect

      You can only move forward in a forward-only cursor, and therefore you cannot access previous records to see if they have changed.

   For more information, see *Choosing a Cursor Type*, page 218.

2. **What happens when a referential integrity violation occurs?**
   A. Your application will continue to execute.

      Incorrect

      If a referential integrity violation occurs, your application will receive a run-time error.

B. You will be prompted to ignore the error and continue working in the application.

Incorrect

If a referential integrity violation occurs, your application will receive a run-time error. Depending on the data source, the command that violates the integrity will fail.

C. The data source will retain its original state and your application must respond accordingly.

Correct

If this type of error occurs, the data source will retain its original state and your application must respond accordingly.

D. The data source accepts the change and your application receives an error message.

Incorrect

If a referential integrity violation occurs, your application will receive a run-time error. Depending on the data source, the command that violates the integrity will fail.

For more information, see *Handling Referential Integrity Errors*, page 230.

3. Transactions can only be managed from which of the following objects?

A. Connection object.

Correct

Only the **Connection** object allows you to manage transactions.

B. **Command** object.

Incorrect

The **Command** object does not support transaction management.

C. Recordset object.

Incorrect

The **Recordset** object does not support transaction management.

D. ADO does not support transactions.

Incorrect

ADO does support transaction management, however, only one object provides this functionality.

For more information, see *Using Database Transactions*, page 226.

4. Which of the following is NOT a feature of SQL Server integrated security?

A. Windows NT groups

Incorrect

Integrated security does support Windows NT groups.

B. Windows NT user names

Incorrect

Integrated security does support Windows NT user names.

C. Non-trusted environments

Correct

Only the Standard Mode security model supports non-trusted environments.

D. Single user name/password combinations for both Windows NT and SQL Server

Incorrect

Integrated security does support single user names/password combinations.

For more information, see *Understanding SQL Server Security*, page 216.

5. Which of the following lock type options must be used with disconnected recordsets?

A. adLockPessimistic

Incorrect

adLockPessimistic is not used for disconnected recordsets.

B. adLockOptimistic

Incorrect

adLockOptimistic is not used for disconnected recordsets.

C. adLockReadOnly

Incorrect

adLockReadOnly is not used for disconnected recordsets.

D. adLockBatchOptimistic

Correct

adLockBatchOptimistic must be used with disconnected recordsets.

For more information, see *Using Record Locking*, page 225.

6. Which is NOT a benefit of stored procedures?

A. They can accept parameters.

Incorrect

Stored procedures can accept parameters.

B. They should only be called once for best performance.

Correct

One of the main benefits of a stored procedure is it performs faster on subsequent calls.

C. They can call other stored procedures.

Incorrect

Stored procedures can call other stored procedures.

D. They encapsulate business functionality.

Incorrect

Stored procedures do encapsulate business functionality, making for easier maintenance.

For more information, see *Overview of Stored Procedures*, page 235.

Chapter 7

1. Which type of binding results in the fastest execution?

A. Late

Incorrect

No information is known about the object at design time. Additional work is required by Visual Basic to access the object at run time, causing a negative impact on the client application's performance.

B. Early

Correct

Visual Basic checks the syntax of calls that use specific object variables. The compiler can produce more efficient code to access the object at run time.

C. Run-time

Incorrect

Run-time is not a type of binding.

D. Mixed

Incorrect

Mixed is not a type of binding.

For more information, see *Declaring Object Variables*, page 248.

2. Which one of the following must be done before an external COM component can be used by an application?

A. You must set a reference to the component's type library in your application.

Incorrect

Although in most cases you will set a reference to a component's type library, it is still possible to use the component from an application without setting a reference to it.

B. You must save and compile the application.

Incorrect

You do not have to save or compile an application before using a COM component.

C. The component must be registered.

Correct

Before a component can be used by another application, the component must be registered.

D. You must view the COM Component in the Object Browser.

Incorrect

Use the Object Browser to view the properties, methods, and events for a component.

For more information, see *Making the Component Available*, page 247.

3. What must you do to make sure the Visual Basic compiler can validate the syntax of a call made to an object at design time?

A. The component must be registered.

Incorrect

Components must be registered, but there is one more step before the Visual Basic compiler can validate the syntax.

B. Set a reference to the component's type library in your application.

Correct

To make the information about the component in the registry available to your Visual Basic client application, set a reference to the component's type library.

C. You must save and compile the application.

Incorrect

You do not have to save or register your application to use a component.

D. You must view the object in the Object Browser.

Incorrect

Use the Object Browser to view the properties, methods, and events for a component.

For more information, see *Making the Component Available*, page 247.

4. **Which of the following ways would you use to create an instance of an object that has been saved to a file?**

A. Use the **CreateObject** function.

Incorrect

If you must use a generic variable in your application because you do not know the specific object type until run time (late binding), use the **CreateObject** function to instantiate the class.

B. Use the **GetObject** function.

Correct

When you want to create an instance of an object that has been saved to a file, use the **GetObject** function.

C. Use the **New** keyword with the **Set** statement.

Incorrect

If you have set a reference to the type library for the external component and can use a specific object variable (early binding), then use the **New** keyword with the **Set** statement to create an instance of the class you want to use in your application.

D. Use the **MakeObject** function.

Incorrect

MakeObject is not a valid function name.

For more information, see *Creating Objects for Components*, page 250.

5. Which Visual Basic tool can you use to find out information about the properties, methods, and events of a COM component you plan to use in your application?

A. The Data View window

Incorrect

You use the Data View window to list and browse all of the database connections currently available to your project.

B. The Visual Data Manager

Incorrect

There is no tool called the Visual Data Manager.

C. The Object Browser

Correct

Use the Object Browser to view the properties, methods, and events you've created for a component.

D. The Visual Component Manager

Incorrect

The Visual Component Manager is a tool to help a team of developers share components.

For more information, see *Creating an Instance of Microsoft Internet Explorer*, page 254.

6. Which of the following declaration statements will allow you to add code to respond to events fired by a COM component?

A. `Dim SampleDoc As New Word.Document`

Incorrect

Use the **New** keyword in the declaration of a component so an instance of the component can be created the first time it is used in code.

B. `Static SampleDoc As Word.Document`

Incorrect

Use the **Static** keyword to extend the lifetime of a component beyond the lifetime of the procedure in which it was declared.

C. `Dim SampleDoc As Object`

Incorrect

Use the **Object** data type when you don't know the specific type of component.

D. `Dim WithEvents SampleDoc As Word.Document`

Correct

To receive notification of COM component events, use the **WithEvents** keyword when you declare the variable for the component.

For more information, see *Using Components*, page 253.

7. What is the name of the type library that contains the InternetExplorer class?

A. Ie4com.dll

Incorrect

There is no component called ie4com.dll.

B. Shdocvw.dll

Correct

The **InternetExplorer** class is exposed from the Microsoft Internet Controls component called Shdocvw.dll.

C. Brwser401.exe

Incorrect

There is no component called Brwser401.dll.

D. InetBrowse.dll

Incorrect

There is no component called InetBrowse.dll.

For more information, see *Creating an Instance of Microsoft Internet Explorer*, page 254.

Chapter 8

1. Which project template would you select to build an in-process COM component?

A. ActiveX Control

Incorrect

Select this template to build an ActiveX control.

B. ActiveX DLL

Correct

Select this template to build an in-process COM component.

C. ActiveX EXE

Incorrect

Select this template to build an out-of-process COM component.

D. Standard EXE

Incorrect

Select this template to build a stand-alone application.

For more information, see *In-Process vs. Out-Of-Process Components*, page 270.

2. Which action results in the registration of a COM component?

A. The COM component is run for the first time.

Incorrect

This is one action that results in the registration of a COM component.

B. The COM component is installed on a computer using Setup.

Incorrect

This is one action that results in the registration of a COM component.

C. The COM component is run with the /REGSERVER command-line argument.

Incorrect

This is one action that results in the registration of a COM component.

D. All of the above.

Correct

All of these actions result in the registration of a COM component.

For more information, see *Registering a Component*, page 278.

3. **Which of the following Instancing property settings should you choose if you want one instance of your component to provide objects to multiple-client applications?**

A. SingleUse

Incorrect

With the **SingleUse** setting, every object of a component that is created by a client application will start a new instance of the component.

B. MultiUse

Correct

With the **MultiUse** setting, one instance of a component can provide objects to many client applications.

C. Private

Incorrect

With the **Private** setting, other applications cannot create instances of a component.

D. PartialUse

Incorrect

PartialUse is not an **Instancing** property setting.

For more information, see *Setting the Instancing Property*, page 274.

4. **When raising errors from a COM component, what constant should you add to the error code you raise?**

A. vbCustomError

Incorrect

There is no constant called vbCustomError.

B. None

Incorrect

If you don't add a correct constant to your custom error code, there is no way to insure it is a unique value.

C. vbObjectError

Correct

Adding the vbObjectError constant ensures that your error numbers do not conflict with the built-in Visual Basic error numbers.

D. vbErrorFromObject

Incorrect

There is no constant called vbErrorFromObject.

For more information, see *Raising Run-Time Errors*, page 288.

5. Which of the following makes a Friend method unique?

A. It will not be available to other classes within the same component or to other client applications.

Incorrect

For a method to not be available to other classes within the same component or to other client applications, it should be declared with the Private keyword.

B. It will be available only to the other classes within the component and not to client applications.

Correct

For a method to be available only to the other classes within the component and not to client applications, it should be declared with the Friend keyword.

C. It will be available to the other classes within the component and to client applications.

Incorrect

For a method to be available to the other classes within the component and to other client applications, it should be declared with the Public keyword.

D. It will not be available to other classes within the component, but it will be available to other client applications.

Incorrect

There is no way to define this scope for a method.

For more information, see *Declaring Friend Properties and Methods*, page 275.

Chapter 9

1. You have created a Setup program for your application using the Package and Deployment Wizard. Which file creates the startup icons?

A. Setup.exe

   Incorrect

   Setup.exe copies the bootstrap files and executes setup1.exe.

B. Setup1.exe

   Correct

   Setup1.exe copies and registers application files, and creates startup icons. Setup1.exe also increments the reference count for shared files in the registry.

C. St6Unst.exe

   Incorrect

   St6Unst.exe is a removal utility that removes the application files and startup icons or groups, and decrements the reference count for shared components.

D. Setup.lst

   Incorrect

   Setup.lst contains the list of files required by your application, and contains general information such as default folders and the required disk space.

For more information, see *Understanding Setup Files*, page 311.

2. Your application uses a complicated graphic to display order status statistics for the production department of your company, and the display is updated whenever an order is entered, constructed, packaged, or shipped. What can you do to improve the performance of your application's display operations?

A. Use a picture box instead of an image control.

   Incorrect

   An image control requires less overhead than a picture box.

B. Set **AutoRedraw** to **True** so your status graphic is redrawn automatically.

   Incorrect

   This will cause your display to be redrawn every time data changes.

C. Make sure you unload rather than hide the status graphic when it is not being used so it will display more quickly when it is needed again.

Incorrect

A hidden graphic will display faster than one that must be loaded.

D. Set **AutoRedraw** to **False** and add code to refresh your status graphic.

Correct

In this scenario, your status might undergo continuous refreshing if **AutoRedraw** is set to **True**. You should set **AutoRedraw** to **False** and add code to refresh the graphic at reasonable intervals.

For more information, see *Tuning Application Performance*, page 301.

3. Your application retrieves data from text files in the form of many long strings. How can you reclaim the memory used by these strings when the data is no longer needed by your application?

A. Set the strings to " ".

Correct

You can reclaim memory from strings by setting the strings to " ".

B. Use **Erase** to remove the strings from memory.

Incorrect

Erase eliminates an array from memory.

C. Use **Remove** to erase the strings from memory.

Incorrect

Remove removes a member of a **Collection** object.

D. Use **PageStrings** to free memory and write the strings to a swap file.

Incorrect

PageStrings is not a valid Visual Basic method.

For more information, see *Tuning Application Performance*, page 301.

4. How can you retrieve an application setting from the registry?

A. Use the **GetAllSettings** function.

Incorrect

Use **GetAllSettings** to retrieve a whole section of the registry.

B. Use the **SaveSetting** function.

Incorrect

Use **SaveSetting** to write an entry to the registry.

C. Use the **GetSetting** function.

Correct

Use **GetSetting** to read a setting from the registry.

D. Use the **DeleteSetting** function.

Incorrect

Use **DeleteSetting** to remove a setting in the registry.

For more information, see *Saving Application Settings*, page 296.

5. Which of the following options does the Package and Deployment Wizard offer when packaging your application?

A. Internet Package

Incorrect

Internet Package is only one of the options the Package and Deployment Wizard offers when packaging your application.

B. Dependency File

Incorrect

Dependency File is only one of the options the Package and Deployment Wizard offers when packaging your application.

C. Standard Setup Package

Incorrect

Standard Setup Package is only one of the options the Package and Deployment Wizard offers when packaging your application.

D. All of the above

Correct

The Package and Deployment Wizard offers the options to create a Standard Setup Package, an Internet Package, or a Dependency File that lists the run-time components required by your application.

For more information, see *Packaging an Application*, page 309.

Chapter 10

1. **Which of the following methods or events of the WebBrowser control do you use to display status information during a Web page download?**

   A. The **Navigate** method

   Incorrect

   Use the **Navigate** method to specify a resource to view. The resource must be identified by a URL.

   B. The ProgressChange event

   Correct

   Use the **DownloadBegin, ProgressChange,** and **DownloadComplete** events to display status information during a Web page download.

   C. The NavigateComplete event

   Incorrect

   Use the **LocationURL** and **LocationName** properties in the **NavigateComplete** event to display the name and URL of a resource in the **WebBrowser** control.

   D. The **Refresh** method

   Incorrect

   Use the **Refresh** method to quickly reload a page that has already been displayed.

   For more information, see *Basic Operations of the WebBrowser Control,* page 329.

2. **Why should you create your Internet or intranet application as an Active document?**

   A. Widely available container

   Incorrect

   A widely available container is only one benefit of creating Active documents.

   B. Immediate visual feedback

   Incorrect

   Receiving immediate visual feedback about the layout of elements in your application is only one benefit of creating Active documents.

C. Execution on a local computer

Incorrect

Execution on a local computer is only one benefit of creating Active documents.

D. All of the above

Correct

All of these are benefits of creating Active documents.

For more information, see *Introduction to Active Documents*, page 330.

3. In a DHTML application, what must you do before you can write code to the elements on your HTML page?

A. Save your HTML page in an external file.

Incorrect

You can either choose to save your HTML page as part of the Visual Basic project or in an external file. Neither choice affects the code you write for your application.

B. Specify a **className** in the Properties window for each element you want to treat as an object in your code.

Incorrect

You do not need to specify a **className** property value for an element on your HTML page in order to write code to that element.

C. Specify an **Id** in the Properties window for each element you want to treat as an object in your code.

Correct

Before you can write code to the elements on your HTML page, you need to specify an **Id** in the Properties window for each element you want to treat as an object in your code.

D. Save your HTML page as part of the Visual Basic project.

Incorrect

You can either choose to save your HTML page as part of the Visual Basic project or in an external file. Neither choice affects the code you write for your application.

For more information, see *Creating the User Interface*, page 339.

4. Which project template should you use to create a Web application that performs its processing on the Internet server?

A. DHTML Application

Incorrect

Use the DHTML Application project template to create a Web application that performs its processing on the Web client.

B. ActiveX Document EXE

Incorrect

Use the ActiveX Document EXE project template to create an out-of-process COM component that runs within an Internet browser window.

C. ActiveX Document DLL

Incorrect

Use the ActiveX Document DLL project template to create an in-process COM component that runs within an Internet browser window.

D. IIS Application

Correct

Use the IIS Application project template to create a Web application that performs its processing on the Internet server.

For more information, see *Steps for Creating an IIS Application*, page 346.

5. Which of the following lines of code would you use to write the contents of the current HTML template webitem, named Welcome, to the Web browser?

A. `Me.WriteTemplate`

Correct

In an HTML template webitem, you use the **WriteTemplate** method of the webitem to write the entire contents of the webitem to the Web browser.

B. `Set Me.NextItem = Welcome`

Incorrect

You use the **NextItem** property of the webclass to navigate between webitems in your application.

C. `Response.Write "<H1>Welcome</H1>"`

Incorrect

You use the **Write** method of the **Response** object to write string information to the Web browser. In this example, the text "Welcome" is written to the Web browser.

D. `Response.Write "<A HREF=" & Me.UrlFor(Welcome).& ">Welcome</A>"`

Incorrect

You use the **URLFor()** function to generate a hyperlink that points to another webitem at run time.

For more information, see *Writing Code in a Webclass*, page 348.

Appendix B:
Lab Hints

Lab Hint 1.1

```
'Exit menu event procedure
Private Sub mnuFileExit_Click()
 Unload Me
End Sub

'About menu event procedure
Private Sub mnuHelpAbout_Click()
 frmAbout.Show vbModal
End Sub
```

Lab Hint 1.2

```
Private Sub txtStudentID_Change()

    ' enable the login button only if numeric student id
    If IsNumeric(txtStudentID) Then
        ' let the user click Login
        cmdLogin.Enabled = True
    Else
        ' not a valid ID - do not allow login
        cmdLogin.Enabled = False
    End If

End Sub
```

Lab Hint 1.3

```
Private Sub cmdLogin_Click()

    ' resize form to show buy button
    frmStateUMain.Height = 5350

End Sub
```

Lab Hint 1.4

```
Private Sub cmdLogin_Click()

    ' resize form to show Ch3 control
    frmStateUMain.Height = 5350

    ' enable Account menu items for all students
    mnuBuyBook.Enabled = True
    mnuGetAccountHistory.Enabled = True

    ' enable bookstore menu items if student works at bookstore
    If txtStudentID <= 5 And txtStudentID > 0 Then
        mnuUpdateInventory.Enabled = True
        mnuOutOfStockReport.Enabled = True
        mnuRefresh.Enabled = True
    End If

    ' disable txtStudentID and command button
    txtStudentID.Enabled = False
    cmdLogin.Enabled = False

End Sub
```

Lab Hint 3.1

```
Private Sub cmdLogin_Click()

    Dim stuCurrent As CStudent
    Dim iValid As Integer

    ' create an instance of the CStudent class
    Set stuCurrent = New CStudent


    ' set the property of the class
    stuCurrent.StudentID = txtStudentID

    ' validate the student
    iValid = stuCurrent.Validate
```

code continued on next page

code continued from previous page

```
            ' handle the return value from Validate
            Select Case iValid
            Case 2
                ' enable the bookstore menu items
                mnuUpdateInventory.Enabled = True
                mnuOutOfStockReport.Enabled = True
            Case 1
                ' disable the bookstore menu items
                mnuUpdateInventory.Enabled = False
                mnuOutOfStockReport.Enabled = False
            Case 0
                ' post an error message
                MsgBox "Not a valid Student ID", , "State University Book-
store"
                txtStudentID.SetFocus
                Exit Sub
            End Select

            ' enable Account menu items for all students
            mnuBuyBook.Enabled = True
            mnuGetPurchaseHistory.Enabled = True

            ' validation from Lab 1
            ' enable bookstore menu items if student works at bookstore
'           If txtStudentID <= 5 And txtStudentID > 0 Then
'               mnuUpdateInventory.Enabled = True
'               mnuOutOfStockReport.Enabled = True
'               mnuRefresh.Enabled = True
'           End If

            ' resize form to show Ch3 control
            frmStateUMain.Height = 5350

            ' disable txtStudentID and command button
            txtStudentID.Enabled = False
            cmdLogin.Enabled = False

        End Sub
```

Lab Hint 3.2

```
Private Sub cmdLogin_Click()

On Error GoTo Login_ErrorHandler

[...]

Exit Sub
Login_ErrorHandler:

    Select Case Err.Number
    Case vbObjectError + 1000, vbObjectError + 1001

        MsgBox Err.Description, , Err.Source
        txtStudentID.SetFocus
        Exit Sub

    Case Else
        ' an unknown error occured
        MsgBox "Error " & Str(Err.Number) & _
               " has occured." & vbCrLf & _
               Err.Description
    End Select

End Sub
```

Lab Hint 4.1

```
Public Sub ShowAbout()

  ' show the about box as Modal
  frmAboutCBL.Show vbModal

  ' remove the about box from memory
  Unload frmAboutCBL

End Sub
```

Lab Hint 4.2

```
'Price Property Procedures
Public Property Get Price() As Double
    Price = CDbl(Val(txtPrice.Text))
End Property

Public Property Let Price(ByVal New_Price As Double)
    txtPrice.Text = Str(New_Price)
    PropertyChanged "Price"
End Property

'BookName Property Procedures
Public Property Get BookName() As String
    BookName = txtBook.Text
End Property

Public Property Let BookName(ByVal New_BookName As String)
    txtBook.Text = New_BookName
    PropertyChanged "BookName"
End Property

'ClassName Property Procedures
Public Property Get ClassName() As String
    ClassName = txtClass.Text
End Property

Public Property Let ClassName(ByVal New_ClassName As String)
    txtClass.Text = New_ClassName
    PropertyChanged "ClassName"
End Property
```

Lab Hint 4.3

```
Private Sub cmdSetClass_Click()
  ClassBookList1.ClassName = txtTestClassName.Text
End Sub

Private Sub cmdShowClass_Click()
  MsgBox ClassBookList1.ClassName
End Sub

Private Sub cmdShowAbout_Click()
  ClassBookList1.ShowAbout
End Sub
```

Lab Hint 4.4

```
Private Sub ClassBookList1_CBLDblClick()
  MsgBox "CBLDblClick received"
End Sub
```

Lab Hint 4.5

```
Sub SetUpDataRepeater()

    ' bind the data repeater control
    '    to the command in the data environment

    ' invoke the command specifiying the parameter
    deStateUBookstore.ClassesPerStudent CInt(txtStudentID.Text)

    ' set the data source of the data repeater
    Set drClassBookList.DataSource =
deStateUBookstore.rsClassesPerStudent

    ' bind the ClassBookList properties to the recordset fields
    drClassBookList.RepeaterBindings.Add "BookName", "BookName"
    drClassBookList.RepeaterBindings.Add "ClassName", "ClassName"
    drClassBookList.RepeaterBindings.Add "Price", "Price"

    ' refresh the data repeater control
    drClassBookList.Refresh

End Sub
```

Lab Hint 4.6

```
Public Property Set Font(ByVal New_Font As Font)

    Set UserControl.Font = New_Font
    PropertyChanged "Font"

    ' set the font for the constituents
    Set txtBook.Font = UserControl.Font
    Set txtClass.Font = UserControl.Font
    Set txtPrice.Font = UserControl.Font

End Property
```

Lab Hint 5.1

```
Private cnStateUBookstore As ADODB.Connection

Private Sub Class_Initialize()

    ' create new connection object
    Set cnStateUBookstore = New ADODB.Connection

    ' open the connection
    With cnStateUBookstore
        .Provider = "SQLOLEDB"
        .ConnectionString = "User ID=sa;Password=;" & _
                            "Data Source=MSERIES1;" & _
                            "Initial Catalog=StateUBookstore"

        .Open
    End With

End Sub

Private Sub Class_Terminate()

    ' close the connection
    cnStateUBookstore.Close

    ' release the connection variable
    Set cnStateUBookstore = Nothing

End Sub
```

Lab Hint 5.2

```
Public Function Authorize(iStudentID As Integer) As Boolean

    ' this method will determine if the student can
    '    purchase a book at this price.
    ' the student's account balance must stay under $500

    Dim rsAccountBalance As ADODB.Recordset
    Dim dBalance As Double
    Dim dPotentialBalance As Double
    Dim strWarning As String

    ' create the recordset object
    Set rsAccountBalance = New ADODB.Recordset

    ' open the recordset using the argument for the Student ID
        rsAccountBalance.Open "Select AccountBalance from Students
    where StudentID = " & Str(iStudentID), cnStateUBookstore,
    adOpenStatic, adLockReadOnly

    ' get the account information from the record returned
    dBalance = rsAccountBalance!AccountBalance

    ' add the value of the book to the balance
    dPotentialBalance = dBalance + mvarPrice

    ' determine if the student can afford to buy the book
    Select Case dPotentialBalance
    Case Is < 450
        Authorize = True
    Case Is <= 499
        Authorize = True
        strWarning = "After this transaction, you will owe the
    University $" & Str(dPotentialBalance)

        ' raise the event that this book purchase will put them
    within $50 of the limit ($500)...
        RaiseEvent Warning(strWarning)

    Case Is >= 500
        Authorize = False
        strWarning = "Over the Limit!  You currently owe the
    University $" & Str(dBalance) & " and are not authorized to buy
    this book."
```

code continued on next page

code continued from previous page

```
        ' raise the event
         RaiseEvent Warning(strWarning)

    Case Else
        Authorize = False
    End Select

    ' close and clean up the recordset
    rsAccountBalance.Close
    Set rsAccountBalance = Nothing

End Function
```

Lab Hint 5.3

```
Public Function Debit(iStudentID As Integer) As Boolean

On Error GoTo Debit_Error_Handler

    ' this method will add the book price amount
    '   to the student's account balance.
    Dim rsStudent As ADODB.Recordset
    Dim dCurrentBalance As Double
    Dim dNewBalance As Double

    ' create the recordset object
    Set rsStudent = New ADODB.Recordset

    ' get the student record for the studentID passed in
    rsStudent.Open "Select AccountBalance from Students where
StudentID = " & Str(iStudentID), cnStateUBookstore, adOpenKeyset,
adLockOptimistic

    ' get the current balance
    dCurrentBalance = rsStudent!AccountBalance

    ' calculate the new balance
    dNewBalance = dCurrentBalance + mvarPrice

    ' update the account balance for this student
    rsStudent!AccountBalance = dNewBalance
    rsStudent.Update

    ' close and release the recordset object
    rsStudent.Close
    Set rsStudent = Nothing

    ' return success
    Debit = True

Exit Function
Debit_Error_Handler:

    RaiseEvent Warning(Err.Description)

    Debit = False

End Function
```

Lab Hint 6.1

```
Function GetBookID() As Integer

    ' call a Stored procedure to get the book ID
    '    for the book being purchased.

    Dim comGetBookID As Command
    Set comGetBookID = New Command

    With comGetBookID

        ' use the connection to SQL Server from the data
environment
        .ActiveConnection = deStateUBookstore.cnStateUBookstore

        ' set this command to be a stored procedure
        .CommandType = adCmdStoredProc

        ' set the command text to the name of the stored procedure
        .CommandText = "sp_GetBookID"

        ' set up the input parameter
        '    use CreateParameter to create the parameter object
        '    use append to add this new parameter to the command
        .Parameters.Append .CreateParameter("@BookTitle", _
                                            adVarChar, _
                                            adParamInput, _
                                            50, _
                    RTrim(drClassBookList.RepeatedControl.BookName))

        ' set up the output parameter
        .Parameters.Append .CreateParameter("@BookID", _
                                            adInteger, _
                                            adParamOutput)

        ' run the stored procedure
        .Execute

        ' return the BookID parameter from this function
        GetBookID = .Parameters("@BookID").Value

    End With

End Function
```

Glossary

action query

A query that copies or changes data. Action queries include append, delete, make-table, and update queries. Delete and update queries change existing data; append and make-table queries move existing data. In contrast, select queries return data records. An SQL pass-through query may also be an action query.

Active document

A Visual Basic application that can be viewed in another container provided by an application, such as Internet Explorer version 3.0 or later or Microsoft Office Binder. Forms created with Visual Basic can be easily converted into Active documents by using the Visual Basic ActiveX Document Migration Wizard.

Active scripting

Microsoft technology for hosting scripts in Internet Explorer and other browsers. The MS Style guide contains the following definition: "Microsoft technology that uses COM to connect third-party scripts to Microsoft Internet Explorer without regard to language and other elements of implementation."

ActiveX

The Microsoft brand name for the technologies that enable interoperability by using the Component Object Model (COM).

ActiveX control

An object that you place on a form to enable or enhance a user's interaction with an application. ActiveX controls have events and can be incorporated into other controls. These controls have an .ocx file name extension.

add-in

A customized tool that adds capabilities to the Visual Basic development environment. You select available add-ins by using the Add-In Manager dialog box, which is accessible from the Add-Ins menu.

aggregate function

A function, such as Sum, Count, Avg, and Var, that you can use to calculate totals. In writing expressions and in programming, you can use SQL aggregate functions (including the four listed here) and domain aggregate functions to determine various statistics.

aggregation

A composition technique for implementing component objects. This technique allows you to build a new object with one or more existing objects to support some or all of the new object's required interfaces.

apartment-model threading

In Visual Basic, apartment-model threading is used to provide thread safety. In apartment-model threading, each thread is like an apartment — all objects created on the thread live in this apartment, and are unaware of objects in other apartments.

append

Add objects, characters, or records to the end of a collection, recordset, or file.

append query

An action query that adds new records to the end of an existing table or query. Append queries do not return records (rows).

application object

The top-level object in an application's object hierarchy. The application object identifies the application to the system, and typically becomes active when the application starts.

application programming interface (API)

The set of commands that an application uses to request and carry out lower-level services performed by a computer's operating system.

application project

Visual Basic project that will be made into an .exe file.

asynchronous call

A function call whereby the caller does not wait for the reply.

asynchronous load

The process of loading and displaying some parts of a document or form before displaying other parts that take longer to load. HTML pages are loaded asynchronously in standard browsers in that elements that load quickly are often displayed while other elements, such as images, are still being processed.

asynchronous processing

A type of I/O in which some file I/O functions return immediately, even though an I/O request is still pending. This enables an application to continue with other processing and wait for the I/O to finish at a later time.

In asynchronous mode, the client issues a request but continues processing until a response is returned. The client may issue multiple requests and can field them in whatever order they return. Asynchronous communications are network independent, and clients can issue requests even if the network or remote system is down.

asynchronous query

A type of query in which SQL queries return immediately, even though the results are still pending. This enables an application to continue with other processing while the query is pending completion.

attached table

A table in one database is linked to another database. Data for attached tables remains in the external database where it may be manipulated by other applications.

Authentication

The level of data integrity guaranteed for communication between two computers across the network.

Automation

A COM-based technology that enables interoperability among components.

Automation object

An object that is exposed to other applications or programming tools through Automation interfaces.

Automation server

An application, type library, or other source that makes Automation objects available for programming by other applications, programming tools, or scripting languages.

banded report

A report that has separate areas that can contain text, data from table fields, calculated values, or user-defined functions as well as pictures, lines, and boxes. Examples include areas for details, headers, footers, titles, and summaries.

base URL

The URL (Uniform Resource Locator) address that brings up the first page of your IIS or DHTML application; in other words, the starting point from which users should access the application.

bind

To associate two pieces of information with one another, most often used in terms of binding a symbol (such as the name of a variable) with some descriptive information (such as a memory address, a data type, or an actual value).

binding

The process of putting an object into a running state so that operations (such as edit or play) supplied by the object's application can be invoked. The type of binding determines the speed by which an object's methods are accessed by using the object variable. See also *early bound, late bound*.

bound control

A data-aware control that can provide access to a specific column or columns in a data source. A data-aware control can be bound to a data source through its DataSource, DataMember and DataField properties. When a data source moves from one row to the next, all bound controls connected to the data source change to display data from columns in the current row.

browse

To walk through data a record or row at a time.

browser

Software that interprets the markup of HTML, formats it into Web pages, and displays it to the user. Some browsers can also contain ActiveX components, and make it possible to play sound or video files.

business object

Representations of the nature and behavior of real-world things or concepts in terms that are meaningful to the business. For example, in an application, a customer, order, product, or invoice can be represented as a business object encapsulated for manipulation by users.

business rule

The combination of validation edits, login verifications, database lookups, and algorithmic transformations which constitute an enterprise's way of doing business. Also known as business logic.

business service

The logical layer between user and data services, and a collection of business rules and functions that generate and operate upon information. They accomplish this through business rules, which can change frequently, and are thus encapsulated into components that are physically separate from the application logic itself.

by reference

A way of passing the address of an argument to a procedure instead of passing the value. This allows the procedure to access the actual variable. As a result, the variable's actual value can be changed by the procedure to which it is passed. Unless otherwise specified, arguments are passed by reference.

by value

A way of passing the value, rather than the address, of an argument to a procedure. This allows the procedure to access a copy of the variable. As a result, the variable's actual value can't be changed by the procedure to which it is passed.

.cab file

A "cabinet" file that contains the files needed to perform an Internet Component Download. You create a .cab file when you want to deploy a control, component, or application to the Web to be downloaded by users. The user's browser expands the .cab file and installs your component.

calling convention

The coding convention used to make a function call.

certificate authority

A firm that can issue a digital signature for a piece of software that a software publisher intends to deploy to the Internet for download. When a user downloads the software, the certificate authority verifies the publisher's identity.

class

The formal definition of an object. The class acts as the template from which an instance of an object is created at run time. The class defines the properties of the object and the methods used to control the object's behavior.

class identifier (CLSID)

A unique identifier (UUID) that identifies an object. An object registers its CLSID in the system registration database so that it can be loaded and programmed by other applications.

class module

A module containing the definition of a class (its property and method definitions).

class name

Defines the type of an object. Applications that support Automation fully qualify class names using either of the following syntaxes: "application.objecttype.version" or "objecttype.version", where "application" is the name of the application that supplies the object, "objecttype" is the object's name as defined in the object library, and "version" is the version number of the object or application that supplies the object, e.g., Excel.Sheet.5.

class of an object

The class or type of an object (for example, Application, WorkSheet, Toolbar).

client

Any application or component that accesses or otherwise makes use of services provided by components.

client batch cursor library

A library that provides client-side cursor support for database applications. This library supports all four types of cursors (keyset, static, dynamic, and forward-only) and provides a number of other features including the ability to dissociate connections and perform optimistic batch updates.

client/server

A term generally applied to a software architecture in which processing functions are segmented into independent collections of services and requesters on a single machine or segmented among several machines. One or more processing servers provide a set of services to other clients on the same or across multiple platforms. A server completely encapsulates its processing and presents a well-defined interface for clients.

code module

A module containing public code that can be shared among all modules in a project. A code module is referred to as a standard module in later versions of Visual Basic.

code signing

A means to certify that code downloaded over the Internet has not been tampered with. Also known as digital signing.

collection

An object that contains a set of related objects. For example, a collection named Tax Preparation Objects might contain the names of objects such as EndOfYear, RoyaltyCalc, and ExemptionCalc. An object's position in the collection can change whenever a change occurs in the collection; therefore, the position of any specific object in the collection may vary.

collection object

A grouping of exposed objects. You create collection objects when you want to address multiple occurrences of an object as a unit, such as when you want to draw a set of points.

column

The visual representation of a field in a grid. A column defines the data type, size, and other attributes of one field of a row (record) of data. All columns taken as a set define a row (record) in the database. An individual column contains data related in type and purpose throughout the table; that is, a column's definition doesn't change from row to row.

COM

See *Component Object Model*.

COM component

Physical file (for example, .exe, .dll, .ocx) that contains classes, which are definitions of objects. You can use these objects in your Visual Basic application.

commit

To make the changes in a transaction permanent.

component

Any software that supports Automation, meaning it can be used programmatically in a custom solution. This includes ActiveX controls (.ocx files), ActiveX documents, and COM components.

Component Object Model (COM)

An industry-standard architecture for object-oriented development. The Component Object Model defines interfaces on which COM components are built.

compound query

A query that is composed of at least one action query (a query that copies or changes data) and at least one select query (a query that returns a **Recordset** without changing data).

connection string

A string used to define the source of data for a database.

constituent control

Control placed on a **UserControl** object's designer.

control

A file in a Visual Basic project with an .OCX file name extension that is associated with a visible interface. The Grid and CommonDialog controls are examples of controls.

control array

A group of controls that share a common name, type, and event procedures. Each control in an array has a unique index number that can be used to determine which control recognizes an event.

cookie

A small packet of information used to store persistent state information on a user's computer.

create an instance

To create an instance of a class (instantiate); that is, to allocate and initialize an object's data structures in memory.

data binding

A notification mechanism that links control properties through the container to a data source, such as a database field.

Data control

A built-in Visual Basic control used to connect a Visual Basic application with a selected data source. Bound controls require use of the Data control as a source of data.

Data Definition Language (DDL)

The language used to describe attributes of a database, especially tables, fields, indexes and storage strategy.

data services

Support the lowest visible level of abstraction used for the manipulation of data within an application. This support implies the ability to define, maintain, access, and update data. Data services manage and satisfy requests for data generated by business services.

data source

The data the user wants to access and its associated operating system, DBMS, and network platform (if any).

data source name (DSN)

Name of a registered data source.

data-aware

Describes an application or control that is able to connect to a database.

data-definition query

An SQL-specific query that can create, alter, or delete a table, or create or delete an index in a database.

database

A set of data related to a particular topic or purpose. A database contains tables and can also contain queries and indexes as well as table relationships, table and field validation criteria and linkages to external data sources.

Database object

A Database object is a logical representation of a physical database. A database is a set of data related to a specific topic or purpose. A database contains tables and can also contain queries and indexes as well as table relationships, table and field validation criteria and linkages to external data sources.

deadlock

Occurs when one user has locked a data page and tries to lock another page that is locked by a second user who, in turn, is trying to lock the page that is locked by the first user. While such occurrences are rare, the longer that a record (or file) is locked the greater the chance of a deadly embrace.

dependent object

Dependent objects can only be accessed by using a method of a higher-level object. For example, the Cells method of the Microsoft Excel Worksheet object returns a Range object.

designer

A designer provides a visual design window in the Visual Basic development environment that enables developers to design new classes visually. Visual Basic provides built-in designers, such as the Data Environment designer and the Webclass designer.

Visual Basic also allows third parties to develop designers for use in the Visual Basic development environment. These designers are collectively known as ActiveX designers.

digital signature

A way of verifying both the contents and the source of a file available for download through the Internet. Verifying the contents allows you to check that the contents of the file you download match the contents of the file when it was made available by the developer. Verifying the source allows you to ensure that the file comes from a reputable source.

DIV

An HTML tag used to group a set of tags together for processing purposes. You can specify an ID for the DIV and refer to that in your DHTML or Visual Basic code. For example, you might use a DIV tag to specify several paragraphs and headings that should be formatted as a unit. You could then apply a style to the DIV tag and all of the items the DIV contains will be formatted identically.

dynamic cursor

A cursor where committed changes made by anyone and uncommitted changes made by the cursor owner become visible the next time the user scrolls. Changes include inserts and deletes as well as changes in order and membership.

Dynamic HTML (DHTML)

A set of innovative additions to HTML that allows page authors and developers to dynamically change the style and attributes of elements on an HTML page, as well as insert, delete, or modify elements and their text after a page has been loaded. Included as part of Internet Explorer 4.*x*.

early bound

A form of binding where object variables are declared as variables of a specific class. Object references that use early-bound variables usually run faster than those that use late-bound variables. See also *late bound*.

Error statement

A keyword used in Error Function, Error Statement, On Error Statement. Error is also a Variant subtype indicating a variable is an error value.

error trapping

An action recognized by an object, such as clicking the mouse or pressing a key, and for which you can write code to respond. Events can occur as a result of a user action or program code, or they can be triggered by the system.

error-handling routine

User-written code that deals with some kinds of errors at run time.

event

An action recognized by an object, such as clicking the mouse or pressing a key, and for which you can write code to respond. Events can occur as a result of a user action or program code, or they can be triggered by the system.

event procedure

A procedure automatically invoked in response to an event initiated by the user, program code, or system. Event procedures are private by default.

event-driven

Describes an application that responds to actions initiated by the user or program code, or that are triggered by the system.

exception handling

Where a service is able to inform their client in some uniform way that an exception was raised or encountered.

exclusive

Indicates whether a database or a table can be shared by other users in a multiuser environment. If the database or table is opened for exclusive use, it can't be shared by other users.

executable code

Code that Visual Basic translates into a specific action at run time, such as carrying out a command or returning a value. In contrast, nonexecutable code defines variables and constants.

executable file

A Windows-based application that can run outside the development environment. An executable file has an .EXE file name extension.

executable statement

A statement that Visual Basic translates into a specific action at run time. Most Visual Basic statements are executable. The main exceptions are declarations, constant definitions, comments, and user-defined type definitions.

explicit declaration

A declaration in which a variable is explicitly declared using DIM, STATIC, PUBLIC, or PRIVATE statements.

expose

To make available to other applications through Automation. An exposed object can be a document, a paragraph, a sentence, a graph, and so on.

foreign table

A database table used to contain foreign keys. Generally, you use a foreign table to establish or enforce referential integrity. The foreign table is usually on the many side of a one-to-many relationship. An example of a foreign table is a table of state codes or customer orders.

form code

All the procedures and declarations saved in the same file as a form and its controls.

form module

A file in a Visual Basic project with an .FRM file name extension that can contain graphical descriptions of a form; its controls and their property settings; form-level declarations of constants, variables, and external procedures; and event and general procedures.

form-level variable

A variable recognized by all procedures attached to a form.

FTP

File Transfer Protocol. An Internet client-server protocol for transferring files between computers.

function pointer

A stored memory location of a function's address.

Function procedure

A procedure that performs a specific task within a Visual Basic program and returns a value. A Function procedure begins with a Function statement and ends with an End Function statement.

general procedure

A procedure that must be explicitly called by another procedure. In contrast, an event procedure is invoked automatically in response to a user or system action.

GUID

Globally unique identifier used to identify objects and interfaces precisely.

handle

A unique integer value defined by the operating environment and used by a program to identify and access an object, such as a form or control.

HTML

Hypertext Markup Language. The language in which Web documents are written. This includes intranet and Internet pages.

HTML template

HTML pages designed to act as templates; some parts of the page are replaced with dynamic content before the page is displayed.

HTTP

HTTP, or Hypertext Transfer Protocol, is a communication protocol used to exchange packets of information between two computers across the Internet using a TCP/IP backbone. In an HTTP transaction, the system opens a connection between a client browser and a Web server, submits a request for data to the Web server, returns the Web server's response to the client, then closes the connection. HTTP is stateless in that no information about the request is maintained after the connection closes.

ID attribute

In HTML, an ID attribute appears inside an opening tag for an element on the page and gives a unique name to the element for use when referencing it in code or script. Both the ID attribute and the NAME attribute perform this function. In Visual Basic Internet applications, elements on a page are required to have IDs or names.

implicit declaration

Declaration that occurs when a variable is used in a procedure without previously declaring its name and type.

inner join

A join in which records from two tables are combined and added to a Recordset only if the values of the joined fields meet a specified condition. For instance, an equi-join is an inner join in which the values of the joined fields must be equal. See also *join*.

installable ISAM

A driver you can specify that allows access to external database formats such as Btrieve, dBase, Microsoft Excel, and Paradox. ISAM is an acronym for Indexed Sequential Access Method. The Microsoft Jet database engine installs (loads) these ISAM drivers when referenced by your application. The location of these drivers is maintained in the Microsoft Windows registration database.

instance

Any one of a set of objects sharing the same class. For example, multiple instances of a Form class share the same code and are loaded with the same controls with which the Form class was designed. During run time, the individual properties of controls on each instance can be set to different values.

instantiate

To create an instance of a class; that is, to allocate and initialize an object's data structures in memory. See *create an instance*.

interface

A set of semantically related functions (methods) used to manipulate data.

Internet

A global, distributed network of computers operating on TCP/IP as a base set of protocols.

intranet

A Web site or series of Web sites that belong to an organization and can be accessed only by the organization's members. Many corporations use an intranet, rather than the Internet, to offer their employees easy access to corporate information, while preventing outside access to that data.

intrinsic constant

A constant provided by an application. Visual Basic constants are listed in the Visual Basic object library and can be viewed using the Object Browser.

ISAM

Indexed Sequential Access Method.

join

A database operation that combines some or all records from two or more tables, such as an equi-join, outer join, or self-join. Generally, a join refers to an association between a field in one table and a field of the same data type in another table. You create a join with an SQL statement.

When you define a relationship between two tables, you create a join by specifying the primary and foreign table fields. When you add a table to a query, you need to create a join between appropriate fields in the SQL statement that defines the query.

key

The Windows Registry stores data in a hierarchically structured tree. Each node in the tree is called a key. Each key can contain both subkeys and data entries called values.

In a database, a key is a column used as a component of an index.

late bound

Object references are late-bound if they use object variables declared as variables of the generic Object class. Late-bound binding is the slowest form of binding, because Visual Basic must determine at run time whether or not that object will actually have the properties and methods you used in your code. See also *early bound*.

locked

The condition of a data page, Recordset object, or Database object that makes it read-only to all users except the one who is currently entering data in it.

locking

A system of ensuring that two processes do not try to affect the same record in a database at the same time.

marshaling

The processing of packaging and sending interface parameters across process boundaries.

MDI

See *multiple-document interface*.

MDI child

A form contained within an MDI form in a multiple-document interface (MDI) application. To create a child form, set its MDIChild property to True.

MDI form

A window that makes up the background of a multiple-document interface (MDI) application. The MDI form is the container for any MDI child forms in the application.

member

A constituent element of a collection, object, or user-defined type.

member function

One of a group of related functions that make up an interface.

menu bar

The horizontal bar containing the names of all the application's menus. It appears below the title bar.

method

A member function of an exposed object that performs some action on the object.

MIME type

An identification code for transmitting non-text files through Internet electronic mail. E-mail was originally designed to handle only ASCII text. However, you can send other types of data including audio, video, and other formats using MIME (Multipurpose Internet Mail Extensions) type encoding. The most common predefined MIME types include GIF and JPEG files, sound files, movie files, postscript programs, and non-ASCII character sets.

modal

Describes a window or dialog box that requires the user to take some action before the focus can switch to another form or dialog box.

modeless

Describes a window or dialog box that does not require user action before the focus can be switched to another form or dialog box.

module

A set of declarations and procedures.

module-level

Describes code in the declarations section of a module. Any code outside a procedure is referred to as module-level code. Declarations must be listed first, followed by procedures. For example:

```
Dim iCounter As Integer    'This is a module-level variable
declaration


Const RO = "Readonly" 'This is a module-level constant declaration


Type Address         'This is a module-level user-defined type
declaration


  Street As String


  State As String


End Type
```

module variable

A variable declared outside of Function, Sub, or Property procedure code. Module variables must be declared outside any procedures in the module. They exist while the module is loaded, and are visible in all procedures in the module.

multiple-document interface (MDI)

An application that provides a single parent window on the desktop which contains other open child windows in the application. When the parent window is minimized or closed, all child windows are minimized or closed with it.

multiple-document interface (MDI) application

An application that can support multiple documents from one application instance. MDI object applications can simultaneously service a user and one or more embedding containers.

multiple-object application

An application that is capable of supporting more than one class of object; for example, a spreadsheet program might support charts, spreadsheets, and macros. See also *single-object application*.

named argument

An argument that has a name that is predefined in the object library. Instead of providing values for arguments in the order expected by the syntax, you can use named arguments to assign values in any order. For example, suppose a method accepts three arguments:

```
DoSomeThing namedarg1, namedarg2, namedarg3
```

By assigning values to named arguments, you can use the following statement:

```
DoSomething namedarg3:=4,namedarg2:=5,namedarg1:=20
```

Note that the arguments need not be in their normal positional order.

non-trusted environment

An environment where authentication information is not shared. For example, SQL Server can communicate in a non-trusted environment because it can use its own security model for user authentication.

Null

A value indicating that a variable contains no valid data. Null is the result of:

♦ An explicit assignment of Null to a variable.

♦ Any operation between expressions that contain Null.

null

A value that indicates missing or unknown data. Null values can be entered in fields for which information is unknown and in expressions and queries. In Visual Basic, the Null keyword indicates a Null value. Some fields, such as those defined as containing the primary key, can't contain null values.

null field

A field containing no characters or values. A null field isn't the same as a zero-length string (" ") or a field with a value of 0. A field is set to null when the content of the field is unknown. For example, a Date Completed field in a task table would be left null until a task is completed.

object

A combination of code and data that can be treated as a unit, for example a control, form, or application. Each object is defined by a class.

An object is an instance of a class that combines data with procedures.

Object Browser

A dialog box that lets you examine the contents of an object library to get information about the objects provided.

object class

A type of object that is registered in the registration database and serviced by a particular server.

Object data type

Object variables are stored as 32-bit (4-byte) addresses that refer to objects. Using the Set statement, a variable declared as an **Object** can have any object reference assigned to it.

> **Note** Although a variable declared with **Object** type is flexible enough to contain a reference to any object, binding to the object referenced by that variable is always late (run-time binding). To force early binding (compile-time binding), assign the object reference to a variable declared with a specific class name.

object expression

An expression that specifies a particular object. This expression may include any of the object's containers. For example, if your application has an Application object that contains a Document object that contains a Text object, the following are valid object expressions:

- Application.Document.Text
- Application.Text
- Documention.Text
- Text

object library

Data stored in a .olb file or within an executable (.exe, .dll, or .ocx) that provides information used by Automation controllers (such as Visual Basic) about available Automation objects. You can use the Object Browser to examine the contents of an object library to get information about the objects provided.

object model

The definition of a hierarchy of objects that gives structure to an object-based application. By defining the relationship between objects that are part of the application, an object model organizes the objects in a way that makes programming easier.

object type

A type of object exposed by an application through Automation; for example, Application, File, Range, and Sheet. Refer to an application's documentation (Microsoft Excel, Microsoft Project, Microsoft Word, and so on) for a complete listing of available objects.

object variable

A variable that contains a reference to an object.

ODBC

See *Open Database Connectivity*.

ODBC data source

A term used to refer to a database or database server used as a source of data. ODBC data sources are referred to by their Data Source Name. Data sources can be created using the Control Panel in Windows or the RegisterDatabase method.

ODBC driver

A dynamic-link library (DLL) used to connect a specific Open Database Connectivity data source with another (client) application.

Open Database Connectivity (ODBC)

A standard protocol that permits applications to connect to a variety of external database servers or files. ODBC drivers used by the Microsoft Jet database engine permit access to Microsoft SQL Server and several other external databases.

The ODBC applications programming interface (API) may also be used to access ODBC drivers and the databases they connect to without using the Jet engine.

out of scope

When a variable loses focus or is out of scope. Scope is defined as the visibility of a variable, procedure, or object. For example, a variable declared as Public is visible to all procedures in all modules in a directly referencing project (unless Option Private Module is in effect). Variables declared in procedures are visible only within the procedure and lose their value between calls unless they are declared Static.

parameter query

A query that requires you to provide one or more criteria values, such as Redmond for City, before the query is run. A parameter query isn't, strictly speaking, a separate kind of query; rather, it extends the flexibility of other queries.

parent project

A project that contains one or more subprojects. A project can be both a parent project and a subproject at once, if it is in the middle of the project hierarchy.

pass-through query

An SQL-specific query you use to send commands directly to an SQL database server (such as Microsoft SQL Server). With pass-through queries, you work with the tables on the server instead of attaching them. Pass-through queries are used to execute SQL queries and system specific commands written using SQL dialects known only to the server.

A pass-through query may or may not return records. If it does, they are always returned in a snapshot.

persisted data

Storage of a file or object in a medium such as a file system or database so that the object and its data persist when the file is closed and then reopened at a later time.

pessimistic

A type of locking in which the page containing one or more records, including the record being edited, is unavailable to other users when you use the Edit method and remains unavailable until you use the Update method. Pessimistic locking is enabled when the Lockedits property of the Recordset object is set to True.

pointer

In programming, a variable that contains the memory location of data rather than the data itself.

primary key

One or more fields whose value or values uniquely identify each record in a table. Each table can have only one primary key. An Employees table, for example, could use the social security number for the primary key.

primary table

A database table used to contain primary keys. Generally, a primary key table is used to establish or enforce referential integrity. The primary table is usually on the one side of a one-to-many relationship with a foreign table.

Private

Private variables are available only to the module in which they are declared.

procedure

A named sequence of statements executed as a unit. For example, Function, Property, and Sub are types of procedures.

Procedure box

A list box at the upper-right of the Code and Debug windows that displays the procedures recognized for the object displayed in the Object box.

procedure call

A statement in code that tells Visual Basic to execute a procedure.

procedure-level

Describes statements located within a Function, Property, or Sub procedure. Declarations are usually listed first, followed by assignments and other executable code. For example:

```
Sub MySub()   ' This statement declares a sub procedure block.

  Dim A    ' This statement starts the procedure block.

  A = "My variable"    ' Procedure-level code.

  Debug.Print A    ' Procedure-level code.

  End Sub   ' This statement ends a sub procedure block.
```

Note In contrast to procedure-level code, module-level code resides outside any procedure blocks.

procedure stepping

A debugging technique that allows you to trace code execution one statement at a time. Unlike single stepping, procedure stepping does not step into procedure calls; instead, the called procedure is executed as a unit.

procedure template

The beginning and ending statements that are automatically inserted in the Code window when you specify a Sub, Function, or Property procedure in the Insert Procedure dialog box.

programmability

The ability of a server to define a set of properties and methods and make them accessible to Automation controllers.

programmable

Capable of accepting instructions for performing a task or operation. A programmable object (Automation object) can be manipulated programmatically with its methods and properties.

project

A group of related files, typically all the files required to develop a software component. Files can be grouped within a project to create subprojects. Projects can be defined in any way meaningful to the user(s) — as one project per version, or one project per language, for example. In general use, projects tend to be organized in the same way file directories are.

project file

A file with a .VBP file name extension that keeps track of the files, objects, project options, environment options, EXE options, and references associated with a project.

Project window

A window that displays a list of the form, class, and standard modules; the resource file; and references in your project. Files with .OCX and .VBX file name extensions don't appear in this window.

Properties window

A window used to display or change properties of a selected form or control at design time. Some custom controls have customized Properties windows.

property

A named attribute of an object. Properties define object characteristics such as size, color, and screen location, or the state of an object, such as enabled or disabled.

A property is a data member of an exposed object. Properties are set or returned by means of get and let accessor functions. See *Property procedure*.

Property list

A two-column list in the Properties window that shows all the properties and their current settings for the selected object.

Property procedure

A procedure that creates and manipulates properties for a class module. A Property procedure begins with a Property Let, Property Get, or Property Set statement and ends with an End Property statement.

property setting

The value of a property.

proxy

An interface-specific object that packages parameters for that interface in preparation for a remote method call. A proxy runs in the address space of the sender and communicates with a corresponding stub in the receiver's address space.

Public

Variables declared using the Public statement are available to all procedures in all modules in all applications unless Option Private Module is in effect; in which case, the variables are public only within the project in which they reside.

query

A formalized instruction to a database to either return a set of records or perform a specified action on a set of records as specified in the query. For example, the following SQL query statement returns records:

◆ SELECT [Company Name] FROM Publishers WHERE State = 'NY'

You can create and run select, action, crosstab, parameter, and SQL-specific queries.

query definition

A formalized instruction to a database to either return a set of records or perform a specified action on a set of records as specified in the query. For example, the following SQL query statement returns records:

SELECT CompanyName FROM Publishers WHERE State = 'NY'

record source

The underlying source of data (a table, query, or SQL statement) for a form or report.

Recordset

A logical set of records.

reference count

The number of instances of an object loaded. This number is incremented each time an instance is loaded and decremented each time an instance is unloaded. Ensures an object is not destroyed before all references to it are released.

referential integrity

Rules that you set to establish and preserve relationships between tables when you add, change, or delete records. Enforcing referential integrity prohibits users from adding records to a related table for which there is no primary key, changing values in a primary table that would result in orphaned records in a related table, and deleting records from a primary table when there are matching related records.

If you select the Cascade Update Related Fields or Cascade Delete Related Records option for a relationship, the Microsoft Jet database engine allows changes and deletions but changes or deletes related records to ensure that the rules are still enforced.

registration

The process of adding a class, container, or object to the registration database.

registration database

Or registry. A database that provides a system-wide repository of configuration and initialization information and information for containers and servers that support Automation.

remote data

Data stored on a server.

remote procedure call (RPC)

A mechanism through which applications can invoke procedures and object methods remotely across a network. Using RPC, an application on one machine can call a routine or invoke a method belonging to an application running on another machine.

reusable code

Software code written so that it can be used in more than one place.

roll back

The ability to remove uncompleted or partially completed transactions after a database or other system failure.

row

A set of related columns or fields used to hold data. A row is synonymous with a record in the Microsoft Jet database engine. A table is composed of zero or more rows of data.

run time

The time when code is running. During run time, you interact with the code as a user would.

run-time error

An error that occurs when code is running. A run-time error results when a statement attempts an invalid operation.

scope

Defines the visibility of a variable, procedure, or object. For example, a variable declared as Public is visible to all procedures in all modules in a directly referencing project (unless Option Private Module is in effect). Variables declared in procedures are visible only within the procedure and lose their value between calls unless they are declared Static.

select query

A query that asks a question about the data stored in your tables and returns a Recordset object without changing the data. Once the Recordset data is retrieved, you can examine and make changes to the data in the underlying tables. In contrast, action queries can make changes to your data, but they don't return data records.

sequential access

A type of file access that allows you to access records in text files and variable-length record files sequentially; that is, one after another.

server

An application or DLL that provides its objects to other applications. You can use any of these objects in your Visual Basic application.

services model

A way of viewing applications as a set of features or services that are used to fulfill consumer requests. By encouraging the developer to model an application as a collection of discrete services, features and functionality can be packaged for reuse, sharing, and distribution across functional boundaries.

services-based architecture

An application model in which the feature set of the business application is expressed conceptually as a collection of services. These services can be grouped based on common characteristics, for example, sematics, behavior, analysis and design techniques. Microsoft Solutions Framework (MSF) identifies three such groupings of services: user services, business services, and data services.

set

To assign a value to a property.

single document interface (SDI)

An application which displays one or more windows on the desktop, each of which can be minimized or maximized independently of each other.

single-object application

An server that exposes only one class of object.

SQL database

A database that can be accessed through use of Open Database Connectivity (ODBC) data sources.

SQL Server

A relational database engine running on a network-accessible server. SQL Servers are responsible for comprehensive management of one or more relational databases residing on the server. They are controlled by and information is passed to and from these servers by way of Structured Query Language (SQL) statements. There are two types of SQL Server: Microsoft SQL Server and Sybase SQL Server.

SQL statement/string

1. An expression that defines a Structured Query Language (SQL) command, such as SELECT, UPDATE, or DELETE, and includes clauses such as WHERE and ORDER BY. SQL strings and statements are typically used in queries, Recordset objects, and aggregate functions but can also be used to create or modify a database structure.

2. A set of commands written using a dialect of SQL used to retrieve or pass information to a relational database. SQL statement syntax is determined by the SQL Server or other relational database engine it is intended to execute on.

stack

A fixed amount of memory used by Visual Basic to preserve local variables and arguments during procedure calls.

stateless

A stateless object is an object that doesn't hold private state accumulated from the execution of one or more client calls.

Static

A Visual Basic keyword you can use to preserve the value of a local variable.

static cursor

Neither the cursor owner nor any other user can change the results set while the cursor is open. Values, membership, and order remain fixed until the cursor is closed. You can either take a "snapshot" (temporary table) of the results set, or you can lock the entire results set to prevent updates. When you take a snapshot of the results set, the results set diverges increasingly from the snapshot as updates are made.

stored procedure

A precompiled collection of SQL statements and optional control-of-flow statements stored under a name and processed as a unit.

Structured Query Language (SQL)

A language used in querying, updating, and managing relational databases. SQL can be used to retrieve, sort and filter specific data to be extracted from the database.

You can use SQL SELECT statements anywhere a table name, query name, or field name is accepted. For example, you can use an SQL statement in place of a table name in the OpenRecordset method.

Sub procedure

A procedure that performs a specific task within a program, but returns no explicit value. A Sub procedure begins with a Sub statement and ends with an End Sub statement.

subroutine

A section of code that can be invoked (executed) within a program.

synchronous call

A function call in which the caller waits for the reply before continuing. Most interface methods are synchronous calls. An operation that completes synchronously performs all of its processing in the function call made by the application. The function returns different values depending on its success or failure.

synchronous processing

When the data interface blocks until an operation is complete or at least until the first row of the results is ready. Opposite of asynchronous processing.

table

The basic unit of data storage in a relational database. A table stores data in records (rows) and fields (columns) and is usually about a particular category of things, such as employees or parts. Also called a base table.

Table object

A type of recordset that is a logical representation of a physical object within a database that contains data about a particular subject. Like all recordsets, a Table object has records (rows) and fields (columns). The Table object is outdated. It is recommended that you use the table-type Recordset instead.

three-tiered architecture

An application model in which the feature set of the business application is expressed conceptually as three layers, each of which supplies services to the adjacent layers: user presentation, core business, and data management. Note that this is a conceptual architecture; while all business applications can be expressed conceptually in terms of the these three layers, the implementation architecture may not be three layers.

transaction

A series of changes made to a database's data and schema. Mark the beginning of a transaction with the BeginTrans statement, commit the transaction using the CommitTrans statement, and undo all your changes since BeginTrans using the Rollback statement.

trigger

Record-level event code that runs after an insert, update, or delete. Different actions can be attached to the different events. Triggers run last, after rules, and don't run during buffered updates. They are most often used for cross-table integrity.

type library

A compound document file that includes information about types and objects exposed by an server. May contain any of the following:

- Information about data types
- Descriptions of one or more objects (each of these descriptions is commonly referred to as a typeinfo)
- References to type descriptions from other type libraries

You can ship a type library in any of the following forms: as a resource in a DLL; as a resource in an .EXE file; as a subfile within a compound document file (sometimes called a 'docfile'); or as a stand-alone binary file.

union query

A SQL-specific select query that creates a snapshot-type Recordset object containing data from all specified records in two or more tables with any duplicate records removed. To include the duplicates, add the keyword ALL.

For instance, a union query of the Customers table and the Suppliers table results in a snapshot-type Recordset that contains all suppliers that are also customers.

update query

An action query that changes a set of records according to criteria you specify. An update query doesn't return any records.

URL

Uniform Resource Locator. A method of indicating the location of a document or other item that is available electronically. Consists of two parts: an identifier for the protocol that should be used to retrieve the document (generally HTTP) and the address from which the document can be retrieved.

validation

The process of checking whether entered data meets certain conditions or limitations.

validation properties

Properties used to set conditions on table fields and records. Validation properties include ValidationRule, Required and AllowZeroLength.

validation rule

A rule that sets limits or conditions on what can be entered in one or more fields. Validation rules can be set for a Field or a TableDef object. Validation rules are checked when you update a record containing fields requiring validation. If the rule is violated, a trappable error results.

VBSQL

Visual Basic library for SQL Server.

WCT file

A modified copy of an HTML file that the system saves after you add an HTML template file to a webclass. The WCT file is saved in the project directory for the IIS application and acts as the source file for the webitem.

Web-based application

An application whose specific implementation technologies are chosen based on official or de facto World Wide Web standards to permit the application to run in an intranet environment or across the Internet.

webclass

A component used in IIS applications. A webclass resides on the Web server and is used to intercept HTTP requests, process associated Visual Basic code, and return a response to the browser. Webclasses contain webitems (usually HTML documents) that can be sent to the browser in response to requests.

webitem

In an IIS application, an item that can be returned to the browser as part of a response to an HTTP request. A webitem is generally an HTML page, but it can be a MIME-type file, such as an image, a .wav file, and so on.

Windows API

The Windows API (Application Programming Interface) consists of the functions, messages, data structures, data types, and statements you can use in creating applications that run under Microsoft Windows. The parts of the API you use most are code elements included for calling API functions from Windows. These include procedure declarations (for the Windows functions), user-defined type definitions (for data structures passed to those functions), and constant declarations (for values passed to and returned from those functions).

Index

A

accessing
  command results, 50
  data, 49
Active Designer files described, 3
Active documents, 268, 330
  containers, 334
  creating, 331
  migrating forms to, 333
  UserDocument object, 332
ActiveX Control Interface Wizard, 124
ActiveX controls, 3, 113, 114, 268
  adding property pages, 142, 144, 146
  classes, 114
  constituent controls, 116
  constituent control properties, 126
  container application interaction, 119
  creating, 114, 116
  customizing, 122
  data-bound controls, 148–52
  data source controls, 153
  deploying. *See* deploying ActiveX controls
  display characteristics, 121
  events, 118, 124, 132
  exposing named constants, 132
  generating code automatically, 124
  HTML templates, 319
  interfaces, 114
  licensing, 315
  methods, 124, 129
  properties, 124, 125
  property values, 130
  signing, 318

ActiveX controls (continued)
  sizing, 121
  templates, choosing, 4
  testing, 134–36
  using, 9
ActiveX Data Objects. *See* ADO
ActiveX DLL, 5
ActiveX documents, 4
ActiveX EXE, 5
adding
  ActiveX controls to HTML pages, 314
  ADO Data controls to toolbox, 57
  ADO objects to projects, 42
  Class Builder to projects, 77
  code to events, 44, 173
  commands, 44, 49
  connections, 43, 44
  controls to Toolbox, 9
  data links, 48
  data to projects, 60
  events to classes, 90
  fields to recordsets, 201
  Help, 81
  items to Webclass designer, 347
  licensing to ActiveX controls, 315
  menus, 19
  methods, 77
  methods, ActiveX controls, 129
  properties, 77
  property pages to ActiveX controls, 142, 144, 146
  records, 194
  UserDocument object to projects, 332
  Visual Component Manager to Toolbar, 282
  WebBrowser control to projects, 328

W

Microsoft®
Mastering Series
Your *Complete* Training Solution

Print Edition: Study at your own pace.

The Mastering Series Print Editions allow you to get up to speed on new technology whenever and wherever you need it. Print Editions provides in-depth, hands-on training in an affordable package. They are designed for the power user who wants to move to the next level.

▶ *More information:* **http://msdn.microsoft.com/mastering/books**

MSDN Training Online: Get in-depth coverage of the latest technology now.

Mastering Series online courses are offered by training centers around the world. They allow you to combine the best of self-study with the advantages of classroom training — without the hassles of travel and being away from work.

▶ *More information:* **http://msdn.microsoft.com/mastering/online**

Classroom Training: Learn from experienced developer/trainers.

Mastering Series instructor-led training classes are the premium way to get training. You learn in hands-on labs with detailed guidance from veteran developers, at thousands of Microsoft Certified Technical Education Centers around the world. The combination of in-depth training and experienced trainers gives you the clearest possible picture of how to use new technology in the real world.

▶ *More information:* **http://msdn.microsoft.com/mastering**

What's right for you?

If you need help sifting through the many training opportunities available for developers, the professionals at any Microsoft Certified Technical Education Center can recommend the most appropriate training program, tailored specifically for you and your needs! They'll help you decide which critical products and technologies are most important to you. And they will assist you in determining what training formats best suit your preferred learning style and resources. To find the Microsoft CTEC near you, visit the Microsoft Find Training web page at:

http://www.microsoft.com/isapi/referral/product_select.asp?train=84

Make the *Career You Deserve* with Microsoft Training Programs

Why get trained?

As a trained IT professional, you can:

▶ Take advantage of extensive opportunities in a growing industry

▶ Stay on top of changes in the industry

▶ Polish old technical skills and acquire new ones

As an IT manager, hiring trained IT professionals provides you with:

▶ Greater assurance of a job well done

▶ Improved service, increased productivity and greater technical self-sufficiency

▶ More satisfied employees and clients

What's right for you?

The professionals at any Microsoft Certified Technical Education Center can recommend the most appropriate training program, tailored specifically for you and your needs! They'll help you decide which critical products and technologies are most important to you. And they will assist you in determining what training formats best suit your preferred learning style and resources.

How do you get the best training?

With instructor-led, online, and self-paced training and instruction available at locations throughout the world and on the Web, you are sure to find what you need among our industry-renowned comprehensive solutions to give you the right method of training to produce the best results. And a combination of training formats sometimes called hybrid training may be more effective than a single methodology.

Where do you get the best training?

Choose from Microsoft Certified Technical Education Centers, Microsoft Authorized Academic Training Program institutions, Microsoft Press, and, Microsoft Seminar Online to get the job done right.

Authorized Academic Training Program

Microsoft Authorized Academic Training Program (AATP) helps full-time and part-time students in participating high schools, colleges and universities prepare for jobs that demand proficiency with Microsoft products and technologies.

For more information, go to: http://www.microsoft.com/aatp/

Microsoft Certified Technical Education Centers (Microsoft CTECs) are full-service training organizations that can deliver system support and developer instruction in a variety of flexible formats.

For more information, go to: http://www.microsoft.com/train_cert/

Microsoft Seminar Online delivers a virtual seminar experience right to your desktop, anytime, day or night.

For more information, go to: http://www.microsoft.com/seminar/

Microsoft Certified Professional Approved Study Guides (MCP Approved Study Guides), an excellent way to stay up to date on Microsoft products & technologies, are rigorously developed & reviewed to ensure adherence to certification objectives.

For more information, go to: http://www.microsoft.com/train_cert/train/mcpasg.htm/

Microsoft Press delivers "anytime, anywhere learning" via a full line of Microsoft Official Curriculum (MOC) self-paced training kits enhanced with print & multimedia that prepare you for the MCP exams.

For more information, go to: http://mspress.microsoft.com/

MICROSOFT LICENSE AGREEMENT

Book Companion CD

user manual, in "online" documentation, and/or in other Microsoft-provided materials. Any supplemental software code provided to you as part of the Support Services shall be considered part of the SOFTWARE PRODUCT and subject to the terms and conditions of this EULA. With respect to technical information you provide to Microsoft as part of the Support Services, Microsoft may use such information for its business purposes, including for product support and development. Microsoft will not utilize such technical information in a form that personally identifies you.

- **Software Transfer.** You may permanently transfer all of your rights under this EULA, provided you retain no copies, you transfer all of the SOFTWARE PRODUCT (including all component parts, the media and printed materials, any upgrades, this EULA, and, if applicable, the Certificate of Authenticity), **and** the recipient agrees to the terms of this EULA.

- **Termination.** Without prejudice to any other rights, Microsoft may terminate this EULA if you fail to comply with the terms and conditions of this EULA. In such event, you must destroy all copies of the SOFTWARE PRODUCT and all of its component parts.

3. **COPYRIGHT.** All title and copyrights in and to the SOFTWARE PRODUCT (including but not limited to any images, photographs, animations, video, audio, music, text, SAMPLE CODE, REDISTRIBUTABLES, and "applets" incorporated into the SOFTWARE PRODUCT) and any copies of the SOFTWARE PRODUCT are owned by Microsoft or its suppliers. The SOFTWARE PRODUCT is protected by copyright laws and international treaty provisions. Therefore, you must treat the SOFTWARE PRODUCT like any other copyrighted material **except** that you may install the SOFTWARE PRODUCT on a single computer provided you keep the original solely for backup or archival purposes. You may not copy the printed materials accompanying the SOFTWARE PRODUCT.

4. **U.S. GOVERNMENT RESTRICTED RIGHTS.** The SOFTWARE PRODUCT and documentation are provided with RESTRICTED RIGHTS. Use, duplication, or disclosure by the Government is subject to restrictions as set forth in subparagraph (c)(1)(ii) of the Rights in Technical Data and Computer Software clause at DFARS 252.227-7013 or subparagraphs (c)(1) and (2) of the Commercial Computer Software—Restricted Rights at 48 CFR 52.227-19, as applicable. Manufacturer is Microsoft Corporation/One Microsoft Way/Redmond, WA 98052-6399.

5. **EXPORT RESTRICTIONS.** You agree that you will not export or re-export the SOFTWARE PRODUCT, any part thereof, or any process or service that is the direct product of the SOFTWARE PRODUCT (the foregoing collectively referred to as the "Restricted Components"), to any country, person, entity, or end user subject to U.S. export restrictions. You specifically agree not to export or re-export any of the Restricted Components (i) to any country to which the U.S. has embargoed or restricted the export of goods or services, which currently include, but are not necessarily limited to, Cuba, Iran, Iraq, Libya, North Korea, Sudan, and Syria, or to any national of any such country, wherever located, who intends to transmit or transport the Restricted Components back to such country; (ii) to any end user who you know or have reason to know will utilize the Restricted Components in the design, development, or production of nuclear, chemical, or biological weapons; or (iii) to any end user who has been prohibited from participating in U.S. export transactions by any federal agency of the U.S. government. You warrant and represent that neither the BXA nor any other U.S. federal agency has suspended, revoked, or denied your export privileges.

DISCLAIMER OF WARRANTY

NO WARRANTIES OR CONDITIONS. MICROSOFT EXPRESSLY DISCLAIMS ANY WARRANTY OR CONDITION FOR THE SOFTWARE PRODUCT. THE SOFTWARE PRODUCT AND ANY RELATED DOCUMENTATION ARE PROVIDED "AS IS" WITHOUT WARRANTY OR CONDITION OF ANY KIND, EITHER EXPRESS OR IMPLIED, INCLUDING, WITHOUT LIMITATION, THE IMPLIED WARRANTIES OF MERCHANTABILITY, FITNESS FOR A PARTICULAR PURPOSE, OR NONINFRINGEMENT. THE ENTIRE RISK ARISING OUT OF USE OR PERFORMANCE OF THE SOFTWARE PRODUCT REMAINS WITH YOU.

LIMITATION OF LIABILITY. TO THE MAXIMUM EXTENT PERMITTED BY APPLICABLE LAW, IN NO EVENT SHALL MICROSOFT OR ITS SUPPLIERS BE LIABLE FOR ANY SPECIAL, INCIDENTAL, INDIRECT, OR CONSEQUENTIAL DAMAGES WHATSOEVER (INCLUDING, WITHOUT LIMITATION, DAMAGES FOR LOSS OF BUSINESS PROFITS, BUSINESS INTERRUPTION, LOSS OF BUSINESS INFORMATION, OR ANY OTHER PECUNIARY LOSS) ARISING OUT OF THE USE OF OR INABILITY TO USE THE SOFTWARE PRODUCT OR THE PROVISION OF OR FAILURE TO PROVIDE SUPPORT SERVICES, EVEN IF MICROSOFT HAS BEEN ADVISED OF THE POSSIBILITY OF SUCH DAMAGES. IN ANY CASE, MICROSOFT'S ENTIRE LIABILITY UNDER ANY PROVISION OF THIS EULA SHALL BE LIMITED TO THE GREATER OF THE AMOUNT ACTUALLY PAID BY YOU FOR THE SOFTWARE PRODUCT OR US$5.00; PROVIDED, HOWEVER, IF YOU HAVE ENTERED INTO A MICROSOFT SUPPORT SERVICES AGREEMENT, MICROSOFT'S ENTIRE LIABILITY REGARDING SUPPORT SERVICES SHALL BE GOVERNED BY THE TERMS OF THAT AGREEMENT. BECAUSE SOME STATES AND JURISDICTIONS DO NOT ALLOW THE EXCLUSION OR LIMITATION OF LIABILITY, THE ABOVE LIMITATION MAY NOT APPLY TO YOU.

MISCELLANEOUS

This EULA is governed by the laws of the State of Washington USA, except and only to the extent that applicable law mandates governing law of a different jurisdiction.

Should you have any questions concerning this EULA, or if you desire to contact Microsoft for any reason, please contact the Microsoft subsidiary serving your country, or write: Microsoft Sales Information Center/One Microsoft Way/Redmond, WA 98052-6399.

Gear Up for Success

Register Today!

Return this
Microsoft® Mastering:
Microsoft Visual Basic® 6.0 Development

registration card today to receive advance notice about
the latest developer training titles and courseware!

For information about Mastering Series products and training, visit our Web site at
http://msdn.microsoft.com/mastering

Microsoft®
Mastering Series
Developer Training

0-7356-0900-4

Microsoft® Mastering:
Microsoft Visual Basic® 6.0 Development

_____ _____ _____
FIRST NAME   MIDDLE INITIAL   LAST NAME

_____ _____
INSTITUTION OR COMPANY NAME   TITLE

_____ _____
MAILING ADDRESS   SUITE/APARTMENT/MAILSTOP #

_____
ADDRESS LINE 2

_____ _____ _____
CITY   STATE/PROVINCE   ZIP/POSTAL CODE

_____ (___) _____
E-MAIL ADDRESS (INTERNET STANDARD, E.G. JOHNSMITH@BUSINESS.COM)   (AREA CODE) PHONE NUMBER

U.S. and Canada addresses only. Fill in information above and mail postage-free.
Please mail only the bottom half of this page.

**For information about Microsoft Press®
products, visit our Web site at
mspress.microsoft.com**

Microsoft Press